Religion in Schools

Religion in Schools

CONTROVERSIES AROUND THE WORLD

R. Murray Thomas

 PRAEGER

Westport, Connecticut
London

Library of Congress Cataloging-in-Publication Data

Thomas, R. Murray (Robert Murray), 1921-
  Religion in schools : controversies around the world / R. Murray Thomas.
     p. cm.
  Includes bibliographical references and index.
  Contents: Varieties of controversy—The nature of belief systems—Tradition, critical
  events, and the exercise of power—France—Japan—England—India—Spain—China—
  Italy—Pakistan—United States of America—Thailand—Australia—Saudi Arabia—
  Answers and trends.
  ISBN 0–275–99061–3 (alk. paper)
  1. Religion in the public schools–Cross-cultural studies.   I. Title.
 LC107.T48   2006
  379.2'8–dc22   2006003362

British Library Cataloguing in Publication Data is available.

Library of Congress Catalog Card Number: 2006003362
ISBN: 0–275–99061–3

First published in 2006

Praeger Publishers, 88 Post Road West, Westport, CT 06881
An imprint of Greenwood Publishing Group, Inc.
www.praeger.com

Printed in the United States of America

The paper used in this book complies with the
Permanent Paper Standard issued by the National
Information Standards Organization (Z39.48–1984).

10 9 8 7 6 5 4 3 2 1

Contents

Preface

In the opening decade of the twenty-first century, reports of controversies over religion in schools were prominently featured by news media around the world. Those reports revealed that a wide variety of issues were topics of public debate, with the issues important in one nation often differing from those important in another. In recent times, each of the following practices has become a topic of protracted debate in one or more societies.

- Teaching religious doctrine that conflicts with the government's political philosophy or state religion
- Displaying religious symbols or writings in schools that are financed by tax moneys
- Allowing students and teachers to wear adornments that identify their religious affiliation
- Celebrating religious holidays in schools
- Using public tax funds to finance—wholly or in part—schools operated by religious groups
- Offering religious-education classes in state-financed schools
- Including the study of humanism, agnosticism, and atheism in religious-education classes
- In state-funded schools, portraying one religion as truer than—or superior to—other religions
- Conducting ceremonies or assemblies during which students and teachers sing religious hymns and repeat religious maxims
- Offering prayers at school functions
- Including religious beliefs in pledges of allegiance to the nation
- Promoting religious beliefs in textbooks, especially in the fields of history and science

- Accounting for the universe's origin by the big bang theory instead of—or in addition to—religious versions of the universe's creation
- Teaching Darwin's theory of evolution instead of—or in addition to—teaching religious interpretations of human beginnings
- Teaching that personified, invisible spirits are the causes of human disease and deformity, earthquakes, volcanic eruptions, deluges, meteor showers, and the like.

The purpose of this book is to illustrate a method of interpreting such conflicts by answering four questions:

1. In recent years, what are typical controversies over religion-in-the-schools that have appeared in various nations?
2. In what ways are the controversies in one nation similar to, and different from, the controversies in other nations? How might we explain why there are such similarities and differences?
3. What interpretive framework can be used for understanding why such controversies assume their particular form in different societies?
4. What attempts have been made to resolve controversies, and how well have those attempts succeeded?

It is important that readers recognize at the outset what this book is intended to be and what it is not intended to be.

The book *is* a description of illustrative religion/school controversies in a variety of societies. By including as many as 12 nations, rather than limiting the focus to one or two, the book offers the advantage of breadth and variety. A particular benefit of using 12 nations is that contrasts and similarities among societies can be more readily demonstrated when numbers of countries are included.

The book *is not* an analysis of likenesses and differences among individual schools or among provinces. In other words, the analysis is limited to the national level—one nation contrasted to another. Consequently, no comparisons are provided for schools, subgroups of religious denominations, or regions of a country. As a result, the breadth of coverage that has been provided by the inclusion of 12 countries has been purchased at the cost of a highly detailed analysis of one or two countries.

Finally, an important consideration in curtailing the book's length was my desire to make the volume affordable for typical readers. Consequently, individual chapters have been limited to a dozen or so pages.

PART I

The Book's Vantage Point

The expression *vantage point*, as intended in these pages, refers to the intellectual perch from which a person views life's events. Thus, a vantage point is a kind of mental watchtower that offers a particular outlook on the world. Or, put another way, a vantage point is like a lens that concentrates on selected parts of the landscape while filtering out or diminishing other parts, thereby producing a special version of the events taking place.

The purpose of the three chapters that comprise Part I is to explain the vantage point from which this book's 12 religion/school controversies are described in Part II.

Chapter 1 introduces the 12 cases of controversy—conflicts that appeared in recent times in France, Japan, England, India, Spain, China, Italy, Pakistan, the United States, Thailand, Australia, and Saudi Arabia.

Chapter 2, entitled "The Nature of Belief Systems," identifies a variety of religious and nonreligious worldviews underlying the conflicts that the 12 cases involve.

Chapter 3—"Tradition, Critical Events, and the Exercise of Power"— sketches elements of the vantage point used in analyzing the 12 cases in Chapters 4 through 15.

CHAPTER 1

Varieties of Controversy

In recent years, conflicts have developed in numerous nations over the role that religion should play in schools—especially over the proper place of religion in government-sponsored schools. Instances of such controversy in various countries demonstrate that the nature of religion/school conflicts can differ significantly from one society to another. For instance, consider the following dozen cases.

France. A 12-year-old Muslim girl's wearing a traditional Islamic head scarf (*hijab*) at a state school prompted officials in 2003 to expel her, saying that the head covering represented a religious statement in a secular school. This incident, and others like it, precipitated vitriolic public debate about the place of religious symbols in the schools of a nation that had prided itself on being a strictly secular state ever since the revolution of 1789. When French President Jacques Chirac supported the girl's expulsion—on the principle that religion should not be permitted in public schools—Islamic leaders protested that the ban was prejudicial, singling out Muslims for discriminatory treatment while Catholic students were allowed to wear crosses in school and Jewish boys were allowed to wear skull caps (Sciolino, 2004).

Japan. Tokyo officials in March 2004 ordered the punishment of more than 200 teachers who had failed to stand during high-school graduation ceremonies for the singing of the anthem *Kimigayo* (His Majesty's Reign), which in 1999 had been declared by law to be the Japanese national hymn. The March order was issued after the teachers refused to sing the Kimigayo because they felt the anthem and the national flag (*Hinomaru*) were too closely linked to Japan's imperial, militarist past. The teachers insisted that the ruling unfairly restricted their constitutional freedom of thought and conscience (Arita, 2004).

England. In 2004, the Qualifications and Curriculum Authority that regulates curriculum content in English schools announced a plan to include humanism, agnosticism, and atheism among the belief systems taught in the nation's required religious-education classes. A spokesman for the authority explained, "It is very much the intention that young people in the context of religious education should be studying nonreligious beliefs. There are many children in England who have no religious affiliation and their beliefs and ideas, whatever they are, should be taken very seriously." The plan included the proposal that the traditional curriculum title *religious education* be changed to *religious, philosophical, and moral education.* The ensuing national debate pitted evangelists, who wanted to strengthen faith teaching in schools, against secularists, who contended that faith teaching was irrelevant to life in modern times (Hinsliff, 2004).

India. The defeat of the ruling Hindu nationalist Bharatiya Janata Party (BJP) by the United Progressive Alliance in June 2004 led to the appointment of a panel of historians assigned to remove Hindu religious beliefs that had been inserted into high-school textbooks during the BJP's reign since 1998—such beliefs as the conviction that ancient Hindu astrology was a valuable tool for predicting earthquakes and other natural disasters (Historians begin work, 2004).

Spain. From 1996 to April 2004, Spain was governed by the People's Party. In keeping with the party's close alliance with the Roman Catholic Church, Prime Minister Jose Maria Aznar in late 2003 issued a decree requiring all students to enroll each year either (a) in a class on Roman Catholic dogma, taught by church appointees and intended for practicing Catholics, or (b) in an alternative class about world religions that education officials said offered a historical view of religion. However, opposition party leaders charged that the alternative was very similar to the Catholicism class.

The reign of the People's Party ended in April 2004 when the Socialists won the national election and took steps toward making Spain an increasingly secular state. In September 2004, the new prime minister, Jose Luis Rodriguez Zapatero, announced a plan to remove religious teaching from all state-run schools, which enrolled 70% of the nation's students. The plan was met with stiff opposition from the country's Roman Catholic bishops who charged that Zapatero's plan would undermine religion and force secularism on Spain (Flamini, 2004).

China. A Hong Kong businessman, Li Guangqiang, was arrested in China's Fujian Province in 2002 on a charge of illegally importing 33,080 Bibles into China for a sect known as the Christian Shouters, so named for the animated nature of the group's emotional prayer meetings. Whereas the Bible is legal reading material in China, evangelical preaching is not. The Shouters had been outlawed in 1995 by the Chinese government for their evangelical form of Christian proselytizing. Mr. Li's arrest was apparently based on the government's objecting not to the Bible itself but to the annotations included in the particular edition of the work, *The New Testament Recovery Version* (Rosenthal, 2002).

Italy. An Italian court in October 2003 ordered the headmaster of a primary school in the town of Ofena to remove the Christian crucifix (a statuette of Christ nailed to a cross) from the wall of a kindergarten in which a 6-year-old Muslim boy was enrolled. The court order came after a 2-year dispute between school authorities and the pupil's father, who was the president of the Italian Muslim Union. Initially the headmaster had agreed to remove the crucifix in that particular classroom. But after a host of complaints from other parents, the crucifix was reinstated. The headmaster then complied with the father's request that the school also display a verse from the Islamic holy book, the Quran: "There is no God but Allah." However, the verse was removed by other parents. This series of incidents set off a highly volatile political and legal confrontation across Italy, particularly because exhibiting a crucifix in schools and public buildings had been required by royal decrees in 1924 and 1928, a ruling reconfirmed in 1984 in an agreement between the Roman Catholic Church and the Italian government (Italian court bans, 2003).

Pakistan. Over the 3-year period 2003–2005, President Pervez Musharraf directed a $255 million educational-reform campaign designed to change the character of Pakistan's 8,000–10,000 madrassas, which were private religious schools where an estimated 600,000 youths spent their time memorizing the Quran. The dual intent of the reform was to (a) expand the madrassas' curriculum to include a variety of secular subjects of practical vocational value and (b) eliminate militaristic teachings that urged students to participate in a holy war against non-Islamic peoples. However, in opposition to Musharraf's campaign, the leader of Pakistan's largest religious political alliance (Muttahid Majlis-e-Amal) charged that the government wanted to control the madrassas and "We will not let that happen—never" (Iqbal, 2003).

United States of America. Early in 2004, the superintendent of schools for the state of Georgia, Kathy Cox, proposed that the word *evolution* be replaced in the state's science curriculum with the phrase *biological changes over time.* She said the term *evolution* should be banned in order to alleviate social pressure on teachers in conservative communities where parents, who subscribed to a biblical explanation of human beginnings, objected to teaching Darwin's theory of evolution. Cox's proposal was strongly opposed by science teachers and by such distinguished citizens as former U.S. President Jimmy Carter who announced that "As a Christian, a trained engineer and scientist, and a professor at Emory University, I am embarrassed by Superintendent Kathy Cox's attempt to censor and distort the education of Georgia's students." In a spirit of compromise, the pastor of a Baptist church said that even though a true Christian could not believe in evolution, both Darwin's theory and the Bible version of creation should be taught so as to "help students understand science" (MacDonald, 2004).

Thailand. In September 2004, the Thai government announced plans to set up government-run Islamic schools in the nation's southern provinces that border on Malaysia. The announcement was condemned by Islamic leaders who charged that Thailand's Buddhist majority was seeking to restrict the religious, cultural, and educational rights of the country's Muslim minority. Thai officials responded that the plan was designed to combat the efforts of radical fundamentalist Islamic teachers in privately run Quran schools who, in the officials' opinion, were "brainwashing" their students to continue the violence that had already led to the deaths of more than 500 people during 2004 (State-run Islamic schools, 2004).

   Australia. The agency responsible for issuing nationwide curriculum guidelines published *A National Statement on Science for Australian Schools* in 1994. The document proposed a wide-ranging set of goals that science teaching would be expected to promote, including "equality of educational opportunities . . . respond to current and emerging economic and social needs of the nation . . . and [develop] skills of literacy." Furthermore, teaching science should foster "a knowledge of languages other than English . . . an appreciation and understanding of, and confidence to participate in, the creative arts . . . a capacity to exercise judgment in matters of morality, ethics, and social justice" (Maratos, 1995, p. 358). In addition to such a broad collection of responsibilities assigned to science teaching, the *Statement* accorded equal scientific status to the worldviews of all cultures, including the belief system of Australia's indigenous people.

Scientific knowledge has been expanded by the cumulative efforts of generations of scientists from all over the world. It has been enriched by the pooling of understandings from different cultures, including western cultures and *indigenous cultures, including Aboriginals and Torres Straits Islanders,* and has become a truly international activity. (Australian Education Council, 1993, p. 3)

This statement was met with protest from members of Australia's scientific community who objected to according any group's belief system the same scientific status as any other group's system. Thus, under the *Statement's* criteria for what qualifies as "science," Aborigine *Dreamtime* beliefs in a spirit world deserved to be honored as "science" as respectable as empirical studies in astronomy, biology, geology, and chemistry. That expanded definition of "science" could then become a guide to the kind of science to be taught in Australian schools (Maratos, 1995).

   Saudi Arabia. Over the latter months of 2001, agents of the Saudi Arabian religious police force arrested 14 foreign workers (ones from the Philippines, Ethiopia, Eritrea, and India) who were accused of teaching Christianity. The arrests were based on a Saudi Arabian law forbidding public expression of any religion other than Islam. The incidents drew widespread criticism from Christian groups in other countries. The 14 foreigners were released from custody at Christmastime and scheduled for deportation (Moore, 2001).

   During the past decade, there obviously have been far more controversies over religion in schools than the ones portrayed in the 12 cases. Then why did I choose to focus on those particular events? My reasons were that the 12 examples:

- Concerned six societies whose cultures are based dominantly on Eastern traditions (Japan, India, China, Pakistan, Thailand, Saudi Arabia) and six based dominantly on Western traditions (France, Great Britain, Spain, Italy, the United States, Australia). Thus, East and West could be equally represented.
- Had been prominently featured in the public press, so they were apparently of considerable public interest.
- Were of recent vintage—representing concerns of the past decade, thereby reflecting present-day interests.
- Involved a variety of belief systems—aboriginal, agnostic, atheistic, Buddhist, Catholic, mainstream Christian Protestant, Christian Evangelical, Hindu, humanist, Islamic, secularist, and Shintoist.

For the purposes of this book, I expanded the concept of *school* to include such learning sites as Sunday schools and similar study groups, as in the China and Saudi Arabia examples.

The types of controversies in the 12 cases support the observation that conflicts over the proper role of religion in schools can vary from one society to another. As a means of emphasizing contrasts between societies, I arranged the chapters of Part II in a sequence that alternates Western and Eastern nations' types of controversies.

A question may now be asked about why a particular type of religion-and-school connection becomes contentious and newsworthy in one society but not in another. In other words, what factors account for similarities and differences across nations in the religion/school relationships that are of public concern? The aim of the following chapters is to suggest how that question might be answered from the vantage point of the book's interpretive framework. In pursuit of that aim, the presentation is cast in a sequence of 15 chapters. As noted in the Part I introduction, Chapter 2—"The Nature of Belief Systems"—identifies principal features of people's worldviews. Chapter 3—"Traditions, Critical Events, and the Exercise of Power"—explains the components of a scheme for interpreting different societies' religion/school conflicts. In Part II, Chapters 4 through 15 illustrate how the 12 cases might be interpreted from the perspective of that scheme. In Part III, Chapter 16—"Answers and Trends"—offers a comparative summary of the 12 cases in terms of a series of themes that run through the Part II accounts of these cases.

CHAPTER 2

The Nature of Belief Systems

Before describing this book's interpretive viewpoint in Chapter 3, I should identify how the terms *belief system*, *religious*, and *nonreligious* are intended in these pages.

A belief system is a collection of convictions a person uses for interpreting life's events. Such a system typically concerns matters of:

- The purpose of life (teleology);
- The nature of existence and reality (ontology);
- The nature of knowledge and how to distinguish fact from fantasy, truth from falsehood (epistemology);
- The origin of the world and of life forms (cosmology);
- Why things happen as they do (causality);
- Rules governing people's treatment of other beings and the physical environment (morality, ethics); and
- People's rights and obligations (privileges, responsibilities).

A distinction is drawn here between *religious* and *nonreligious* belief systems.

RELIGIOUS BELIEF SYSTEMS

A religious system (a religion) typically includes faith in the reality of (a) invisible spirits (gods, angels, genies, ancestral shades, jinns, or the like) that influence events and affect people's destinies, (b) a continuation of spiritual life after physical death, and (c) rituals people can perform to influence the actions of spirits. For convenience of discussion, religions can be divided into three major clusters: (1) the Hindu-Buddhist-Jain-Sikh line, (2) the

Judaic-Christian-Islamic line, and (3) a catchall category of many hundreds of religious persuasions that do not fit into either of the first two clusters.

The Hindu-Buddhist-Jain-Sikh Line

Hinduism traces its beginnings back perhaps 4,000 years. At present, there are an estimated 837 million Hindus throughout the world, most of them in India. Buddhism appeared 2,500 years ago as a protest to aspects of traditional Hinduism that the creator of Buddhism—a Hindu of noble birth named Gautama Siddhartha—judged to be both false and harmful. At present, there are an estimated 373 million followers of Buddhism, mostly in China, Myanmar (Burma), and Thailand. Jainism also originated about 2,500 years ago as a further variant of Hinduism designed to alter what Jainists considered to be faulty features of traditional Hindu doctrine. Jains currently number around 4 million. Sikhism, which appeared 500 years ago, was a further attempt to remedy what its founders viewed as mistaken aspects of Hinduism. Today there are more than 24 million members of the Sikh community, most of them in the Punjab region of India (Barrett & Johnson, 2004).

What these members of the Hindu line share in common is the belief that humans are constructed with a body and a soul. Following death, the body decomposes into the four elements from which all physical matter is composed—earth, air, fire, and water. The soul, in contrast, was not created anew at the time the person was conceived and born. Rather, each person's soul was generated at some indefinite time in the far distant past. Across the centuries, that soul has inhabited numerous bodies, periodically passing out of one deceased physical frame to enter another newly created one. This process of a soul's vivifying one body after another over eons of time is known as *metempsychosis* or *transmigration of the soul*. The doctrine of each of these faiths specifies the kinds of behavior that people should exhibit if they want the body that their soul will next inhabit to be more desirable than bodies inhabited in the past. Hinduism and its derivatives are polytheistic faiths that include multiple invisible spirits or gods who influence people's lives.

The Judaic-Christian-Islamic Line

The Jewish-Christian-Islamic sequence of religious ideologies consists of an initial religion—Judaism—followed by two major reformation movements that today exist as separate doctrinal and organizational systems. Judaism was founded well over 3,000 years ago and today is credited with 13.5 million adherents around the world. Christianity was the first great reform movement, intended to correct ostensible shortcomings of Judaism as that faith was being practiced 2,000 years ago. Today there are an estimated 2.1 billion Christians worldwide. The second major reform, Islam, was launched 1,300 years ago to remedy putative doctrinal errors and improper practices of both the Judaism and Christianity of that era and of other minor religious persuasions. At present there are an estimated 1.1 billion members of the international Islamic community (Barrett & Johnson, 2004).

Among the beliefs held in common by members of the Judaic-Christian-Islamic line is the conviction that there is a single supreme being or personified power that created the universe and its inhabitants and that continues to guide events in the universe. The all-powerful, omniscient being of Judaic-Christian-Islamic monotheism was originally called Yahweh by Jews, God by Christians, and Allah by Muslims. Humans, in Judaic-Christian-Islamic belief, are composed of a physical body and a spiritual soul. The soul is embedded in the body at some point between the individual person's conception and birth. Upon the death of the body, the soul continues to live eternally in either a state of pleasure (heaven) or a state of misery (hell), or perhaps in some indeterminate condition (limbo or Catholicism's purgatory). During people's lives on earth, how well they abide by church doctrine may affect where their soul will end up after their body's demise.

Other Religious Traditions

There are hundreds of other religions throughout the world. Among the more prominent is China's Confucianism, whose early formulation is credited to the sage Confucius in the fifth century BCE.[1] As originally conceived, Confucianism was a plan for the proper organization of society and not a religion with unseen spirits and an envisioned life after death. But in later times such religious elements were added by some of the system's followers. Another traditional Chinese faith is Taoism (with Tao meaning *Heaven's Path* or *The Way*). Taoists see life and death as simply different manifestations of Tao or Nature's Way of Life. Taoists recommend that people study nature in order to live a serene life that accords with Nature's Way. A third significant East Asian denomination is Shinto, the traditional philosophical foundation of Japanese society.

Many religions that are outside the mainstream faiths can be subsumed under the label *ethno-religions.* The membership of each ethno-religious faith is limited to the people of a particular clan or tribal group. Ethno-religionist systems are found in 144 countries (Barrett & Johnson, 2004). By 2000, an estimated 3.8% of the world's peoples were followers of such belief traditions, but the number of adherents was on the decline as tribes' members increasingly joined a major faith or else abandoned religion. Geographically, such persuasions have ranged from the Zulus' faith in South Africa to Voodoo on the island of Haiti, to Navajo belief in the Southwestern United States, and to the Dreamtime conceptions of Australian aborigines. Although widely separated from each other, these diverse faiths tend to share four features in common. They all:

1. Envision the universe as consisting both of tangible, visible entities (such as people, animals, places, objects) and of unseen spirits that affect events in the visible world.

2. Propose that when the elements of the universe are in proper balance, nature is at peace and people are free of pain and stress. When the elements are out of balance, natural disasters occur (earthquakes, floods, drought, and the like) and people suffer social disorder, illness, injury, and emotional stress.

3. Contend that the disrupted harmony of the universe can be remedied by people (a) performing rites and austerities that mollify the offended spirits and (b) displaying the moral values considered proper for adherents of the faith. Whereas some values are embraced in all such belief systems, others are specific to a particular faith.

4. Hold that the goal of human development is that of promoting the harmony of the universe. The precise nature of that harmony and how order can be restored can differ somewhat from one of the belief systems to another (Thomas, 1997, p. 261).

NONRELIGIOUS BELIEF SYSTEMS

Nonreligious persuasions do not include a theology that recognizes such things as invisible spirits, life after death, and rituals intended to influence events. Five well-known nonreligious philosophical positions are *humanism* (sometimes referred to as *secular humanism*), *agnosticism, atheism, materialism*, and *rationalism.*

The variety of humanism of interest here proposes that people are responsible for fashioning their own destinies through their own efforts, limited only by their innate ability and the physical and social environments they inhabit. A typical humanist is convinced that people can lead fitting lives (a) without believing in God, in a soul that lives on after a person dies, or in the universe having been created by an intelligent being, and (b) believing that quite suitable lives and proper behavior can be based on reason, goodwill, and experience (Mason, 2004).

Agnostics hold that questions about invisible spirits or life after death are unanswerable—at least by any method presently available. In effect, agnostics say, "We just don't know." Atheists, on the other hand, reject outright the idea of invisible spirits and life after death, which are notions they regard as ridiculous.

One popular variety of materialism asserts that there is only one substance in the universe and that substance is physical, empirical, or material. Everything that exists consists of matter and energy. Thus, the idea of spiritual substance is a delusion. There are no such things as supernatural, occult, or paranormal experience or after-death existence. Those things are either delusions or can be explained in terms of physical forces.

Rationalism, in the form proposed by the French philosopher René Descartes (1596–1650), is based on four laws governing the proper investigation of any problem:

Accept nothing as true that is not recognized by the reason as clear and distinct. First, analyze complex ideas by breaking them down into their simple constitutive elements, which reason can intuitively apprehend. Next, reconstruct complicated problems by beginning with simple ideas and working synthetically to the complex. Finally, make an accurate and complete enumeration of the data of the problem, using in this step the methods of both induction and deduction. (Adapted from The philosophy of René Descartes, 2005)

An estimated 15% of the world's 6.3 billion people qualify as nonreligious—including humanists, agnostics, atheists, materialists, rationalists, and those who are simply nonbelievers (Barrett & Johnson, 2004).

In summary, people throughout the world subscribe to diverse belief systems that determine how they interpret events and how they act as a result of those interpretations. Controversies occur over religion in schools whenever influential groups in a society disagree about which worldview should be the basis of school practice. The nature of such belief-system confrontations in 12 societies is described in Chapters 4 through 15.

CHAPTER 3

Tradition, Critical Events, and the Exercise of Power

What I propose in this chapter is that understanding the religion/school relationships in the 12 cases of controversy can be fostered by analyzing those relationships from a vantage point focusing on:

1. the nature of belief constituencies,
2. the influence of cultural tradition,
3. events that significantly threaten and/or change tradition, and
4. the exercise of power by the main belief constituencies engaged in confrontations over religion in schools.

The essence of that vantage point is reflected in this proposition:

Traditions and critical events from the past have contributed to the present status of a belief constituency and thereby affect that constituency's exercise of power during confrontations over religion in schools.

To clarify the rationale behind such a proposition, the following discussion explains what is meant by the four concepts that form the core of this book's interpretive perspective—*belief constituencies, tradition, critical events,* and *the exercise of power.*

BELIEF CONSTITUENCIES

A *belief constituency* is a collection of people who subscribe to the same cluster of convictions. Consider, for example, the belief that the world was created and is controlled by a single supreme being—God, Allah, Yahweh—who knows all (omniscient), is everywhere at once (omnipresent), and is all-powerful (omnipotent). As noted in Chapter 2, such a conviction is held in common by faithful Christians, Muslims, and Jews. Thus, members of those three religions form a belief constituency relating to the monotheism that is at the center of Judeo-Christian-Islamic doctrine. However, such a notion is not accepted by Hindus and Shintoists, who believe in multiple gods or spirits that display varied traits. But within any broadly encompassing constituency there can be groups that disagree about other sorts of belief than the one that binds them together. For instance, the Christian conviction that Jesus was divine (the son of God who was sent to the world to save humankind) is rejected by Jews and Muslims. Thus, in terms of Jesus's divinity, Christians form their own constituency. It is also the case that even within such a limited group as Christians there can be divisions of opinion about additional matters, so the group divides itself into subgroups of belief on those matters. For instance, some Christians believe that every passage in their Bible is the literal truth as dictated by God, whereas others believe the Bible is a history of wise writers' understanding of life, an understanding inspired by God but not a literal revelation of God's words.

Controversies over religion in schools occur only in societies that have more than one belief constituency competing for people's allegiance. The nature and intensity of that competition can depend on how the belief constituencies compare with each other in terms of such characteristics as their (a) size and cohesiveness, (b) societal ideals, (c) sources of supporting evidence, (d) command of resources, and (e) quality of leadership.

Size

A constituency's size is determined by the number of people subscribing to a particular cluster of beliefs. Other things being equal, the greater the percentage of people holding a belief, the greater the likelihood that those peoples' ideas about the proper role of religion in schools will prevail. For instance, Brazil's population is 97.5% Christian (74.3% Catholic, 23.2% Protestant), whereas Turkey's population is 97.2% Muslim. And even though neither nation has an official religion, we might expect religion/school relationships to be more heavily influenced by Christian opinions than Muslim opinions in Brazil, and quite the opposite in Turkey. However, "other things" are never equal, so constituency size must interact with further conditions—cohesiveness, societal ideas, resources, quality of leadership—for determining the role that a given belief system will assume in schools.

Cohesiveness

It is apparent that all members of a belief system are not alike in how strictly they subscribe to their professed faith's doctrine and practices. Within the total number of people affiliated with a particular constituency, some may abide by all of the faith's teachings, whereas others may accept only a portion of the denomination's doctrine.

On the assumption that the most devoted followers of a religion will be those who spend more time attending church services, we can estimate the cohesiveness of religious groups by learning about their frequency of church attendance. Note, for instance, a comparison between Sweden and Ireland. Among Sweden's residents, 86.5% are reported to be affiliated with the Church of Sweden (a variety of Lutheranism). However, at least 30% have been identified as *nonpracticing* and only 4% said they went to church regularly. In contrast, among the 88.4% of Ireland's residents who associate themselves with Roman Catholicism, 84% have claimed that they participate in church services at least once a week (Europe: Religion, 2004; Sparks, 2004, pp. 604, 704). In Canada, where 77.1% of the population has been listed as Christian, only 38% of a survey's respondents said they went to church regularly. However, the team that conducted the survey cautioned that such a figure was unrealistically high. A more direct measure of church attendance suggested that the actual proportion was closer to 10%.[1]

Thus, I would suggest that the greater the proportion of adherents of a religion who hold fast to that religion's tenets and practices, the more likely the members of that denomination will voice a consistent attitude about religion/school relationships.

Societal Ideals

All modern societies have ideals representing what the members of the society—or, more accurately, what the people in power—believe are the rules of organization, of rights, and of responsibilities that make for the good and proper life. On the national level, these ideals are typically in the form of a constitution (France, India, Japan, the United States, Pakistan) or a succession of agreements and traditions (England). Or influential ideals may be found in a religious or philosophical persuasion that goes beyond national borders (Christianity, Islam, Judaism, Shinto, Confucianism). Thus, in controversies over religion/school relationships, constituencies often appeal to such ideals in order to support the position they advocate.

Sources of Supportive Evidence

Belief constituencies can differ in the kinds of evidence on which they base their convictions. Types of evidence can include:

- A person's word—parent, priest, teacher, chieftain, astrologer, mystic, television personality, scientist, or someone with an academic degree or professional certificate.
- A revered religious document, a textbook, an encyclopedia, an academic journal, a newspaper, or a magazine.

- Empirical data—results of an experiment, archeological excavations, a collection of biological specimens, or a survey of events.
- Personal experience through participation in, or observation of, activities that lead to inferences about what is true and what is false about life.
- Intuition, revelation, or inspiration, in the sense of ideas that come to mind either spontaneously or during meditation.

An important difference among belief systems is in the kind of evidence adherents accept for verifying the truth or falsity of a system's tenets and practices. Devoted evangelical Christians accept the literal meanings of passages in the Christian Bible, Muslims accept the verses of the *Quran* and the sayings in the *Sunnah*, Hindus accept the *Manu Smriti* and *Upanishads*, Confucians accept *The Analects* and *The Book of Mencius*, and Jews accept the *Torah*. Devoted Roman Catholics accept the word of the Pope and of priests, Muslims accept the word of an imam, Voodoo advocates accept the word of a practitioner.

Proponents of nonreligious belief systems may trust conclusions published in an encyclopedia, academic journal, or textbook. Atheists may accept what Karl Marx, the creator of a dialectical-materialism belief system, wrote about religion—that religion is "the opiate of the masses." Humanists may rely on such writings of Robert Green Ingersoll (1833–1899) as *Secularism* and *Liberty in Literature*.

Frequently, adherents of a nonreligious system test the truth of assertions by applying principles of scientific inquiry. Although there is no single scientific method of investigation to which all scientists subscribe, there are principles they hold in common. One such principle is that conclusions about life and reality should be founded on empirical evidence derived from the direct study of events—from observations of the world that are collected and summarized. Then logical interpretations are drawn about what the collected information means. Those interpretations may be cast in the form of a scientific theory.

A second principle is that all interpretations are subject to revision on the basis of additional empirical evidence and its analysis. In contrast to the everlasting conclusions offered in most—if not all—religions, no conclusion drawn from scientific inquiry is considered final and definitive. Each answer about reality is assumed to be no more than an approximation of the truth, an approximation that requires more data, further testing, critical review, and refinement.

A third principle concerns *sampling*. Whenever someone studies a limited number of events or people (a sample), and then wishes to apply the conclusions from that study to a broader range of events or people (a population), it is necessary to offer convincing evidence that the significant characteristics of the sample are the same as those of the population. For instance, great caution should be observed in inferring that the pattern of beliefs of people in one village of a region forms the same pattern as the beliefs in every other village.

In summary, controversies over questions of religion in schools often result from the contending groups basing their beliefs on different sources of evidence. And whether a person will adopt a particular belief system can depend heavily on whether that person agrees with the system's choice of supporting evidence.

Command of Resources

The phrase *command of resources* refers to the ability of a constituency to assemble the means of influencing policies and practices bearing on religion/school relationships. The most obvious resource is money. However, it is not money itself but, rather, what money can buy that affects schooling policies. Money can (a) buy books and periodicals that promote a religion; (b) purchase the services of specialists (public relations experts) in ways of communicating beliefs to the public; (c) command space and time in such communication media as newspapers, books, radio, television, and the Internet; and (d) provide goods and services for people in order to obtain their support (often considered to be a form of bribery).

Quality of Leadership

The belief constituency's success in affecting a society's religion/school policies is strongly influenced by the social status and skills of persuasion of the group's leaders. Valued leadership characteristics include:

- *Social status*—a respected reputation and popularity
- *Vision*—a clear conception of the group's values and goals
- *Skills of persuasion*—eloquence as a speaker, debater, writer
- *Organizational acumen*—ability to attract workers, define their assignments, establish a plan for efficient interaction among workers, and foster workers' morale
- *Persistence*—the capacity to sustain effort even under unfavorable circumstances

It is not necessary that each member of the leadership corps displays all five traits. Rather, the traits can be distributed among the members.

Summary

The five characteristics identified in the foregoing paragraphs do not exhaust the ways in which belief constituencies can differ from each other. However, I think those five play a significant role in controversies over religion in schools, and so the five are used in the interpretations of the 12 cases of religion/school conflicts offered in Chapters 4 through 15.

TRADITION

The term *tradition* means "the usual way things are done." So, for the purposes of this book, tradition refers to the dominant belief system of a constituency—a pattern of convictions followed by a group of people for at least several decades and often for a great many generations. The description of a tradition can be found in both written and unwritten forms. Written forms include the key documents of a religious or philosophical persuasion, such as the Jewish *Torah*, Christian *Bible*, Latter Day Saints' *Book of Mormon*, Confucian *Analects*, Islamic *Quran*, Sikh *Guru Granith Sahib*, and Marxism's *Communist Manifesto*.

Unwritten forms of tradition are found in customs—in the ways people act in daily life. People adopt customs from observing others' behavior and from what they are told to do and not to do by parents, ministers, teachers, companions, law enforcement personnel, and mass communication media.

CRITICAL EVENTS

An event is deemed *critical* when it performs one of more of the following functions:

- *Introduces a belief system that differs from, and competes with, a traditional system.* Example: Growing numbers of North African Muslims who immigrated to France after World War II introduced an ever-increasing Islamic worldview to compete with a traditional Roman Catholic worldview.
- *Interrupts the practice of an existing tradition.* Example: After United States military forces took control of the Japanese government in 1945, the schools' curricula were no longer allowed to include traditional military drill or the Shinto religion.
- *Shifts the dominant power from one belief constituency to another.* Example: In the 2004 Spanish election, authority to govern the nation changed from the pro-Catholic People's Party to the secularist Socialist Party, thereby eliminating obligatory religious instruction in public schools.
- *Solidifies the strength of a belief constituency whose traditional power has been threatened by a competing tradition.* Example: A 1924 law in Italy strengthened Catholicism's presence in schools by requiring the display of a Christian crucifix in every classroom.

Critical events can include such happenings as a public election, a military invasion, the colonization of a region, the death of a leader (king, president, pope, head of a political party) that leads to a successor, the publication of a document (*The Declaration of Independence*, Marx's *Das Kapital*, Darwin's *The Origin of Species*, Rousseau's *Social Contract*), a series of speeches (Jesus's sermons, the Buddha's teachings), or an invention (Galileo's telescope, Gutenburg's movable type).

It is apparent, however, that a new departure which is set off by a critical event may not be accepted by everyone in the society. Many people may remain faithful to their established tradition, thereby producing a conflict between the old and the new, a conflict that may be reflected in controversies over religion in schools.

Obviously, no society is static. All societies are in a state of transition, either rapid or slow. Transitions can be interpreted as struggles among forces, some of which press for change (transformative forces) and some of which resist change and seek to maintain the status quo (conservative forces). Transformative forces can arise either within the society or from outside. An example of a within-society force (a critical event) would be an invention introduced by someone who is already a member of the society. Confucius was such a person in China, Gautama Siddhartha (the Buddha) in India, Jesus in Judah, Muhammad in Arabia, Thomas Jefferson in America, Karl Marx in Germany. An example of outside forces is the conquest (a series of critical events) of Africa, Asia, and the Americas by European colonialists between 1500 CE and the mid-twentieth century—conquest that led to the introduction of European culture into the colonized regions. In addition to aggressive intrusions into a society by outsiders are more peaceful ones by missionaries or by immigrants seeking a better way of life. Further examples of external forces are mass communication media—newspapers, movies, radio, television, the Internet—that acquaint members of a society with beliefs and ways of life previously unfamiliar in that society.

Many of the cases described in Chapter 1 involved confrontations between worldwide forces of change and societies' usual ways of life. The following are four examples of worldwide forces that have pressed for change in religion/school linkages.

- *Scientific progress.* Increasing numbers of people have been adopting more scientific standards for judging the sort evidence needed to support claims of "fact" or "truth" rather than depending solely on documents from ancient times. This trend has been partly the result of scientific and technological advances that offer empirically supported answers to questions that previously depended on religious lore—questions about the earth's age and beginnings, the creation and development of life forms, historical events recounted in holy books, and tales of miraculous happenings.

- *Declining religious participation.* As noted earlier, many nations have witnessed a decrease in attendance at religious services, a trend interpreted to imply that many people have become less interested in religious doctrine because of new social and recreational pursuits as well as expanded sources of knowledge provided by convenient modes of travel, books, radio, television, and the Internet.

- *Increasing cultural diversity.* Advances in communication technology have enabled people all over the earth to learn about ways of life and of opportunities in places other than where they themselves live. This extended awareness has combined with advances in land, sea, and air travel to make people's moving away from home to distant sites a practical venture. Particularly since World War II, such changes have contributed to increasing the cultural heterogeneity of societies. Countries whose religious composition was dominated in the past by a limited number of faiths have been obliged to accommodate a growing diversity of belief systems.

- *International agreements.* Ever since the United Nations was created in the mid-twentieth century, increasing international social pressure has been exerted on governments to become signatories to such covenants as the United Nations *Universal Declaration of Human Rights*, which is a document affirming that

everyone has the right to freedom of thought, conscience and religion; this right includes freedom to change his [or her] religion or belief, and freedom, either alone or in community with others and in public or private, to manifest his [or her] religion or belief in teaching, practice, worship, and observance. (Universal Declaration, 1948)

Not only have such bodies as the United Nations obtained the formal commitment of governments to such social principles, but they have also monitored progress toward the stated ideals and have publicized how faithfully governments have lived up to their pledge. The publicity and, in some cases, economic sanctions have motivated governments to alter traditional religion/school policies so as to conform with the values reflected in such documents.

In the country cases analyzed in Chapters 4 through 15, the interaction between forces of stability (tradition) and forces of change (critical events) is cast as a historical description, a chronicle that helps explain why each chapter's controversy has assumed its particular character.

THE EXERCISE OF POWER

The expression *exercise of power* means the extent to which the behavior of one person (or group) influences the beliefs or behavior of another person (or group). For example, if Person A thinks or acts differently because of Person B's presence (bodily or symbolic), then Person B has power over Person A. But if Person A thinks or acts just the same, whether or not Person B is present, then B has no power over A. The amount of power B exerts over A is indicated by how drastically or inevitably A's belief or behavior is altered by the presence of B.

The concept *exercise of power* is essential to the analyses of controversies in Chapters 4 through 15, because the interpretations offered in those chapters are cast as power struggles between competing belief constituencies that attempt to have their notions of proper religion/school relationships prevail.

The amount of power a constituency can exert in religion/school controversies depends on how the competing constituencies compare with each other in such influential characteristics as size, cohesiveness, attractive ideals, supportive evidence, command of resources, and quality of leadership. A further factor of particular importance is a constituency's position of authority. The word *authority* refers to the official power held by an individual or group. There are various ways by which authority is assigned to a person or group: (a) by the order of a conqueror who has bested foes in battle; (b) by rules written by persuasive leaders, with the rules published in a revered document (a religion's holy scripture, a nation's constitution); (c) by the majority of the populace that are qualified to vote in elections; or (d) by the population's chosen representatives. Constituencies in positions of authority typically enjoy special access to resources not available to ones without such official power.

A critical event affecting religion/school relationships may consist of an incident that changes the basis for determining who will hold the authority. Thus, the overthrow of a democratic government by a military junta can change the basis for assigning authority from the voting public to a coterie of military officers. In contrast, an election in a stable democratic government will not likely change the basis for assigning authority; if the election ousts the reigning political party from office, only the individuals or groups that occupied positions of authority will likely be changed and the system remains intact.

CONCLUSION

The analysis of the 12 cases of religion/school controversies in Chapters 4 through 15 is based on a scheme that features interactions among four concepts—*belief constituencies, tradition, critical events,* and *the exercise of power.* I am not assuming that this way of interpreting controversies is the only reasonable approach to understanding religion-and-school relationships. A variety of other perspectives can also provide useful insights into religion/school issues. But I adopted the model described in this chapter because it is easy to grasp and it yields explanations that I find persuasive.

With this chapter's proposal in mind, we are now ready to use it for interpreting conflicts over religion/school relationships in the 12 country cases.

PART II

Analyses of the Twelve Cases

To facilitate readers' efforts to compare the 12 cases with each other, all chapters from 4 through 15 are organized in the same pattern. Each begins with a brief paragraph identifying the basic nature of the chapter's controversy, and then continues with

- A chronicle of traditions and critical events leading up to the controversy (*Historical Roots*),
- Influential characteristics of the principal groups (constituencies) that engaged in the conflict (*The Contending Constituencies*), that is, characteristics affecting the contending groups' power and strategies, and
- An estimate of how the case was settled or might be settled (*Resolving the Controversy*).

CHAPTER 4

France

The religion/school controversy in France was precipitated by Muslim girls being forbidden to wear headscarves in public schools, although they were permitted to do so in private schools and public universities. The most obvious contending groups in the case were (a) the French government currently in power and (b) leaders of the country's five million Muslims (the largest number of Muslims in any European country).

HISTORICAL ROOTS

The significance of the headscarves episode is perhaps best understood when viewed against the history of relations between successive French governments and (a) two religious communities—Roman Catholics and Muslims—and (b) nonreligious secularists.

Roman Catholicism

The origin of today's awkward and sometimes conflict-ridden relationship between the French government and the Roman Catholic Church goes back more than two centuries. Well into the eighteenth century, France continued to be a traditional Catholic nation, with the French monarch sharing religious authority with the pope in Rome. At that time, Christian Protestants and Jews were still denied religious rights. When Luis XVI at age 20 became king of France in 1774 upon the death of his grandfather, Luis XV, he enjoyed quasi-priestly privileges. One privilege was that of appointing bishops and abbots, thus enabling the king to secure the loyalty of impoverished or ambitious members of the aristocracy by assigning them religious posts. Other kingly functions were those of extracting funds from churches and of reforming monasteries. However, the Catholic Church's traditional social prestige and doctrinal rights suffered a decisive blow on the occasion of a critical event—the outbreak of the French Revolution in 1789, and especially with the passage of the new regime's legislation. Under the motto "Liberty, Equality, Fraternity," the revolutionary forces intended to place the nation's affairs in the hands of the common people (in practice, the middle-class bourgeoisie) rather than continue in the hands of the nobles and clergy. The nation henceforth would be a secular, democratic republic. A newly convened National Assembly ended feudalism by stripping nobles, the clergy, towns, and provinces of their special privileges. Church lands were confiscated, monastic vows were abolished, and in 1790 Luis XVI was forced to sign a Civil Constitution of the Clergy that turned any remaining churchmen into employees of the French state by requiring them to take an oath of loyalty to the new republic's constitution. Thus, the Church of France was no longer under the jurisdiction of the Roman Catholic Church but was merely a French national establishment in defiance of the pope's authority. The papal leadership in Rome never accepted this new arrangement.

Over the next two-and-a-quarter centuries, the spirit of the French Revolution was retained in a succession of constitutions that carried the original motto of *liberty, equality, fraternity*. The most recent version (1958, with subsequent amendments) affirms that

the French people hereby solemnly proclaim their dedication to the Rights of Man and the principle of national sovereignty as defined by the Declaration of 1789, reaffirmed and complemented by the Preamble to the 1946 Constitution. . . . France is an indivisible, secular, democratic, and social Republic. It ensures the equality of all citizens before the law, without distinction as to origin, race, or religion. It respects all beliefs. . . . Its principle is government of the people, by the people, and for the people. (France: Constitution, 2004)

As the history of religion in so many societies has amply demonstrated, government edicts do not eliminate deep-seated belief systems from the populace. Thus, Roman Catholicism has continued over the decades to be embraced by a large portion of the French people—with nearly two-thirds of French residents currently identified as professed Catholics. Many of the devout present-day Catholics feel that their traditional position of respect and power in the French society is threatened by both Muslims and secularists.

Islam

The credit—or blame—for the large number of Muslims now living in France goes to French colonial practices of yesteryear. As part of European nations' colonization efforts in the nineteenth and twentieth centuries, France acquired North African territories, sent French settlers to those new colonies, and aggressively promoted French culture among North Africans, who were principally adherents of Islam. Specifically, in 1830 Algeria became a French territory and in 1848 became a *département* attached to France. In the spring of 1881, France invaded Tunisia, claiming that Tunisian troops had crossed the border into Algeria. Tunisia then became a French protectorate. In 1904 Morocco was divided into spheres of French and Spanish influence, with a 1912 treaty establishing the two zones as protectorates of Spain and France.

Subsequently, as the decades advanced, the intimate ties between France and its colonies across the Mediterranean led to a growing flow of French settlers going to North Africa and of Algerian, Moroccan, and Tunisian Muslims going to France. Because in the colonies the indigenous peoples had been taught French language and culture, the ones who emigrated to France could readily adjust to life there. Even after the colonies won their political independence following World War II, the immigration of Muslims continued at an accelerating pace as indigenous peoples in the former colonies sought a better way of life in France. Once the newcomers settled in France, their high birth rates quickly added to their numbers. Therefore, by the early years of the twenty-first century there were more than five million Muslims in France, about half of them French citizens. In terms of national origin, an estimated 35% were from Algeria, 25% from Morocco, and 10% from Tunisia. The remaining 30% were from many other nations or were French converts to Islam that numbered perhaps 30,000 (Islam in France, 2004). A recent survey reported that France's Muslims had come from 53 different countries, spoke 21 different languages, and represented multiple Asian, Middle Eastern, African, and European cultures (Taheri, 2003).

For the French society, the 2004 headscarf incident was of little importance in itself. The true significance of the event was its symbolizing deep-seated troubles between Muslims and the majority of the French people. The headscarf controversy had started in 1989 with the first cases of Muslim school girls refusing to uncover their heads. Over the next 15 years, the issue periodically waned, yet always revived again through a series of bans, rules, waivers, overturnings, and decrees. Curiously, by 2003 there were 1,200 cases of veiled girls attending state schools, but only four were expelled. Consequently, wearing headscarves could appear to be little more than a dress code infraction in just a few schools (Caldwell, 2004). Why, then, the impassioned public fuss set off by the April 2004 event? Apparently it was because the episode was a symptom of a serious underlying problem: amicable coexistence between doctrinaire Muslims and the rest of the French population proved painfully difficult when key tenets of fundamentalist Islam seemed so at odds with the belief systems of the nation's Catholics, secularists, Protestants, and Jews.

In such confrontations as the head-covering controversy, critics from the Muslim community accused the French government and the non-Islamic public of

• Discriminating against Muslims in employment opportunities.
• Failing to respect Muslims' religious beliefs and practices.

- Failing to integrate Muslims into the nation's political system, so that near the end of the twentieth century there were no influential politicians capable of speaking on Muslims' behalf. In the entire country only "300 or so" Muslims served as elected city officials, no more than a few had been elected to regional positions, and none was in parliament (Gurfinkiel, 1997).

Non-Muslims, in response to such charges,

- Accused Muslims of lawlessness that threatened public peace and safety, with this charge supported by statistics showing that Muslims comprised only 7% of the general population but 50% of the nation's prison inmates.
- Suggested that while a minority of Muslims held positions of importance in French society, "a very high proportion are in the underclass, that segment of the population that relies not so much on education and work as on welfare and predatory activities" (Gurfinkiel, 1997).
- Warned that France, over the next half-century, might well become dominantly Islamic as a result of the high growth rate of French Muslims, their aloofness from mainstream society, their increasing religious assertiveness, and the growing appeal of Islam to non-Muslims (Gurfinkiel, 1997). Such a development would result in the destruction of traditional French culture—that way of life so highly treasured over the decades by the nation's "truly French" inhabitants.

Secularism (*Laïcité*)

In Henri Astier's analysis of the headscarf episode, he wrote, "Secularism is the closest thing the French have to a state religion. It underpinned the French Revolution and has been a basic tenet of the country's progressive thought since the eighteenth century" (Astier, 2004). Because secularism has been a key player in the headscarf controversy, understanding its nature is essential to an interpretation of the event.

What historians refer to as the Age of Enlightenment or Age of Reason came to the fore in Europe during the 1700s and reached its height in the writings of such French philosophers as Jean Jacques Rousseau (1712–1778) and Voltaire (1694–1778). The French Revolution produced a bitter clash between the traditional French belief system—with its Roman Catholic foundation—and the new enlightenment. Proponents of an enlightenment worldview rejected claims that religious zealots (the pope, Catholic priests, Protestant pastors, Jewish rabbis, Muslim imams) and writers of holy books (Bible, Torah, Quran) received orders from God about what is true about the world and what behavior is proper. Instead, advocates of the Age of Reason contended that life's decisions should be made by people carefully observing events and then using those observations to decide—by means of common sense and logic—what is true about the world and how best to act.

Over the two-and-one-quarter centuries since the Revolution, relationships between churches and the French government have taken several turns that involved critical events. After the Revolution, a succession of popes in Rome sought to block French republic influence over other European states. In response, French troops on two occasions marched to Rome and abducted the pope who was currently in office. Napoleon Bonaparte in 1801 worked out a compromise (a *concordat*) with the Vatican in which the Catholic Church could continue activities in France so long as it limited its attention to spiritual concerns. That agreement lasted until 1905 when antichurch leaders in the Third French Republic declared a strict separation of church and government. Their legislation decreed that (a) no religion could be supported financially or politically by the state; (b) everyone had the right to follow a religion, but no one was obligated to do so; (c) no religious education would be permitted in schools; and (d) no new religious symbols could be displayed in public places (French secularism, 2004). Across the decades, those rules have guided relationships between the state and the Catholic Church, Protestant denominations, and Judaism. In 1937 the minister of education warned the nation's teachers to keep all religious symbols out of their schools. Since the late 1960s, diligence in applying such rules has become particularly evident (White, 2003).

In summary, the purpose of French secularism or *laïcité* has been to ensure that citizens' primary loyalty is to the state and to its principles of freedom of conscience for individuals against the intervention of the authorities, neutrality of public services and their agents, and personal religious freedom that is in harmony with the rights and obligations of French citizens (Dord, 2003). Loyalty to religious beliefs and practices is thus relegated to a position of secondary importance.

Other Belief Systems

Additional worldviews bearing on the headscarf case are those of Protestantism and Judaism. However, because there are relatively small numbers of Protestants and Jews in France, people who are dedicated to those two religions have played only a peripheral role in the headscarf controversy.

As a means of summarizing the relationship of key critical events to three belief constituencies, Figure 4.1 depicts two timelines. The timeline in the upper tier of the figure offers a highly simplified long-range sketch of key events—1700 to 2005. The timeline in the lower tier identifies several critical events of recent years—2000 to 2005.

THE CONTENDING CONSTITUENCIES

As noted earlier, the principal adversaries in the head-covering episode have been the secularist government and Muslims. A minor role has also been played by two sorts of vocal bystanders—other religious groups in France (Catholics, Protestants, Jews) and concerned groups outside the country. The following paragraphs identify significant characteristics of each of these groups and the strategies they adopted for pursuing their goals. In preparation for the

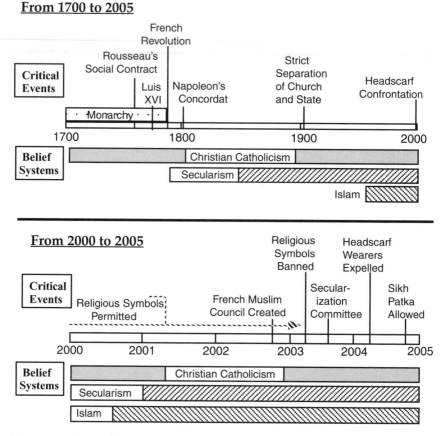

Figure 4.1 Critical events and belief systems in the French case.

discussion, it is helpful to note the reported distribution of present-day belief systems in France's population of 59 million: Catholics 65%, the nonreligious (including atheists) 20%, Muslims 7%, Protestant Christians 1%, Jews 1%, and others 6% (Sparks, 2004). It is also helpful to recognize that those gross percentages fail to reflect significant differences in the beliefs among the individuals who compose a particular group. That is, each constituency includes doctrinaire traditionalists, moderates, and individuals who are members in name but rarely in belief or practice.

The Secularist Government

The most powerful of the contending constituencies in the headscarf conflict was the French government. The government's strength was due to its position of official authority, to the nation's tradition of governmental secularism, and to the support of that tradition within the populace, regardless of the citizens' religious persuasions.

The attitude of the conservative/centrist government that held office during the head-covering case was most clearly reflected in the actions of President Jacques Chirac, a Roman Catholic whose primary allegiance was to secularism. As already mentioned, the springtime headscarf crisis in 2004 was not an unexpected event but simply an opportune occasion for exposing to public view a confrontation that had been brewing for years. Since even before the revolution of 1789, successive French governments had been successful— and sometimes rather brutal—in bringing religious bodies under state control through organizing them into official groups that the government could conveniently monitor.

In late 2002, after two decades of attempts to create a similar body for Muslims, Chirac succeeded in collecting the nation's varied Islamic communities within a newly created French Council of the Muslim Religion that was expected to cooperate willingly with the government. Like similar organizations that already existed for Catholics, Jews, and Protestants, the council would enable the government to deal systematically with issues of education, style of dress, work activities, and the administration of places of worship. The state also announced its intent to take over the training of Islamic educators (imams) through providing the necessary funding for departments of Muslim theology. Prime Minister Jean-Pierre Raffarin explained the need for the state to control imams: "It is important that the imams exercise their ministry on our territory having a full knowledge of French society, . . . [including] the laws of secularism" (White, 2003).

The formation of the council helped set the stage for the government's next step toward assuming control over Muslims' activities. In February 2003, the French parliament approved (494 for, 36 against, 31 abstentions) a law banning "all obvious religious symbols" from schools. Forbidden symbols included an Islamic veil (head scarf, bandanna, beret), a Jewish skullcap, a large Christian cross, a Sikh turban, or excessive hairiness that "immediately makes known a person's [Sikh's] religious faith" (White, 2003). In Cirac's support of the law, he said, "We cannot allow people to shelter behind a deviant idea of religious liberty in order to defy the laws of the republic or to threaten fundamental principles of a modern society such as sex equality and the dignity of woman" (French schoolgirl expelled, 2003).

The secularity law had been drafted in response to an official 2003 report warning about the danger of society breaking apart into racial and faith-based groups. The report recommended the removal of religious symbols from classrooms as well as steps to hasten integration of the growing North African minority. The law did, however, give individual schools leeway in deciding which symbols might be acceptable. Strong agreement within the French government over the religious symbols ban is suggested by the fact that in the parliamentary vote on the ban, 88% of the lawmakers were in favor of the ban and only 6% against it (another 6% abstained). The late-February 2004 headscarf event was set off in a school whose personnel decided that girls wearing a head covering were in violation of the new legislation.

Back in July 2003, the government had taken a further step toward gaining control of religious bodies by Chirac's announcing the formation of a Secularization Commission, affirming that secularism was a duty: "There are no laws in France higher than the laws of the republic" (White, 2003).

Pinto (2004) has suggested that the support of the new religious symbols law by many Catholics, Protestants, Jews, and French Muslims reflected most citizens' belief that the legislation was "the only possible response to a long and tormented French political past, rife with religious tragedy, a story in which Islam is simply the latest arrival." And the importance of keeping schools free from any hint of religion has been explained by Abdussalam (2003) as French secularists' conviction that the public school is "the voice of the nation and the place of total justice and goodness," which gives the school the right to "impose its values and visions that are supposed to be the general values of the society."

In the headscarf controversy, the elected officials in the Cirac-led government enjoyed the greatest formal authority of any constituency involved in the case. The officials also commanded the most resources (public funds, the right to pass laws, access to the public press). As experienced politicians, they likely had the most leadership experience.

In rationalizing their ban, government officials could turn to the formal statement of ideals for French society—the nation's constitution that promised liberty for all citizens in a secular, democratic, social republic. The constitution envisioned a society that respected all belief systems and ensured the equality of all citizens before the law, "without distinction as to origin, race, or religion." The government's decision to forbid religious symbols in state schools could thus be defended as a proper implementation of the "without distinction" tenet. But, as some critics of the ban suggested, allowing all pupils to display symbols of their religious affiliation in school would also fulfill the "without distinction" requirement.

Although the religious symbols ban had been overwhelmingly endorsed by members of parliament, there remained a vexing question about whether such a regulation was the wisest way to deal with ethnic and religious groups' practices in an increasingly multicultural nation, particularly in the midst of France's efforts to fit amicably into an expanding multicultural European Union.

Muslims in France

Analysts classify France's Muslims in several ways. One way is to divide Muslims by citizenship, with half of them being French citizens and half not. Another way is by generation—an older generation and a younger one. Older Muslims are apt to have assimilated themselves into French life and wish to get along amiably with the rest of the population, obeying the country's laws without open complaint. Younger Muslims—and particularly immigrants of recent years—have been prone to resent their being treated as undesirable inferiors, with that resentment expressed in word and deed. Young, antisecular, radical Muslims speak much louder than older and more moderate members of the Islamic community. Prominent among radical activists have been ones apparently guided by, and perhaps financed by, fundamentalist Muslim organizations in the Middle East. A third way to classify Muslims is by how faithfully they adhere to Islamic doctrine. Studies by the National Center for Scientific Research in Paris suggest that less than 13% of France's Muslims regularly engage in daily prayers, attend services at a mosque, and abide by other dictates of the faith. However, nearly all of the nation's Muslims appear to consider Islam part of their personal identity (Taheri, 2003).

French Muslims' reaction to the headscarf ban reflected this complex, heterogeneous nature of the nation's Islamic populace. Older, more assimilated members of the Islamic community accepted the ban without objecting, seeing such acceptance as reasonable, or at least as judicious. Younger militant Muslims defied the ban by urging girls to cover their heads, by accusing the government of prejudicial treatment of Muslims, and by promising scarf wearers legal aid in defending their religious rights.

Prior to the passage of the secularity law, schools could cater to Muslim students' beliefs by allowing the creation of student religious committees, sex segregation in gym classes, prayer breaks during the baccalaureate exams at the end of high school, the exclusion of pork in school cafterias, and students' absenting themselves from classes on human reproduction. But under the new law, such provisions would be inadmissible (Adelore, 2004). The success of the government's ban in bringing students into line was reflected in a report by Minister of Education Francois Fillon that only 240 schoolgirls in all of France wore headscarves at the opening of the 2004 school year compared to over 1,200 in 2003 (Ganley, 2004).

As a source of political power, the number of Muslims in recent decades had increased rapidly, as had such resources as funds and political guidance from the Middle East that strengthened the leadership role of aggressive militants from the younger generation. Thus, in the early twenty-first century, Islamic forces in France wielded more power over public policy than they had at any time in the past.

In summary, the response of French Muslims to the no-religious-symbols legislation was mixed, reflecting the variegated composition of the country's Islamic community. Many accepted secularism in the schools as realistic. Others resented restrictions on students' displays of their religious beliefs. Despite the highly vocal complaints of Muslim activists, the secular government's decision prevailed, so the new law was implemented.

Other Religious Denominations

As indicated earlier, the politically noteworthy non-Muslim religions in France are Catholicism, Protestantism, and Judaism. A further faith of significance for the no-religious-symbols case has been Sikhism, because of the turban that Sikh males are required to wear.

The resources (money, influence over mass communication media) that the Catholic Church could bring to bear on decisions about religion in public schools had diminished over the years as the number of devout followers declined. Although the authority of the Catholic priesthood over matters within the church remained strong, churchmen had no official power over institutions outside the church, including the public schools.

The lingering influence of Catholic tradition in school policies was perhaps the most important factor in conserving elements of religion in public schools. Since early times, religious symbols (Christian crosses, stars, paintings of biblical scenes) and observances (time off for Christian holidays, celebrations during Christmas and Easter seasons) had been common in state schools. As long as the general population consisted almost exclusively of dedicated Catholics, those religious trappings posed no problem, despite the secular nature of the government. However, the arrival of growing numbers of Muslims set off fears within the French population that their traditional way of life was threatened. Muslim girls' head coverings were increasingly viewed as a symbol of that threat. However, forbidding headscarves at school while allowing Christian crosses and Jewish skullcaps would violate the equal rights principle in the French constitution. Hence, parliament was obliged to bar students of every faith from any ostentatious display of their religious affiliation. In effect, the motivation to conserve traditional practices (allowing Christian symbols) came from within French society, whereas the pressure to change those practices came from outside (Muslim immigration).

France's Catholics have been a diverse collection of adherents. For example, even though two-thirds of French people are identified as Catholics, surveys suggest that less than 10% go to mass regularly and only 6% go to confession at least once a year (The spirit yes, 1993). In December 2003, the French newspaper *Le Figaro* reported that 45% of the people who describe themselves as Catholics could not explain what event Easter celebrates (Caldwell, 2004). The decline in religious fervor among Catholics had apparently accelerated since the 1960s. In 2001, the French scholar Yves Lambert observed that

many practicing Catholics stopped going to church and some lost their religion. In turn, they passed on their lack of belief to their children. Given that only half of children with church-going parents retain their religion, it's easy to see why secularization advances so rapidly. (Lambert in White, 2003)

Thus, at the time of the headscarf confrontation, Catholics did not comprise a cohesive group that held fast to religious doctrine and practices. Instead, Catholics seemed to be a collectivity that would support the government's secularization position. Nominal Protestants and Jews, who each represented only 1% of the French population, might well fit a similar pattern of diversity of belief. Consequently, it appears unlikely that the bulk of French citizens who identified themselves with Catholicism, Protestantism, and Judaism would object to the banning of religious symbols in schools. Pinto (2004) has proposed that those groups "perceived the proposed law as a badly needed return to order after a decade when Islam had become in their eyes, a far too privileged interlocutor of the French state, even though Muslims were in the front line of [the populace's] social and political prejudice."

However, some vocal Christian and Jewish church leaders objected to the secularity law. They claimed that preventing students from wearing religious symbols would "exacerbate emotions" and damage the integration of students in schools (French clerics, 2003).

One unintended effect of the anti-religious-symbols law was that its implementation exposed remaining influences of Catholicism in the schools. For instance, even though a 1905 law had separated church and state, public schools had been allowed to keep chaplains, most of them Catholics who taught catechism classes, so long as they were not paid by the state. In 1960 a law even defined a process for creating new chaplain posts and permitted existing ones to continue. But now, under the 2004 secularist legislation, catechists—garbed in religious cassocks—should no longer be acceptable (Catholic chaplains, 2004). Furthermore, as school officials started to implement the no-symbols law early in the 2004 school year, they hoped to resolve all problems before the school break for the Catholic All Saints' Day. Muslims then asked why such a Catholic school holiday was provided if there was strict separation of state and religion (Decide turban issue, 2004). Consequently, the headscarf episode revived dormant concerns about what true separation of church and state meant for public schools.

The estimated 5,000–7,000 Sikhs in France posed a particular problem for the government. Sikh males who are true to their faith are obliged to wear a turban to cover their uncut hair. Unlike Muslim girls who insisted that Islam requires them to wear head coverings, Sikhs argued that their turbans and headcloths were simply intended to cover their hair that they refused to cut for religious reasons. Consequently, if they failed to cover their heads, their uncut hair would itself be a religious sign in violation of the new law. But, as the law was first implemented, the Sikhs' reasoning failed to yield an exception. Turbans were still forbidden, as Education Minister Fillon announced that the "very small Sikh community causes us no problems, but the law applies to everyone" (Decide turban issue, 2004).

The Nonreligious Constituency

Most of France's nonreligious inhabitants (20%) would probably endorse the religious symbols ban on the grounds that public schools should not promote religion.

Outsiders

People outside of France who sought to influence the French government's headscarf decision included foreign Muslims and non-Muslim commentators.

Supporting the Ban | Opposing the Ban

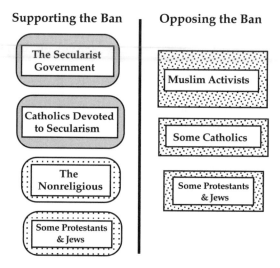

Figure 4.2 Principal constituencies in the head-scarf case.

In early 2004, nearly 10,000 Muslim women marched through Paris in protest against the headscarf ban, with that demonstration repeated in such places as Cairo, Beirut, London, Baghdad, India's Kashmir region, Stockholm, Oslo, Jordan, and Kuwait (Ganley, 2004). Among the foreign commentators who chided the French for banning headwear was a high official in the United States government. In addition, many journalists in other countries suggested that the French government was helping the Islamic terrorists by convincing Muslim youths that their adopted homeland—France—would not allow them to follow the rules of their faith. However, none of the criticism from abroad altered the ban that apparently had been welcomed by the majority of French citizens. In effect, personal freedom to follow one's own choices, though important in France, came second to preserving the strict neutrality of the state (French Secularism, 2004).

Summary

As a way of summarizing the lineup of belief constituencies in the headscarf case, Figure 4.2 offers a graphic estimate of the opposing constituencies that participated in the debate.

RESOLVING THE CONTROVERSY

The matter of settling the headscarf issue can usefully be divided into *immediate* and *ultimate* solutions. An immediate solution is a current settlement of the conflict. An ultimate solution is a permanent—or at least a long-term—settlement that serves to keep the controversy from again becoming a public issue.

The French government's immediate solution was to introduce and implement the no-religious-symbols law. However, quite clearly, the angry dissatisfaction voiced by Muslims in France and abroad—and by Sikhs—indicated that the law would not likely settle the matter in the long term.

The attempts of the French government to solve the problem permanently included the establishment of a new type of school. In the midst of the headscarf debate, the government in September 2003 had opened a private, state-funded Muslim secondary school, the first of its kind for Muslims, where head coverings would be allowed. This new Lycée Averroés—similar to private schools that Catholics, Jews, and Protestants had operated for years—began with eight boys and six girls who would follow the country's national curriculum but who could also elect courses in Arabic language and Islamic culture. However, concerns were expressed by both Muslims and non-Muslims about how well that type of school might achieve its goal of assimilating Muslims into the French society. Some observers feared that such an arrangement might isolate and radicalize Muslim students (Blignaut, 2003).

An adjustment in applying the law was also made in late 2004 by the government's still banning the Sikh turban but allowing Sikh schoolboys to substitute a discreet sash—*patka*—to control their unshorn hair. Or, as an alternative, Sikhs could enroll in private schools not governed by the religious-symbols law (Nath, 2004).

In speculating about the long-term influence of the secularity law, Pinto observed that

it is too early to tell whether these secular forces in French society are right or wrong. With time, so-called backward, nonmulticultural France could be in the forefront of a new intellectual current in Europe that will stress a shared future over any exaggerated ethnic and religious identity. (Pinto, 2004)

CHAPTER 5

Japan

The Japanese case described in Chapter 1 involved a confrontation between Tokyo government officials and secondary school teachers who refused to stand and sing the country's national anthem. In the following pages, the interpretation of the case begins with (a) a look into the past to identify events that significantly affected the nature of the recent confrontation, and then continues with (b) a description of the principal adversaries in the case and (c) an estimate of how the issues underlying the conflict might be resolved.

HISTORICAL ROOTS

Twice during the past two centuries, radical changes have been wrought in the Japanese system of governance and in key features of Japanese society. The relevance of those critical events for the government-versus-teachers confrontation is reflected in the answer to a fourfold question.

What were the characteristics of three successive historical eras in terms of (a) the nation's system of governance and the goals of the leaders, (b) forces that precipitated the change from one era to another, (c) the nature of schooling, and (d) the nation's dominant religion—especially, the role of religion in schools?

Three Successive Forms of Governance

Over the first half of the nineteenth century, Japan was still ruled under the Tokugawa or Edo regime that had been in power since 1603. The regime featured a feudal system of governance that located the control of power and property in a warrior class (*samurai*) that comprised 6% of the population. The remaining 94% of the people were commoners who filled descending social class strata as farmers, artisans, and traders. The nation's emperor continued to be revered as in the past, but he served as nothing more than a figurehead without political power. Actual control throughout the Tokugawa era was wielded by the nation's preeminent military leader, the *shogun*, and his fief lords and their troops.

The Tokugawa tradition was marked by a strict international political isolationism imposed by a succession of shoguns who feared the intrusion of Western culture, and particularly feared the Catholicism introduced into China by Portuguese and Spanish missionaries. Throughout the reign of the shoguns, the European and North American powers that were bent on extending their trade and colonial control would periodically seek to penetrate the barriers of Japanese isolationism. This endeavor finally succeeded in the mid-1800s, chiefly through a show of naval force by American Commodore Matthew Perry in 1853–1854, eventuating in 1858 in a commercial treaty that opened trade between Japan and the United States. During this same period, skirmishes between Japanese naval forces and a fleet of British, Dutch, and French warships forced Japan's rulers to extend entry privileges to those three nations as well as to Russia.

The ineffectiveness of the last of the Tokugawa shogunates in repulsing the incursions of Western foreigners precipitated a political crisis in the 1860s, a critical event that brought an end to the Tokugawa tradition and launched the Meiji tradition that would last until 1945 with the close of World War II.

The new leaders that came to the fore in the Meiji era adopted a radically different approach to governance and foreign relations than the shoguns had followed. The period was inaugurated with the restoration of Emperor Mutsuhito in 1868 as the head of state. Under the new Meiji constitution, the emperor held sovereign power, a political and military control that was theoretically close to absolute. However, the real power was wielded by generals and admirals. Japan now aggressively sought aid from the West to renovate the nation's military establishment and its commercial and industrial practices. In contrast to the Tokugawa goal of rejecting European and American influences, the Meiji copied the methods that had made Western nations so strong—methods that might transform Japan into a world-class military and economic empire-builder. That strategy proved remarkably successful. In 1894 a brief war between Japan and China over trade and political rights in Korea ended in defeat for China and in the transfer of Formosa (Taiwan), the Pescadores Islands, and the Liaotung Peninsula to Japanese control. A decade later a disagreement with Russia over rights in Manchuria precipitated the Russo-Japanese war, won by Japan. Russia was forced to evacuate Manchuria, turn over other territories to Japan, and recognize Japan's sphere of influence in Korea, a country Japan would adopt as a colony in 1910. Following World War I, Germany's interests in China and the Pacific Islands were transferred to Japan. By 1937, open warfare had broken out between Japan and China and continued until the end of World War II, driving Chinese forces into the back country so as to leave Japan in somewhat uneasy control of China's coastal provinces. This accelerating parade of military triumphs emboldened

Japanese rulers in 1941 and 1942 to take on the United States, Britain, France, and the Netherlands as enemies. Japanese planes attacked American naval ships in Hawaii, and Japanese armies captured European colonies in Southeast Asia, including French Indochina (Cambodia, Laos, Vietnam), British holdings in Burma and the Malay Peninsula, the Dutch East Indies (Indonesia), and the Philippines.

By the early 1940s, the aim of the Meiji leadership had, indeed, been fulfilled. The citizens of Japan could be proud of their ever-expanding empire. These were days of honor and glory, with Japan's military victories proving the preeminence of the nation and its people.

But whatever euphoria Meiji rulers and the populace enjoyed would end in August 1945 after atomic bombs destroyed the cities of Nagasaki and Hiroshima, and Japanese military leaders surrendered to United States military officers. This event introduced the third major era of the past two centuries—that of present-day Japan, 1945–2005.

Under the direction of the Americans who would supervise the reconstruction of Japan, a new constitution was formulated in 1946. The document began with the following commitment, quite the opposite in spirit from the constitution of Meiji times.

We, the Japanese people, desire peace for all time and are deeply conscious of the high ideals controlling human relationships, and we have determined to preserve our security and existence, trusting in the justice and faith of the peace-loving peoples of the world. We desire to occupy an honored place in an international society striving for the preservation of peace, and the banishment of tyranny and slavery, oppression, and intolerance for all time from the earth. We recognize that all peoples of the world have the right to live in peace, free from fear and want. (Constitution of Japan, 1946)

The American administrators forbid the Japanese to have an army, navy, or air force, so that the nation's protection from attack would henceforth depend on American military units stationed in the country, a condition that continued into the twenty-first century. Being prevented from maintaining fighting units was clearly humiliating to the Japanese, in view of their many military triumphs of the previous half-century. They were being told that they could not be trusted and thus required foreign supervision. The humiliation was partially compensated for by the government being freed of the great expense of supporting an army, navy, and air force. Thus, over the 60 years following 1945, a new Japanese democratic form of government, coupled with the ingenuity and hard work of the populace, transformed the nation into an internationally envied economic giant.

In summary, during the period 1800–1945, Japan moved from an isolated existence under the shoguns into the Meiji 78-year period with the intent to create a world-class empire that would be the pride of the people—respected, envied, and feared by other nations. But the days of glory ended with the Japanese armed forces' surrender in 1945 and the mortifying experience of being forced to admit blame for a militaristic past, to adopt a foreign form of government, and to lose the right to defend their own country against attack.

It is useful to note that there had been two sources responsible for the major change in governance in the 1860s—an external force (Western nations' military and commercial intrusions) and an internal force (Meiji leaders who fashioned the society that would produce a vast empire of which the Japanese people could be proud). The 1945 change, in contrast, was effected entirely by external intervention, that of U.S. military forces and their allies who dismantled the empire, leaving the Japanese in control of no more territory than their original islands.

Schooling

Each of the three eras—Tokugawa, Meiji, and present-day—provided distinctively different educational provisions.

The Tokugawa period witnessed the development of two types of schools—those for the samurai ruling class and those for commoners. In more than 270 samurai schools, boys were taught calligraphy, elementary arithmetic, some Chinese and Japanese history, self-discipline, and martial arts. In tens of thousands of primary schools for commoners, boys learned reading, writing, calculating with the abacus, moral precepts for common people, and suggestions for daily conversation (Japan's modern education system, 1980, pp. 4–8).

After 1860, educational reform initiated by the Meiji regime was guided by the Government Order on Education, developed by a commission well versed in British, French, German, and U.S. American schooling practices. The Order charted a future course for education that departed radically from the socially stratified schools of Tokugawa times. The new system would consist of three tiers of schools—elementary, middle, and higher—under the direction of a Ministry of Education. Girls would receive schooling opportunities equal to those for boys, and children of all social classes would attend the same institutions, a provision that promoted the social equality which continues to mark Japanese society in modern times. Thus, the new Meiji educational policies and curricula reflected a combination of (a) innovations from Western nations and (b) continued dedication to Japanese moral precepts, pride in the country's heritage, glorification of Japanese culture, and devotion to the emperor (Cummings, 1980).

The Meiji education system was enthusiastically embraced by the people so that enrollment among school-age children rose from 46% in 1886 to 64% by 1896, then increased to 97% in 1906 and 99% in 1916. Since then it has continued at the 99% level or above (Japan's modern education system, 1980, pp. 464–465). The curricula emphasized moral education, Japanese language and history, mathematics, science, physical fitness, and—for boys—vocational skills and military drill. Drawing, singing, and handicrafts were included in the primary schools' offerings.

In sum, the Meiji education system produced the highly literate, well-trained population essential for the regime's empire-building—a population well pre-pared in both vocational skills and dedication to the Meiji leaders and their goals. Particularly during the 1920s and 1930s, the school system was de-signed to promote the government's plan of military preparedness and national supremacy (Thomas, 1983).

Following World War II, the U.S. occupation government did not require major changes in the basic schooling structure or in most of the subject matter taught, because Japanese education already operated under an organizational pattern adopted decades earlier from the West. Therefore, mandatory changes focused primarily on moral education, civics, military drill, and interpretations of twentieth-century history that had characterized schooling during the Meiji era. Military drill was eliminated and history books were rewritten to corre-spond more closely to views held by the U.S. occupation government. Moral studies stressed the occupation forces' conception of a democratic society. That conception included a form of Western-liberal individualism that dif-fered from the traditional Japanese concern for the good of the group over the good of the individual. Whereas the Meiji constitution had emphasized the need for citizens to place the emperor and the nation's welfare above self-interest, the 1946 constitution, as required by the occupation government, stressed individuals' rights.

All of the people shall be respected as individuals. Their right to life, liberty, and the pursuit of happiness shall, to the extent that it does not interfere with the public wel-fare, be the supreme consideration in legislation and in other governmental affairs. All of the people are equal under the law and there shall be no discrimination in political, economic, or social relations because of race, creed, sex, social status, or family origin. Freedom of thought and conscience shall not be violated. Freedom of religion is guaranteed to all. No religious organization shall receive any privileges from the State, nor exercise any political authority. No person shall be compelled to take part in any religious acts, celebration, rite, or practice. The State and its organs shall refrain from religious education or any other religious activity. (Constitution of Japan, 1946)

Consequently, the postwar era significantly altered the role of religion in Japanese schools.

The Shinto Religion

Shinto or Shintoism (*The Divine Way* or *The Way of the Gods*) is an ancient indigenous belief system that assumed four principal forms over the centuries: (a) *imperial Shinto*, practiced in the family of the Japanese emperor; (b) *shrine Shinto*, consisting of festivals and of pilgrims visiting shrines to obtain blessings at key junctures of life (birth, marriage); (c) *folk Shinto*, an amalgam of super-stitious, magico-religious rites practiced by the common people; and (d) *basic Shinto*, a stratum of beliefs undergirding not only the other three types but all of Japanese society, including the portion of the population that were officially Buddhist (Agency for Cultural Affairs, 1972, p. 32).

By the early twenty-first century, the religious affiliation of Japan's 128 million people was as follows: Shinto 54%, Buddhist 40%, Christian 1%, and other types 5% (Sparks, 2004).

Unlike most major religions, Shinto has no revered holy book and no specific commandments to be obeyed. However, like other faiths, Shinto does recognize the existence of invisible spirits, known as *kami*, whose behavior offers some guidance about how people should conduct their lives. Whereas most kami are benevolent and foster people's welfare, a minority are malevolent, responsible for misfortune in individuals' lives and for such widespread disasters as drought, earthquake, famine, and flood. The common traits shared by all kami are not those of kindness or compassion but, rather, power and cleverness, which humans are wise to respect, especially in the malevolent kami. The majority of kami—the benevolent ones—also hold in common such virtues as kindness, compassion, faithfulness, and generosity (Spae, 1972).

Shinto teaches a situational or conditional moral philosophy that eschews such commandments as "don't cheat, don't lie, don't kill" and, instead, judges the propriety of behavior on the ultimate result of actions rather than on the virtue of the actions themselves. Hence, deceit, stealing, and killing are proper if they lead to desirable ends. Shinto's ethic is one of intention, emphasizing that one's acts should arise from noble intent (Ross, 1965, p. 109). This situational feature of Shinto fitted nicely into the Meiji regime's plans, since any method that worked could be used to achieve the nation's goals.

Shinto is also an ethnically restricted religion, binding the Japanese together in opposition to people of other racial origins, on the grounds that all Japanese trace their ancestry back to the earliest ancient deities—the original kami—from which every Japanese has descended. In effect, all Japanese are members of a single, extended family. Therefore, from the Meijis' perspective, it was proper for the Japanese—self-recognized as superior—to perform as a unit in controlling and guiding foreign peoples.

Unlike many religions, Shinto does not focus on people preparing for a life after death where they will find peace and happiness. Instead, Shinto is concerned with the here and now. Life on earth is seen as good, whereas death is seen as evil—a dreaded curse (Ono, 1962, p. 108). Whatever rewards people are to earn must be found in the present and not in a life hereafter.

With this sketch of Shinto now in hand, we are prepared to consider (a) the form that Shinto assumed over successive political eras and (b) changes in the place assigned to Shinto in the schools.

After the mid-nineteenth century, with the rise to power of the Meijis, a new constitution identified the Japanese emperor as "sacred and inviolable," thereby officially endorsing the millennium-old legendary belief that the emperor was a god. The Meiji government, bent on turning Japan into a world political power, fused the several types of Shinto into a state system that would form the philosophical core of the society. State Shinto not only portrayed the emperor as divine, but also cast the Japanese as people par excellence, destined to rule territories beyond their shores. To disseminate that belief among the young, State Shinto was taught in schools as part of history and moral education. Thus, over the first four decades of the twentieth century, State Shinto helped generate popular support for the Japanese military conquest of Korea, Taiwan, Manchuria, Pacific Islands, much of China, the Philippines, and Southeast Asia. But when conquest was halted in late 1945, Emperor Hirohito was compelled by the U.S. military commanders to renounce the claim that he was divine. The new 1946 constitution, at the insistence of the U.S. occupation government, guaranteed religious freedom, outlawed any form of state religion, required strict separation of governmental and religious functions, and forbid any religious instruction in public schools.

So, with the foregoing brief historical review as background, we are now ready to speculate about significant characteristics of the adversaries who participated in the recent conflict over the requirement that students and teachers sing the Japanese national anthem in Tokyo's schools.

THE CONTENDING CONSTITUENCIES

The most obvious adversaries in the Tokyo case were (a) the city's school board and (b) a collection of more than 200 teachers who refused to stand and sing Japan's official national anthem at high-school graduation ceremonies, with those teachers supported by the teachers union. However, those two groups were only the immediate representatives of two far larger behind-the-scenes constituencies. The first consisted of people who yearned for the spirit of the Meiji era and the opportunity for the nation to conduct its own affairs free from monitoring by foreigners. These pronationalism patriots endorsed the board of education's actions. The second constituency, represented in the Tokyo incident by the recalcitrant teachers, consisted of people who embraced the individualism and freedom-of-choice expressed in the 1946 constitution and who regretted the nation's military aggression during the Meiji period.

In addition to the pair of actively participating adversaries in the anthem-and-flag confrontation was a silent group of Japanese—perhaps quite large in number—who were undecided about the desirability of requiring teachers and students to sing the anthem and honor the flag. They served as onlookers, a somewhat puzzled audience witnessing the drama being played out between government officials and the resistant teachers and some of the students.

The following paragraphs identify characteristics of the two main constituencies that played an active role in the conflict.

The Nationalism Constituency

Over the 60-year period between 1945 and 2005, signals of a Japanese nationalism reminiscent of the Meiji era appeared with increasing frequency and intensity. The April 2004 confrontation between Tokyo school officials and teachers was only one of a widening range of incidents that reflected a resurgent nationalist spirit.

Consider, for example, the significance of the 1999 adoption of the *Kimigayo* as the national anthem and the *Hinomaru* as the nation's flag. The words of the Kimigayo (The Emperor's Reign) are from a tenth-century 31-syllable poem, translated into English as

May the reign of the Emperor continue for a thousand, nay, eight thousand generations and for the eternity that it takes for small pebbles to grow into a great rock and become covered with moss. (Japanese National Anthem, 2004)

The poem was set to music in 1880 by an imperial court musician, Hiromori Hayashi, and then adopted as the national anthem for the Meiji regime in 1888. During that same period, the Hinomaru—a red disk on a white background—became the nation's official flag. The disk represented the sun, which in Shinto lore symbolized the supreme kami-goddess and Ruler of Heaven—*Amaterasu-o-mi-kami* (Kendall, 2004).

The government in 1999 recommended the singing of the anthem at school ceremonies and the display of the flag at all schools. However, that regulation was often loosely implemented. Students or teachers who disagreed with the ostensible "thought control" that the requirement represented were allowed to absent themselves from such ceremonies. However, as the years advanced, boards of education—and their monitors who were often referred to as "religious police"—moved to strictly enforce the rule. Resistance to the anthem-and-flag law was particularly stiff in Tokyo, where 90% of the schools in 1999 displayed the flag but only 10% of the schools sang the anthem. Thus, in 2004 the board of education moved to force compliance by requiring each high school to issue a seating chart before graduation day, with the chart showing each teacher's chair, thereby making it easy for the board's monitors to identify by name any teachers who failed to stand and sing (The flag and the anthem, 2004).

Stern methods were also adopted in other school districts. Patriotism supervisors from the board of education in the southern Japanese city of Kurume visited 40 elementary and junior high schools to judge the degree to which students and teachers sang the Kimigayo with gusto. The monitors rated participation as *quiet, medium,* or *loud.* Six schools failed to meet the standard (Kendall, 2004).

In addition to the anthem and flag incidents, a growing list of other events signaled a rising nationalism that cast a shadow of State Shinto over the schools. A controversial middle-school history book published in 2001 by the ultra-conservative Japanese Society for History Textbook Reform (Tsukurukai) was sharply censured by the Chinese and Korean governments for what they considered serious misrepresentations of Japanese soldiers' behavior in those nations before and during World War II. Despite criticisms of the book, the

Tokyo school board in 2004 adopted the text for two dozen of the city's several hundred public schools (China steps up criticism, 2004). In 2005, a revised version of the textbook that cast Japanese military conquests in an even more admirable light than had the earlier edition was endorsed by Japan's ministry of education, despite angry protests from the Chinese, South Korean, and North Korean governments. Furthermore, in 2005 the ministry adopted other texts for the 2006 school year that

were toned down in additional ways. The term "comfort women," a euphemism for wartime sex slaves, mostly from Korea, China, and the Philippines, disappeared from all eight junior high history textbooks approved by the national government. . . . One book maintained a vague reference to wartime comfort stations for Japanese soldiers. Up to 2001, however, all of them contained specific references to the practice of forced sexual slavery. . . . The Japanese Society for History Textbook Reform, which drafted the most controversial of the new textbooks, hailed the approvals as being in step with current thinking in Japan. Some schoolbook publishers and government officials have argued that it is time to remove "self-deprecating" historical references. (Faiola, 2005)

The 2001 version of the textbook had been adopted by less than 1% of school districts nationwide, but Tsukurukai and its supporters hoped to raise that number to 10% with the revised edition. In late 2005, the board of education for the city of Otawara became the first municipal government to adopt the latest edition of the disputed textbook (Tokyo school board, 2005).

A further example of a nationalist trend appeared in the Japanese-style comic book *Manga*, read by both children and adults. Highly popular editions of *Manga* in recent years dealt with Meiji military exploits on the Asian mainland. "Most notable among these [editions] is the popular 'On War' by Yoshinori Kobayashi, which paints the Japanese Army as liberator rather than occupier (sentiments publicly shared by [Tokyo's] Governor Ishihara) and whitewashes or ignores many of the wartime atrocities committed in China and on the Korean peninsula" (Weston, 2004).

In the confrontation between the Tokyo government and the refractory teachers, what factors contributed to the power of the faction led by the Tokyo government? That faction appeared to draw its strength from the

- Tokyo officials' superior position to that of the teachers in the school system's authority and leadership hierarchy,
- 1999 official adoption of the national anthem and flag,
- government's top-level leaders' unyielding position in the Kimigayo incident,
- older generation's nostalgia, with many people still revering the emperor as divine and recalling with pride the days of Japan as a world-class military power, and
- humiliation of the nation's leaders having been forced by the American military to accept the 1946 constitution.

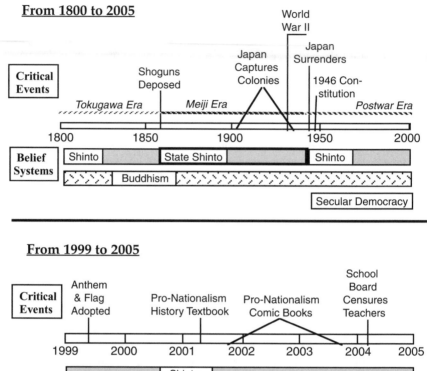

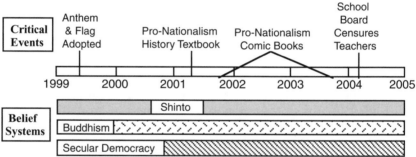

Figure 5.1 Critical events and belief systems in the Japanese case.

To support its cause, the Tokyo government could draw on ages-old Japanese tradition—including earlier Japanese constitutions—to buttress its efforts to promote a revived Japanese nationalism as the proper direction in which the nation should be headed. The Japanese have a long history of respect for authority—for official power—as demonstrated in the population's obedient support of the Meiji regime. That tradition might be expected to work in favor of the government's actions in the Kimigayo dispute.

The proportion of the Japanese population that would endorse the Tokyo government's position is unknown. In modern times, public-opinion polling serves as a popular means of discovering people's beliefs about controversial issues. However, in the national anthem conflict, the ministry of education quashed any proposals that an opinion survey be conducted.

The historical setting of the Japanese controversy is summarized in Figure 5.1 as a pair of timelines. The timeline on the upper tier identifies a few critical events and belief systems from the year 1800 to 2005. The timeline on the lower tier shows four influential events during the 1999–2005 period.

The Individualism Constituency

The teachers and students who refused to stand and sing the Kimigayo were not alone in resisting the Tokyo government's order to honor the anthem. Teachers' and students' right to "follow their conscience" by not venerating symbols of Meiji militarism was openly supported by organizations as diverse as the Japanese Communist Party, evangelical Christians, and the Buraku Liberation League (a 200,000-member alliance of individuals whose ancestors during the sixteenth and seventeenth centuries had been officially relegated to the bottom of the Tokugawa social class system and whose descendents were treated in a prejudicial manner up to the present day). The supporters also included citizens—chiefly of the younger generation—who placed high value on the individual rights emphasis of the 1946 constitution. A group of the reprimanded teachers claimed that the board of education's action was "drawing heavy, severe criticism from parents, students, and sensible citizens, as well as teachers" (Statement on the second appeal, 2004).

The tenor of the teachers' defense of their behavior is suggested by the following passage from a statement by 42 of the reprimanded teachers who filed appeals protesting their treatment by the Tokyo board of education.

[On graduation day] the education board sent several inspectors to each school and forced us to stand up and sing Kimigayo . . . by intimidation. The ceremony celebrating students' graduation was transformed into an event which forced students, their parents, and teachers to stand up and sing Kimigayo while facing the national flag hoisted at the center stage. It is not exaggerating to say, nowadays, that schools have been changed into "prisons" without the freedom of education and conscience guaranteed by Article 19 of the [1946] Japanese Constitution. (Statement on the second appeal, 2004)

So, the constitution imposed after World War II had been embraced by a large body of teachers and students, thereby threatening the revival of the Tokyo government's version of nationalism that smacked of Meiji times.

As for the teachers' fear of sanctions, the government had already demonstrated that it would punish students or teachers who failed to sing the anthem and honor the flag, so that such a fear was well founded. The "religious police" had ferreted out teachers and students who did not stand and join in the Kimigayo or who neglected to do so with sufficient enthusiasm, and such recalcitrants were punished. Subsequently, most of Tokyo's teachers, students, and school administrators did comply with the government edict. But the likelihood that many of them did so out of fear rather than true conviction is suggested by the fact that prior to the crackdown on teachers in 2004, the 1999 order that the Kimigayo and Hinomaru be openly honored had been very laxly applied in schools. Thus, it seemed that a substantial portion of the school population—teachers, principals, and students alike—might well have

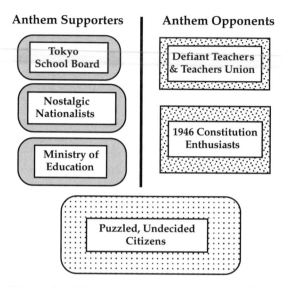

Anthem Supporters | **Anthem Opponents**

Tokyo School Board

Nostalgic Nationalists

Ministry of Education

Defiant Teachers & Teachers Union

1946 Constitution Enthusiasts

Puzzled, Undecided Citizens

Figure 5.2 Main adversaries in the national anthem controversy.

subscribed to the individualism/antimilitarism theme of the 1946 constitution but were unwilling to act on that preference if it meant they would be disciplined for doing so. Thus, the number of people who would endorse the refractory teachers' actions in spirit but not in action might have been rather large.

From what sources did the disobedient teachers and students apparently draw their strength? Three likely sources were (a) the 1946 constitution's emphasis on individuals' rights, (b) the 380,000-member teachers union opposing the requirement that teachers sing the anthem, and (b) such international documents as the United Nations Declaration of Human Rights to which Japan was a signatory.

Each side in the conflict sought popular support for its stance through pronouncements in the mass media—newspapers, radio, television, and the Internet. However, the government enjoyed greater resources than the teachers for pressing its cause by virtue of access to public funds and the ability to distribute directives through the network of the government bureaucracy.

Summary

A graphic estimate of the constituencies' positions in the anthem-and-flag conflict is shown in Figure 5.2. The Ministry of Education has been included in the diagram because its endorsement of the 2005 textbook revisions appears to be in keeping with the spirit of the anthem-and-flag ruling.

RESOLVING THE CONTROVERSY

The original controversy had occurred in March 2004. By August that year, the confrontation ostensibly had been resolved by the Tokyo Board of Education compelling the dissident teachers to attend lectures about their obligations of service and about legal consequences they could suffer. Around 200 teachers participated in the training sessions. Some had their pay cut, and several dozen others resigned from their jobs. An attempt in July by a group of teachers to get an injunction against the board's actions had been rejected by a district court; however, the judges did add a cautionary proviso: "Should an identical training program be forced repeatedly on teachers and their freedom of thought infringed, it may violate the Constitution or law" (Rebel teachers, 2004).

Although the Kimigayo issue supposedly had been laid to rest by the Tokyo board's "teacher reeducation" efforts, obviously the controversy had not been permanently settled. The ministry of education's refusal to allow the public to be polled about the anthem-and-flag issue implied that ministry officials feared a survey might reveal that their actions were not generally acceptable to the public or, at least, that the citizens were seriously split over the matter.

By 2006, it seemed likely that the nationalism revival would continue to build in the future, with the government increasingly adopting coercive methods to reinstate attitudes and practices of Meiji times. What such a movement might mean for State Shinto in the schools and for revisions of the 1946 constitution was unclear.

CHAPTER 6

England

The English case in Chapter 1 involved a confrontation between (a) government curriculum planners, who proposed a multifaith version of religious education for schools, and (b) traditionalists, who defended the Christian-faith-advocacy approach, which had been the mainstay of the schools' religious-education classes, past and present. The case was the most recent episode in an extended tale of how religious tolerance—or, more accurately, *belief system tolerance*—evolved in a nation (a) that still had an official state religion, (b) whose monarch was the titular head of that religion, and (c) whose schools were required by law to include religious education as a regular part of the curriculum. The beginnings of that tale can be traced back to the early decades of the sixteenth century.

HISTORICAL ROOTS

The following glance back through history focuses on two developments, those of religious tolerance and of religious education.

Backgrounds of Religious Tolerance

The Anglican Church (Church of England) was part of the Catholic Church network under the pope in Rome until 1536 when the English king, Henry VIII, dissolved the country's monasteries and abbeys and declared the Church of England an independent institution, headed by the English sovereign rather than the pope. That critical event marked a break with Rome that reflected the same spirit of reform expressed by Martin Luther 19 years earlier when he nailed his 95 theses to a church door in Wittenburgh, Germany. Today there is still a public perception that Henry created the Anglican Church over his anger at the pope's failure to annul Henry's marriage to his first wife, Catherine of Aragon. But historical records suggest that "Henry spent most of his reign challenging the authority of Rome, and that the divorce issue was just one of a series of acts that collectively split the English church from the Roman church" (Church history, 2004).

Before Henry divested England's Roman Catholic priests and monks of their properties and positions, there had been little tolerance in England for people who subscribed to belief systems other than Catholicism. And following the establishment of the independent Anglican Church, there was still no greater acceptance of religious diversity. Churches outside the Anglican fold were unwelcome. Nevertheless, one denomination that would flourish in the seventeenth century was the Puritan variety of Calvinism, a Protestant creation of the French-born John Calvin, whose disciples in England stripped away the ceremonial vestiges of Catholicism that had been retained by Anglicans and simplified church organizational structure. By the mid-seventeenth century, under the leadership of Oliver Cromwell, Puritans had taken control of the English government, but displayed no greater tolerance of other faiths than had the Catholics and Anglicans before them. Cromwell's troops damaged Anglican places of worship, destroyed treasured art works, and persecuted both Anglicans and Catholics.

The first signs of official religious tolerance appeared in the reign of Charles II, who assumed the position of English king after Cromwell's death. Charles ruled from 1660 until his own demise in 1685. He had personally favored Catholicism, yet recognized the strength of both Puritanism and the Anglican tradition, so he urged religious tolerance and, in particular, spoke out against the persecution of Puritans. His broad-mindedness in religious matters has been recognized as "more from political wisdom than overwhelming morality" (Charles II, 2004). But when, as head of the Anglican Church, he offered civil liberties to Roman Catholics by appointing some to public office, Parliament responded with the Test Act that prohibited Catholics from holding government posts. Thus, there was religious tolerance in theory, but rarely in practice.

By the eighteenth century—despite the dominance of the reinstated Anglican Church which meant that no one who was not an Anglican could hold public office—an increasing variety of religious faiths appeared in England. In 1733, when the French philosopher and social critic Voltaire (1694–1778) was living in London, he wrote that England was "a country of sects"—Catholics, Jews, Presbyterians, Lutherans, Baptists, Methodists, Quakers, and more. He noted that the Anglican clergy were prone to generate among their followers "as much holy zeal against nonconformists as possible" (McElroy, 1998). However, he also observed that in the world of business, the English showed a remarkable acceptance of each other's religious beliefs. Voltaire attributed this tolerance in everyday life to Britishers' overriding interest in commerce—their conviction that religion should not get in the way of financial gain.

Go into the Exchange in London, that place more venerable than many a court, and you will see representatives of all the nations assembled there for the profit of mankind. There the Jew, the Mahometan, and the Christian deal with one another as if they were of the same religion, and reserve the name of infidel for those who go bankrupt. (Voltaire in McElroy, 1998)

During the nineteenth century, Britain's colonial empire reached its height as the nation's closely linked military and commercial forces brought greater numbers of the world's territories under British control. The interaction between Britain and the colonies sent the English, Scotch, Irish, and Welsh to service overseas and brought peoples from the far-off colonies to the British Isles for education, business, visiting, and work opportunities. British scholars translated Asian religious works into English, resulting in such volumes as Max Muller's *Studies in Buddhism* (reprinted 1999) and Buhler's Hindu *Laws of Manu* (1886) becoming available to English readers. Thus, religious diversity in England grew, as did the population's opportunity to learn of beliefs other than their own. Such events increased the social pressure to become tolerant of religions other than the official Anglican Church of England. Those trends continued through the first four decades of the twentieth century.

World War II would be the critical event that spelled the end of the British colonial empire in its prewar form. Over the decades after the war, nearly all colonized territories would be granted their political independence. Thereafter, the future relationship between England and former colonies would be that of equals within a commonwealth. Because members of the commonwealth retained special rights to settle in England, during the half-century following World War II hosts of immigrants from former colonies in Asia, Africa, and the Caribbean came to live in the British Isles, markedly increasing the number of people practicing religions other than the Anglican faith or other Christian callings.

In parallel with the arrival of more people from non-English religious traditions, the Christian population declined rather rapidly—from 38.6 million in 1990 to about 37.8 million in 2000, while the general population increased from 56.9 million to 59.0 million (Key statistics, 2004). According to the 2001 census, slightly more than three-quarters of the nation's residents reported having a religion. Of the total, 72% identified themselves as Christians and 3% (1.6 million) as Muslims. There were also sizable groups of Hindus (559,000), Sikhs (336,000), Jews (267,000), Buddhists (152,000 thousand), and people subscribing to a variety of other faiths (179,000) (Religion in Britain, 2004).

Among the English, religion in recent decades has rapidly assumed a diminishing role, with more individuals becoming Christians in name only or turning to secular humanism, agnosticism, atheism, or free thinking for their beliefs. In 1990, only 17.3% of avowed Christians were church members and just two-thirds (4.4 million) actually attended church services. By 2000, the figures dropped to 15.6% members and 3.8 million attenders. Davie (in Crabtree, 2002–2003) estimated that "between 1960 and 1985 the Church Of

England . . . was effectively reduced to not much more than half its previous size." Between 1980 and 2000, the Anglicans suffered a further 27% drop in attendance, while Roman Catholic attendance at mass declined a similar amount (Crabtree, 2002–2003). However, the Christian population's beliefs in the existence of God, heaven, and life after death held up better than church membership and attendance. A study by Robin Gill suggested that, in a sample of the English general population,

74% [of respondents admitted] to belief in God in the 1970's, compared with 68% in the 1990's. Belief in life after death rose from 37% in the 1970's to 43% in the 1990's, with belief in heaven being roughly constant, at 52% of the population in the 1970's, and 51% of the population in the 1990's. (Key statistics, 2004)

Summary

By the early years of the twenty-first century, English society had become a combination of tradition and change. The tradition had started in the mid-sixteenth century with Henry VIII expelling Catholicism from the realm, creating the Church of England as the country's official religious body, and appointing himself head of the church. That tradition remained intact at the beginning of the twenty-first century, when Anglicanism was still England's official religion and the monarch—now Queen Elizabeth II—was still head of the church. Furthermore, "The Anglican Church alone is protected from expressions of contempt for its beliefs. The common law offences of blasphemy and blasphemous libel limit free speech only when the Church of England is the subject" (The church of privilege, 2004).

In Henry's days, and for many decades thereafter, intolerance toward other religious faiths was the norm. Strong measures were adopted to maintain the Church of England's ecclesiastical and political dominance—measures that included social persecution and laws favoring Anglicans over followers of other faiths. But by the twenty-first century, that tradition had changed dramatically so that religious tolerance had become the expected ideal. In 2004, the English government's new religious-education curriculum would be one indicator of that change.

Several societal trends—particularly over the last half of the twentieth century—contributed to the marked decline in the Church of England's influence and to the diminished role that religion in general assumed in people's lives. Those trends included:

• Greater cultural diversity, as a growing number of people from former British colonies settled in England, thereby adding larger proportions of adherents of other faiths to the general population.
• People (a) adopting more scientific standards for judging the sort of evidence needed to support claims of "fact" or "truth" rather than (b) depending solely on documents from ancient times. This trend was partly the result of scientific and technological

advances that offered empirically supported answers to questions that previously had depended on religious lore—questions about the earth's age and beginnings, the creation and development of life forms, historical events recounted in the Christian Bible, and biblical miracles. Increased formal education throughout the United Kingdom over the decades contributed to the populace learning of scientific explanations for phenomena for which earlier generations had accepted religious accounts.

- A decrease in church attendance as other sources of entertainment and socialization drew people's attention away from the church—such sources as television, athletic contests, amusement parks, and pubs.
- Britain's becoming a signatory to such international agreements as the United Nations *Universal Declaration of Human Rights* which affirmed that

everyone has the right to freedom of thought, conscience and religion; this right includes freedom to change his [or her] religion or belief, and freedom, either alone or in community with others and in public or private, to manifest his [or her] religion or belief in teaching, practice, worship, and observance. (Universal declaration, 1948)

Backgrounds of Religious Education

Today's required religious-education classes in English schools are a continuation of a long tradition. In England, the first schools were established by Christian denominations and charitable organizations with the aim of propagating religion while teaching the young to read and calculate. Hence, religious content formed the central core of the curriculum. As Derek Gillard (2001) has explained,

The earliest schools in England were the 'Song Schools' of the Middle Ages, where the church educated the sons of gentlefolk and trained them to sing in cathedral choirs. By the sixteenth century the church had began to set up Elementary Schools to cater for other sections of the community. Indeed, until about 1880 virtually all education in England was provided by the church.

The study of religion and morality was then retained when, in the Education Act of 1870, England introduced state-supported elementary schools for the general population, operated under local school boards. Over the following decades, as more subjects were added to the course of study, religious education continued in the form of a separate subject as well as part of schoolwide daily worship sessions, assemblies, and such special occasions as Christmas and Easter.

The Education Act of 1944 cast the religious-education provision in more specific terms by requiring all state-supported and state-aided schools (ones operated by religious groups) to provide religious instruction and to begin each school day with collective worship in which all elementary and secondary pupils participated. Although the act applied only to schools in England and Wales, similar legislation in Scotland and Northern Ireland made religious education there a mandatory subject of study. In 1988 the Education Reform Act established a national curriculum of 10 subjects, plus religious education as the one subject from which pupils or teachers could withdraw. In effect, parents who objected to teaching religion—which in most cases would be some form of Christianity—could exclude their children from such instruction. Although religious study is still obligatory, the opportunity for parents to absent their children from religious education continues in effect today.

Whereas central education authorities have required the study of religion, they have not mandated the content of that study. Decisions about the substance of religious instruction have been the province of local education authorities and of religious denominations that sponsor schools. In the case of state-aided voluntary schools (ones operated by church groups but financed by the government), instruction could be designed to propagate the sponsors' particular faith—Anglican, Catholic, Methodist, Hindu, or the like. During the early twenty-first century, about 7,000 (28%) of England's 25,000 schools were "faith-based," with the Church of England running nearly 5,000 schools in England and Wales, while Roman Catholics operated most of the remaining 2,000. Among 40 non-Christian religious schools, 32 were Jewish (Gillard, 2001). Almost one million children attended state-financed Anglican schools in England and Wales (National Society, 2004).

Focusing entirely—or primarily—on a particular faith's own doctrine and practices is known as the *confessional* aim of instruction that has dominated religious education in the past. However, in both secular state schools and faith schools, the more modern approach has become that of *comparative religions*, offering learners an overview of various religious persuasions so students might understand different faiths and make up their own minds about which, if any, they preferred. The comparative-religion mode is the one urged by the government's curriculum planners. It is also the basis for the standardized tests administered to assess students' achievement, and so it has become a more common type of instruction. However, each school or local education authority is still allowed to determine the specific content of its religious education. That decision has been influenced by the religious composition of the surrounding community and by the parents of the pupils enrolled. Consequently, in most schools the primary focus has been on Christianity and on the one or two Christian denominations most prominently represented in the local population.

Such, then, has been the history of religious education in England. It was against this historical background that the country's Qualifications and Curriculum Authority (QCA) in late 2004 introduced its national framework for teaching religious education in English schools—the first such national plan ever produced. And, by including humanism, agnosticism, and atheism as part of religious instruction, the government took the ultimate step toward belief system tolerance in the mandated religious-education program.

Now consider some key provisions of the new plan. In October 2004, the government's Secretary of Education and Skills, Charles Clarke, introduced England's first national framework by proposing that

religious education can transform pupils' assessment of themselves and others, and their understanding of the wider world. I see it as vital in widening inclusion, understanding diversity, and promoting tolerance. Last year, following consultation with key stake-holders, I asked the QCA to look at how this could be achieved and I am delighted to be launching this framework. I know that all the major faith and belief groups and the RE [religious education] community are supportive of the framework and I would like to thank them for their invaluable contribution throughout its development. (Clarke launches, 2004)

The purpose of the framework was to establish national expectations that could help local schools develop consistently high standards of religious in-struction. The framework set attainment targets for learning and described how performance should be assessed and reported in order to develop in learn-ers a clear understanding of the knowledge and skills that the schools should promote. The framework reaffirmed that religious matter

must be taught according to a locally agreed syllabus except in voluntary aided schools with a religious character [that devise their own syllabi]. Each local education authority must convene an Agreed Syllabus Conference to produce a syllabus that sets out what local pupils should be taught. The Education Act of 1996 states that an agreed syllabus must reflect the fact that the religious traditions in Great Britain are mainly Christian, whilst taking account of the teachings and practices of the other principal religions represented in the country. (Clarke launches, 2004)

Thus, the plan gave privileged status to Christianity in an effort to

counter fears that Christianity has been sidelined in religious education as merely another faith taught as part of a wider study of beliefs. The new framework calls for children to study Christianity throughout their school careers. The other five major religions—Buddhism, Hinduism, Islam, Judaism, and Sikhism—should all be studied by pupils by age 14, the guidelines say. But [children] should also study "other religious traditions" such as Baha'i, Jainism, and Zoroastrianism, and "secular philosophies such as humanism." (Cassidy, 2004)

The introduction of the framework in 2004 came in the wake of an ear-lier controversy over faith-based schools when Prime Minister Tony Blair (a staunch Anglican) in 2001 announced a plan to expand single-faith schools financed from public moneys. The proposal was founded on Blair's claim that schools operated by "faith-based organizations" were better at both (a) pro-moting spiritual and moral values in their students and (b) producing higher academic performance (as reflected in standardized test scores) (Gillard, 2001). In general, members of the clergy were delighted with Blair's plan, with the

Church of England planning to establish 100 additional schools. However, the prime minister's announcement also drew harsh criticism from members of parliament, secularists, state schools, and the public press who challenged the claim that single-faith schools were better than secular schools at producing moral, well-taught youths. One commentator attributed the Anglicans' and Catholics' enthusiasm for Blair's plan to their considering the proposal a lifeline they could grasp to slow the decline in faithful churchgoers.

Few who first meet religion in adulthood are able to take it seriously; priests know that to keep the old faiths alive, they have to get their hands on children. (A. C. Grayling in Gillard, 2001)

Critics countered Blair's assertion that faith-based schools were academically superior to secular schools by noting that religious schools selected their students more often from well-to-do families and usually avoided enrolling children with special needs. Research from The Institute for the Study of Civil Society in 2001 revealed "an enormous and unacceptable variation in standards between schools across England that was as marked in church schools as it was in local authority schools" and that "churches were failing to monitor the standards being achieved in their schools" so "parents should not assume church schools equaled a quality education" (Marks in Gillard, 2001).

Opponents of the expansion of single-faith schools also charged that such a move would exacerbate divisions in the society, resulting in greater religious segregation, denominational antipathy, and social disorder in an increasingly multicultural England.

In effect, public interest in faith-based schools, their tradition of public funding, and the type of the education they offered had been newly stirred up prior to the appearance of the 2004 religious-education framework. In the debate, pressure on policymakers to conserve the religious-education practices of the past came from fundamentalist members of the nation's long-established church groups, especially Anglicans and Catholics. At the same time, pressure to broaden the schools' mandatory religious instruction appeared from both inside traditional English society and outside. The inside forces included liberals within the Christian community and proponents of the increasingly popular nonreligious belief systems. The outside forces appeared in the form of immigrants from Asia and Africa who sought recognition in the schools' religious education for their Islamic, Hindu, Sikh, and Buddhist convictions.

Summary

Critical events, modes of national governance, and significant belief systems in the English case are depicted as two timelines in Figure 6.1. The timeline

From 1500 to 2000

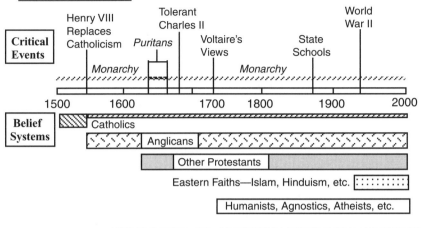

From 1940 to 2005

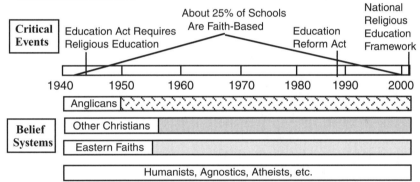

Figure 6.1 Critical events and belief systems in the English case.

on the upper tier extends from 1500 to 2000. The timeline on the lower tier focuses on the 65-year period between 1940 and 2005.

With the foregoing historical sketch of English religious education in mind, we now consider the lineup of principal constituencies that actively participated in the debate over England's first national religious-education curriculum guidelines.

THE CONTENDING CONSTITUENCIES

The adversaries in the debate can be divided into two groups—the framework's proponents and the framework's critics.

Framework Proponents

The vocal supporters of the government's 2004 national religious-education guidelines included (a) the ruling Labor Party's education secretary, Charles Clarke; (b) the Church of England's top education official, Canon John Hall; (c) the Church of England's Board of Education; (d) the Catholic Education Service; and (e) representatives of other religious groups that had been consulted while the plan was being formulated. Furthermore, because adherents of humanism had participated in preparing the national plan, the publication of the framework was welcomed by the British Humanist Society as "a significant step forward for religious education" (Cassidy, 2004).

The framework would also enjoy the support of members of the public who were nominal Christians and who thought students should learn the beliefs of people who differed in their convictions about how best to guide their lives.

In size and cohesiveness, Anglicans and Catholics were rapidly losing their dominant political power, while secularists and Asian religious groups became more influential. Consequently, Church of England and Roman Catholic leaders were obliged to accept the 2004 multicultural approach of the religious-education framework even though that approach worked against the churches' traditional indoctrination mode of instruction. It seems improbable that Anglican and Catholic clergy were overjoyed with the multiple-belief-systems approach of the government's plan. But by endorsing the scheme, the clergy would appear to be reasonable and tolerant as they struggled for survival in a society that was rapidly losing its religious fervor. And, in the religious denominations' favor, accepting the framework in word did not necessarily mean accepting it in deed, since the framework was not obligatory, so church schools could teach whatever they wished.

France and Japan, like most nations, have written constitutions that express a set of cherished ideals in the form of (a) a description of government structure and (b) people's rights and responsibilities in the sort of society envisioned by the framers of the document. England is unique in that it is governed under an unwritten or uncodified constitution consisting of documents and customs in various forms—statutes (such as the Magna Carta of 1215 and the Human Rights Act passed by parliament in 1999), common law (decisions of courts that affect the general population), conventions (accepted ways of doing things that are not written down but are well-established practices), and international agreements (such as the United Nations Declaration of Human Rights). The creators of the 2004 religious-education framework could easily defend the constitutionality of the multiple-belief-systems feature of their plan by citing statutes, common law, and international agreements that guaranteed freedom of belief and equal educational opportunities for all segments of the population. At the same time, the plan's creators could also defend the somewhat incongruous favored-status accorded Christian denominations by their citing the long-established convention of requiring Christian religious instruction in the schools. Curiously, both the supporters and critics of the 2004 plan could find evidence among a multitude of laws and conventions to buttress their positions in the debate over the framework.

Framework Critics

Two groups that opposed the framework, or at least parts of it, were unusual bedfellows—(a) resolute, doctrinaire advocates of a particular religious tradition and (b) fervent secularists.

Resolute Religious Devotees

Some Anglican and Catholic officials—with their church membership and attendance declining rapidly—objected to the framework's proposal that religious education involve comparing belief systems of various religions as well as humanism, agnosticism, and atheism. Because the traditional purpose of schools sponsored by religious groups had been to teach children the tenets of the denomination operating those schools, that purpose would be defeated—or at least seriously weakened—if equal attention were given to beliefs other than that of the schools' patrons. Devotees of a given religion typically doubt the wisdom of spending time describing other creeds when it is obvious that their own religion is "the true one" and deserves to be studied in depth.

Fervent Secularists

The National Secular Society condemned the framework as "a charter for indoctrination." The Society predicted that implementing the plan would cause nonreligious parents to withdraw their children from religious-education lessons because the framework portrayed religion as "a truth to be embraced" instead of "something to be questioned." A Society spokesman warned that "Non-believing children are to have their philosophy challenged at every turn in RE [religious education class]. Many parents who do not want their children to be taught that superstition is a good basis for a rational life will be horrified" (Cassidy, 2004).

For years, secularists had been distressed at including any religious education at all in publicly financed schools. They argued that religion was the antithesis of education because

[Teaching religion] harms individuals by distorting human nature through repressive moralities and the inculcation of false beliefs, fears and hopes. . . . Children should emphatically not be taught as "facts" the myths and legends of ancient religious traditions. To do this to anyone unable to evaluate [the myths'] credibility is a form of brainwashing or even abuse. Public funds should never be used to that end. (A. C. Grayling in Gillard, 2001)

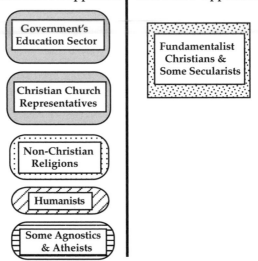

Figure 6.2 The adversaries in the religious-education controversy.

Summary

In the 2004 religious-education debate, pressure on policymakers to conserve the religious-education practices of the past came from fundamentalist members of the nation's long-established church groups, especially Anglicans and Catholics. At the same time, pressure to broaden the schools' mandatory religious instruction appeared from both inside traditional English society and outside. The inside forces included liberals within the Christian community and proponents of the increasingly popular nonreligious belief systems. The outside forces appeared in the form of immigrants from Asia and Africa who sought recognition in the schools' religious education for their Islamic, Hindu, Sikh, and Buddhist convictions.

The arguments adduced by religious groups in support of their desire to teach their beliefs in schools were typically founded on faith that their holy books (Bible, Quran, Upanishads, Torah) offered the infallible truth. In contrast, the arguments put forward by the nonreligious humanists, agnostics, and atheists questioned the worth of beliefs that lacked empirical support—that is, lacked perceptible evidence that such things as invisible spirits (gods, angels, devils), heaven, hell, or an afterlife actually existed. The 2004 framework, by providing a place in religious education for studying nonreligious worldviews, implied that matters of evidence could become important foci of discussion. Thus, it seems reasonable to expect that faith in ancient writings versus faith in empirical observations would become an issue of discussion in classes that compared religious and nonreligious belief systems. Whether that would be true in practice was a question to be answered only by an inspection of learning materials and visits to classrooms.

Figure 6.2 shows a graphic estimate of the contending constituencies that participated in the 2004-curriculum-framework debate.

RESOLVING THE CONTROVERSY

The 2004 framework was, itself, a device aimed at settling a long-fought conflict over the proper nature of religious education in schools that were supported by public moneys. The framework sought to achieve such resolution by proposing the nationwide adoption of a curriculum that gave every belief system a chance to be heard. And the plan did seem to achieve that goal (at least on paper) of accommodating everyone, because the proposal was endorsed by representatives of diverse religions and by humanists as well. As a result, the framework had few outspoken opponents—mostly disgruntled secularists and adamant Anglican and Catholic zealots. However, because the government's program was only advisory, not mandatory, local schools and denominations could still teach whatever they liked. Consequently, the framework did not settle the underlying disagreements that had always divided belief constituencies and prevented nationwide accord regarding the content of school instruction that focused on religion.

CHAPTER 7

India

The case of India mentioned in Chapter 1 concerned the appointment of a panel of historians assigned to remove from secondary-school textbooks the Hindu religious beliefs that had been inserted by the Bharatiya Janata Party (BJP) before it was voted out of office in June 2004. The following interpretation of that event begins with (a) an inspection of the episode's ancient roots, and then continues with (b) an analysis of the constituencies involved in the confrontation and (c) speculation about how the conflict over schoolbooks' contents might be settled.

HISTORICAL ROOTS

The four historical periods on which the following discussion focuses are those of (a) the establishment of Hinduism, (b) the Muslim era, (c) the years of British colonialism, and (d) India's political independence.

The Birth and Growth of Hinduism

According to the most widely accepted version of India's ancient past, Aryan tribes invaded Northern India in a series of waves, perhaps around 1500 BCE, where they confronted, battled, and eventually conquered the region's smaller, darker-skinned Dravidian people and other indigenous tribes. The ancestors of the invading Aryans apparently had originated in the steppes of Southern Russia and, over a long period of time, had passed through Iran to arrive finally in India. The Aryans brought with them the Sanskrit language and an evolving religious tradition which, when settled into Northern India, became the Vedic faith, deriving its name from the Sanskrit word *veda*, meaning "sacred knowledge." Across the centuries following the Aryans' arrival, Vedic belief expanded in two ways, geographically and philosophically. From its introduction into Northern India, Vedaism gradually spread south and east, eventually pervading the entire subcontinent. At the same time, its character changed significantly, causing some present-day scholars to conclude that the period around 700 BCE marked the end of the Vedic era and the start of true Hinduism (Renou, 1961, p. 21).

Two features of Hinduism particularly important for understanding the recent case of high-school textbook revision are Hinduism's (a) way of explaining life's events and (b) social caste structure.

Ways of Explaining Life's Events

Devoted, doctrinaire Hindus—past and present—have viewed life through the lens of ancient holy writings. The origin of the universe, the causes of daily events, the purpose of life, the structure of society, the kinds of human behavior and their consequences—all are interpreted from a worldview formulated two or more millennia ago. Consequently, Hindu fundamentalists explain such phenomena as earthquakes, floods, and droughts in astrological terms (Jyotish Vedic astrology), reasoning that the relationships among stars and planets determined the events. Furthermore, dedicated Hindus accord Vedic mathematics (an early style of mental calculating) the same status in schooling as modern-day chemistry and astronomy. They recommend ancient Ayurvedic medical practices (herbs, panchakarma cleansing) for treating illness and disease (Baldauf, 2004). And they insist that these beliefs, along with a Hindu version of history, be featured in school textbooks.

Hindu Social Caste Structure

A potent scheme Aryan leaders invented for guarding their favored position of privilege and power in Indian society was a social caste system that they asserted was of divine origin—a structure authorized by the gods. That system, which has dominated social life in India over the centuries and up to the present day, is founded on the conviction that one's social status in the world is determined by a celestially created hierarchy of social classes or castes. An infant is born into the caste of his or her parents and is destined to remain in that caste throughout life. The caste structure in its most basic form consists of four well-defined upper strata, plus one almost ignored lower stratum that continues to be occupied today by the least respected, least privileged members of society.

The four main castes, ranging from the most advantaged and honored at the top to the least advantaged at the bottom, follow this order: (a) the Brahmins (sometimes called Brahmanas) are priests who exercise spiritual power and are experts in teaching the holy scriptures, (b) the Kshatriyas (Ksatriyas) or warriors and administrators wield the secular power needed for governing the society, (c) the Vaisyas or artisans and cultivators perform business and production functions, and (d) the Sudras (Shudras) serve the three higher castes. The three upper castes are considered to be Aryan, occupied by descendents of the original tribes that arrived in Northern India, whereas the Sudras are considered to be non-Aryan. According to the ancient *Bhagavad Gita* scriptures,

the works of Brahmins, Ksatriyas, Vaishyas, and Shudras are different, in harmony with the powers of their born nature. The works of a Brahmin are peace; self-harmony, austerity, and purity; loving-forgiveness and righteousness; vision and wisdom and faith. The works of a Ksatriya are a heroic mind, inner fire, constancy, resourcefulness, courage in battle, generosity, and noble leadership. The works of a Vaishya are trade, agriculture, and the rearing of cattle. The work of the Shudra is service. (Quoted in Ross, 2004)

Beneath the formal caste structure is a region occupied by Hindu society's despised outcasts, traditionally referred to as *untouchables* but, in more recent and less derogatory terms, have been called members of *scheduled castes* and *scheduled tribes*. According to modern-day estimates, almost 20% of India's Hindus form the upper three castes, nearly 60% are Sudras, and slightly more than 20% are in the lowest stratum (15% in scheduled castes and 7.5% in scheduled tribes) (Daniel, 2004; Shinn et al., 1970, p. 154).

Theoretically, the caste system consists of only the top four strata or "colors" (*varna*), kept pure by restrictions against marriage across caste boundaries. But in reality, ever since the Aryan tribes entered India 3,500 years ago, there has been a substantial amount of intermarriage, as recognized by a special name assigned to each mixed caste. Consequently, today there are about 3,000 recognized subcastes produced by complex permutations of marriage across class lines, with most of the subcastes associated with particular occupations (Renou, 1961).

When India achieved political independence after World War II, the new constitution outlawed the caste system. However, government edicts can hardly eliminate a centuries-old social structure by a single stroke of the pen. Thus, in the course of daily life, the caste system is still very much alive today.

In India's recent textbook controversy, the traditional Hindu caste system was endorsed—at least by implication—in the revisions to textbooks ordered by the Hindu nationalist government that was in power over the 1998–2004 era. Those textbooks then became an issue of contention in the further revisions of texts ordered by the government that ousted the nationalists from office in 2004.

The Muslim Era

Over two-and-one-half millennia (1500 BCE to 1000 CE), Hinduism—along with such Hindu offshoots as Buddhism and Jainism—dominated religious, political, and social life throughout the South Asian subcontinent. Then, around 1000 CE, Muslims successfully invaded India from the north and eventually ended the rule of Hindus in most areas of the country through military conquest that established powerful sultanates in region after region. By the late seventeenth century, the Islamic Mughal Empire extended over virtually all of India.

Throughout the seven-century Muslim reign, adherents of the two distinctly different religious traditions lived side by side—Hinduism with its caste system and multiple gods, Islam with its basically egalitarian social structure and its single, all-powerful god, Allah. The literatures on which the two faiths based their beliefs were markedly different—the Vedas, Upanishads, Manu Smriti, Mahabharata, and Ramayana for the Hindus; the Quran (Allah's revealed word) and Sunnah (sayings and deeds of Prophet Muhammad) for the Muslims. Such contrasting core features of the two religions rendered them incompatible, so there was always tension between their constituents. In its total number of followers, Hinduism was substantially larger than Islam, a condition that would eventually affect the modern-day composition of India's population. When India would become a politically independent sovereign nation after World War II, Muslims made up around 25% of the population, with most of the rest being Hindus. The postwar bloody strife between the two religious groups was settled only when two northern portions of the country were separated from India to form a new Islamic nation, Pakistan (the eastern sector of which would become the independent nation of Bangladesh in 1971). Many Muslims from various parts of India migrated to Pakistan. However, a substantial minority remained in India so that by the early twenty-first century India's 1.1 billion people included 77% Hindus (and devotees of such derivatives of Hinduism as Buddhism, Jainism, and Sikhism), 12% Muslims, 3% Christians, 3% tribal traditionalists, and 5% followers of other belief systems (Sparks, 2004).

When the nationalist BJP headed the government over the 1998–2004 period, the party's pro-Hindu revision of history textbooks depicted the Muslim era of 1000–1700 as a "dark age of Islamic colonial rule which snuffed out the glories of the Hindu empire that preceded it. One textbook claimed that the Taj Mahal, the Qu'tb Minar, and the Red Fort—three of India's outstanding examples of Islamic architecture—were designed and commissioned by Hindus" (Ramesh, 2004). Such a denigrating portrayal of the Islamic era in the BJP's textbooks resulted in members of the Muslim community endorsing the re-revision of history texts ordered by the government that took office upon the defeat of the BJP in March 2004.

British Colonialism

The vast South-Central Asian territory that is now occupied by India, Pakistan, and Bangladesh was governed by a multitude of princedoms within the Mughal Empire before British military forces and commercial venturers—from the mid-eighteenth century through the mid-twentieth century—politically unified the region as a British colony so that India became the crown jewel of Britain's worldwide colonial empire. Several innovations that the British introduced into the colony would significantly affect governance of the region when India finally became an independent nation after World War II. One influence was the system of administration that included a civil service which employed many Indians, particularly at the regional and local levels. Thus, when independence finally arrived, there were already experienced indigenous civil service personnel in place to maintain government operations. A second influence was the introduction of European-style schooling which the British provided for a portion of upper-class Indians who would then play important roles in the movement for Indian independence during the first half of the twentieth century. A third influence was the British model of democratic voting for selecting government officials at both local and national levels. As it turned out, the mode of education and the system of voting would serve the Indians well in their successful effort to end Britain's rule over the region.

The history textbook revisions introduced by the Hindu nationalist BJP over their 1998–2004 reign not only depicted nearly eight centuries of Muslim control as social/cultural deterioration, but also portrayed the two centuries of British hegemony as a deplorable distortion of a properly ordered Hindu society.

India's Political Independence

In the final years of the nineteenth century, a gradually accelerating movement for India to become a politically independent nation was launched by British-schooled Indians whose efforts were abetted by such English citizens as Annie Besant, a widely respected woman's rights advocate and convert to Hindu Theosophist belief. Under the direction of such British-educated Hindus as Mohandas Gandhi (1869–1948) and Jawaharlal Nehru (1889–1964), the home-rule movement gained momentum throughout the early decades of the twentieth century and resulted in the creation of elected regional legislatures—a start toward self-governance. However, stiff resistance by the British prevented the granting of full independence until 1947.

Following the partitioning of the colony into the nations of India and Pakistan in 1947, Indian leaders formulated a constitution that was ratified in January 1950. The document included elements from Western democracies, along with provisions devised specifically for Indian society. Examples of the borrowings were the British model of parliamentary democracy, several principles of the United States Constitution (separation of major powers of government, a supreme court, federal/state structure), and the French Revolution's themes of liberty, equality, and fraternity.

We, the People of India, having solemnly resolved to constitute India into a sovereign socialist secular democratic republic and to secure to all its citizens:

Justice—social, economic and political;

Liberty of thought, expression, belief, faith and worship;

Equality of status and of opportunity; and to promote among them all;

Fraternity, assuring the dignity of the individual and the unity and integrity of the Nation.

The State shall not discriminate against any citizen on grounds only of religion, race, caste, sex, place of birth or any of them.

Article 45. The State shall endeavor to provide, within a period of ten years from the commencement of this Constitution, free and compulsory education for all children until they complete the age of fourteen years. (Constitution of India, 2004)

The highly popular leader of the Indian Congress Party, Jawaharlal Nehru, became the new nation's first prime minister. Since then, India's political scene has featured a great number of parties. Thus, no single party can carry an election. Whereas both the BJP and the Congress have had the largest numbers of members, in order to gain control of the government each has had to attract others whose policies were sufficiently similar to their own to form an acceptable coalition. For most of the half-century after India gained political independence, the Congress Party and its allies controlled the government. But before the 1998 election, the Congress lost many of its followers in the aftermath of corruption charges and ineffective leadership. Hence, in 1998 the growing popularity of the BJP and its partners enabled the party to topple the Congress from its traditional position of authority. The BJP promoted Hinduism, in contrast to the secularism advocated in the nation's constitution and supported by the Congress Party. The aim of the BJP was not only to recapture the past (prior to 1000 CE) by preventing changes brought by social and scientific innovations from outside India's Hindu culture, but also to revise history so that the ancient culture appeared both idyllic and well suited to the present day.

However, the Congress Party and its allies in the 2004 national election toppled the BJP from power and ordered the revision of textbooks that had been written during the BJP's years in office. The BJP's defeat in the March 2004 election was

attributed to popular discontent with the BJP's record on economic policy, notably its perceived inability to extend the benefits of strong economic growth to a broader range of the populace. Disaffection was particularly evident amongst the rural electorate, suffering under the pressures of drought, a dearth of infrastructure investment, and relative impoverishment. (Rashtriya Swayamsevak Sangh, 2004)

Summary

The foregoing sketch of India's history has ranged across a period of 3,500 years.

- 1500 BCE to 1000 CE: The Hindu religion, with its caste system, evolved out of Vedic belief brought by the Aryan invaders from the steppes of Russia. Hinduism dominated political and cultural life throughout the Indian subcontinent.

- 1000 CE to 1750 CE: Mughal invaders, with their Islamic belief system, conquered ever-greater portions of the subcontinent, yet most inhabitants continued to live according to Hindu religious doctrine and the caste system.

- 1750 CE to 1947 CE: British commercial and military forces by gradual stages gained control over the region and exploited the country's resources, making India the most important component of the British worldwide collection of colonies.

- 1947 CE to 2005 CE: India became a sovereign socialist secular democratic republic dedicated to justice, liberty, equality, and fraternity for all citizens, regardless of their religion, race, caste, sex, or place of birth. During the 6-year period that the BJP was in control of the government (1998–2004), school textbooks were rewritten to promote a Hindu nationalist view of the world. But upon the defeat of the BJP in March 2004 by the Congress Party and its allies, the new government ordered a further revision of textbooks to expunge what critics judged to be BJP distortions of Indian history.

To illustrate several high points in the history behind the Indian case, Figure 7.1 presents two timelines. The upper-tier timeline depicts 3,500 years of critical events and forms of governance, along with dominant belief systems of successive periods. The lower-tier timeline displays the same features for the most recent century-and-a-quarter, 1875–2005.

THE CONTENDING CONSTITUENCIES

The most obvious political adversaries confronting each other in the textbook-revision controversy were the Congress Party and the BJP. Each was supported by its collection of minor political groups and by sympathizers in the general population. Inspecting the two parties' backgrounds and aims can help explain why they acted as they did in the schoolbook case.

The Congress Party—Multicultural Secularists

In the final years of the nineteenth century, an incipient Indian national-ist movement coalesced in the formation of the Indian National Congress in 1885, an organization initially loyal to the British colonial government but, with the passing years, ever more vociferous in demanding the right to self-governance. Although some freedoms were granted by the British in 1919, the Congress leadership felt the changes were insufficient. Consequently, during the 1920s and 1930s, the party sanctioned campaigns of noncooperation and civil disobedience that were led by Mahatma Gandhi, who voiced the convic-tion that "Nonviolence is the greatest force at the disposal of mankind. It is mightier than the mightiest weapon of destruction devised by the ingenuity of man" (Attenborough, 2004).

By the time the British granted full independence to India in 1947, Jawaharlal Nehru was the leader of the Congress Party and was selected as the nation's first prime minister. Although the party was clearly dominated

From 1500 BCE to 2000 CE

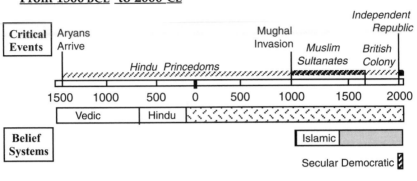

From 1875 to 2005

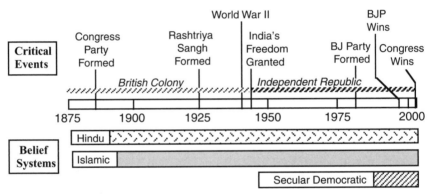

Figure 7.1 Critical events and belief systems in the Indian case.

by Hindus and continues so today, its leaders were intent on establishing a secular, democratic republic with equal opportunities and status for all citizens, as defined in the constitution—a dramatic contrast to the centuries-old caste-bound society. The ideal of liberty and equality continued to guide party decisions over the decades after 1947. When the Congress Party won the 2004 election, its dedication to the ideals of the nation's constitution provided the motive behind the appointment of historians in late 2004 to rewrite the textbooks that had been revised when the BJP was in charge during the 1998–2004 era.

The Bharatiya Janata Party—Hindu Nationalists

In 1925 an Indian physician, Dr. Keshav Baliram Hegewar (1889–1940), founded the Rashtriya Swayamsevak Sangh (National Self-Service Organization), dedicated to promoting Indian independence and Hindu religious practices and culture. Leaders of the Sangh favored an aggressive militaristic approach to freeing the country from British control in contrast to Mohandas Gandhi's nonviolent methods. Over the three-quarters of a century since the Sangh's birth, the organization grew to become what supporters claimed was the world's largest volunteer organization. By the early twenty-first century, the Sangh listed more than 25,000 branches (*shakhas*) across India. Each shakha's program was conducted for one or two hours every morning in a public place. The program consisted of physical activities (yoga, training in stick fighting), discussions of social topics, prayers to Mother India (*Bharat Mata*), and lectures on Indian history, philosophy, culture, and ethics (Rashtriya Swayamsevak Sangh, 2004). The Sangh also administered 14,000 schools.

To serve as the political-action arm of the Sangh, the Bharatiya Janata Party (Indian People's Party) was created in 1980, the successor to an earlier series of bodies that had promoted the Sangh's political agenda. As one important resource, the BJP profited from the organizational skills and long-established good-works reputation of the party's parent body, the philanthropic Rashtriya Swayamsevak Sangh, which could supply large quantities of volunteer workers and experienced leaders. By the late 1990s, the BJP had become one of India's largest political parties. Although the BJP presented itself as nonpartisan, advocating the development of "Indianness" rather than promoting the Hindu religion, its particular kind of Indianness required faithful adherence to a belief system rooted in ancient Hindu scriptures—the Vedas and Upanishads. BJP spokespersons openly expressed their disappointment with the secular, multicultural nature of the nation's constitution. As one BJP proponent wrote in 2004, "It would have been logical for our post-1947 rulers to restructure national life in keeping with our [original Hindu] culture. Sadly, that golden opportunity was lost" (Rashtriya Swayamsevak Sangh, 2004). Some BJP writers even suggested that only Hindus should be accorded Indian citizenship.

After the BJP gained control of the government in 1998 as the leader of a 23-party coalition, the group's innovations in the field of education drew sharp criticism from liberal Hindus, secularists, and adherents of other religions, who charged that the BJP was attempting to "saffronize" the nation's public schools—a reference to the saffron hue of the Sangh's flag. The innovations included such acts as (a) authorizing graduate university degrees in Hindu astrology, (b) giving government subsidies to universities that offered ancient Vedic mathematics and Vedic rituals, (c) extolling Hindu priest craft, and (d) decreeing that every state educational function should open with the singing of the Saraswati Vandana, a hymn in praise of Saraswati, the Hindu goddess of learning and wisdom.

But the BJP's opponents saved their most strident criticism for textbook revisions wrought during the period 1998–2003. The new texts depicted Aryans as the original people of India—"indigenous geniuses who created the Indus Valley civilization"—rather than accepting evidence that Aryan nomads had entered India from the Russian steppes (Ramesh, 2004). In addition, the texts minimized the pernicious effects of the caste system and entirely omitted such "awkward facts" as a Hindu nationalist's assassinating Mahatma Gandhi in 1948 (Panikkar, 2005).

The revised eleventh-grade science text stated that during the ancient Hindu "golden age," India was ahead of all other countries in science and medicine, with such knowledge thereafter borrowed by Arabs and passed on to Europeans. In effect, India was portrayed as the birthplace of science. The history books' discussions of architecture during the Muslim era of 1000–1700 failed to recognize the merging of Hindu and Islamic styles to form the syncretic mode found in so many of the nation's historic structures. Such was the nature of the many changes in science, social studies, and history books during the BJP's tenure of office.

In assessing the significance of the BJP textbook program, K. N. Panikkar proposed that the revisions were

inspired by the political project of Hindu fundamentalism, to transform the multicultural and multireligious Indian nation into an exclusively Hindu state. What the textbooks have attempted is to reshape the Indian past to derive legitimacy for this political project and to communally reconstruct the historical consciousness of the coming generations. In the process, the generally accepted norms and methods of historical discipline have irreparably suffered. (Panikkar, 2005)

The philosophical support for the BJP's program derived from ancient Hindu scriptures—Vedas, Upanishads, and the like. In contrast, the Congress Party and its coalition partners drew their ideals from the 1947 constitution as well as from constitutions of other modern nations and from such internationally endorsed commitments as United Nations statements about human rights.

Summary

An estimated lineup of constituencies on the two sides of the textbook conflict is displayed in Figure 7.2. The term *Secularists* in the figure refers to groups that advocated a nonreligious, multicultural government in which no creed was favored over any other. The term *Hindu Nationalists* refers to proponents of a government that would impose fundamentalist Hindu beliefs and social structures on the nation's citizenry and would use the public schools to propagate those beliefs.

RESOLVING THE CONTROVERSY

The Indian textbook case illustrates the importance of a constituency having the formal authority to dictate educational policies and practices. That authority is acquired by a political party winning enough seats in parliament to qualify as the nation's governing body until the next election. When the BJP

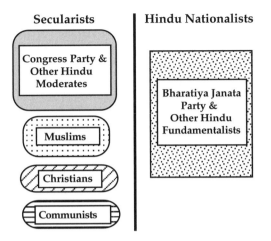

Figure 7.2 Adversaries in the textbook-revision controversy.

won the 1998 election, it received the needed authority and thus could legally order the rewriting of textbooks to suit the party agenda. When the Congress Party led the United Progressive Alliance to victory in 2004, the authority shifted to the Alliance.

The tactics that contending constituencies adopt to further their cause can differ between the time they are in office and the time they are out. For instance, the Hindu nationalists, after taking charge of the government in 1998, could not only order the rewriting of textbooks but could use official government directives, ceremonial occasions, and press releases to laud and defend their actions. In contrast, constituencies currently out of office were obliged to pursue their goals by lawsuits and newsworthy events that cast doubt on the competence of the people in power. The nature of this give-and-take between the adversaries in the textbook case is illustrated by the following events.

When the BJP instituted the practice of singing the Saraswati Vandana hymn at the opening of educational conferences, secularists at such gatherings walked out in protest and publicized their objections in newspapers (Gurumurthy, 1998). The BJP's proposal that students in public schools sing the hymn at school gatherings was followed by a rash of articles in periodicals objecting to forcing a Hindu hymn on Muslim pupils (Sachar, 1999).

Whereas each of India's individual states has been free to decide its own educational policies and practices, a federal body—the National Council of Educational Research and Training—has played a key role in determining curriculum content nationwide. When the BJP came into power, it changed the membership of the council to further Hindu nationalist aims, which were then reflected in new curriculum guidelines that led to the textbook revisions. In protest, the Congress Party in 2002 filed a lawsuit, claiming that the new curriculum included Hindu material that violated the nation's constitution. However, the Supreme Court ruled that India's secular constitution did not prohibit academic lessons on religion, adding that "Students should know about their own religion and religions of others." Subsequently, in the public press critics charged that religious lessons based on the guidelines would be socially divisive since the proposed curriculum praised Hindus while denigrating Muslims (India's Supreme Court, 2002). Christian educational leaders publicly voiced their dismay that the National Council would issue such curriculum directives without consulting the Christian denominations that managed 20,000 educational institutions attended by nearly 10 million students (Akkara, 2001).

Thus, during the BJP's time in office, secularists were outsiders complaining of the government's curriculum changes. Then, with the BJP's defeat in 2004, the tables were turned. The Congress Party's secularist coalition was in a position to require the rewriting of texts, whereas the BJP and its compatriots were left to use public communication media to advance their cause.

In 2004 the order from the secularist government to re-revise school books provided no more than a temporary resolution of the controversy, since matters could change if Hindu nationalists again came into office. Thus, it seems unlikely that there will ever be a permanent settlement. Instead, there would only be periodic temporary arrangements that reflected the desires of whichever political coalition is currently in office.

It might first appear that textbook revision at the national level would seriously affect schooling throughout India. However, Panikkar (2005) has pointed out that history texts produced by the National Council have been used in only 3% of the nation's schools, because individual states and private schools are free to choose the books they will use. Thus, the textbook case is more significant symbolically than in how well it reflects religious bias in the curricula of India's entire school system. In effect, the importance of the case is primarily in its exposing the deep-seated division in Indian society over the role religion should assume in public education.

CHAPTER 8

Spain

The Spanish case mentioned in Chapter 1 concerned the Socialists defeating the ruling People's Party (*Partido Popular*) in the 2004 national election. With the Spanish Socialist Workers' Party (*Partido Socialista Obrero Español*) now in power, their prime minister, Jose Luis Rodriguez Zapatero, revoked the schools' compulsory religious-education legislation that had been sponsored in 2003 by the leader of the People's Party, Jose Maria Aznar. This rejection of mandatory religious education in schools set off a bitter confrontation between Roman Catholic authorities and the secularists who were now in charge of the government. The nature of the confrontation and reasons that it assumed its particular form are described in the following pages.

The Spanish case is an example of conflict resulting from conservatives attempting to sustain past laws and customs in the face of changing public attitudes. The case also illustrates how important it is for advocates of a belief system to win the political authority that enables them officially to alter the role of religion in the schools. In addition, the tale includes faint echoes of a Christian/Muslim conflict from the far distant past.

HISTORICAL ROOTS

The following review identifies two historical trends that contribute to understanding the Spanish case: (a) the connection between religion and the political control of a society and (b) the place of religion in the schools.

Religion and Political Control

For nearly 1,700 years Roman Catholicism was the most influential religion in Spain, and so it continues today. Although the dominance of the Catholic faith over the centuries was interrupted by Islamic forces from about 720 to

1492 CE, Catholicism would return stronger than ever and continue dominant even through the twentieth century. The following review suggests the importance of religious belief for successive periods of political control of Spanish society, beginning with Roman Emperor Constantine's conversion to the faith in the fourth century CE and culminating with the Socialists' triumph in the 2004 election.

Constantine's Conversion

During the five centuries of the Roman Empire's control over its western region (from about 0 CE to around 500 CE), the Iberian Peninsula (today's Spain and Portugal) was one of the empire's valued possessions. Christianity had been introduced into the peninsula in the first century CE, and by the second century it had won a measure of popularity among the indigenous Iberians living in the cities. But Christianity did not become widespread until after Roman Emperor Constantine (306–337 CE) converted to the faith and declared Roman Catholicism the empire's official religion. Whereas prior to Constantine's time Christian churches had operated mainly as individual congregations, from his conversion forward Christianity would be unified into a hierarchical system with headquarters in Rome. Today's structure of Roman Catholicism, with a pope at its pinnacle, is a legacy of Constantine's effort. Thus, under Constantine's rule, Catholicism was adopted by the peninsula's population, the *Hispano-Romans*, who were a combination of indigenous peoples, Roman occupation forces, and the offspring of their intermarriage. The emperor's conversion was the critical event that launched the Catholic tradition.

By the fifth century, the western portion of the Roman Empire was crumbling under attacks by barbaric tribes from Central Europe. The Huns, under their leader Atilla, attacked not only the Romans but also such Germanic tribes as the Visigoths, who retreated into the Iberian Peninsula where they would gain political control and rule the Hispano-Romans. Religion was a divisive issue between the Visigoths and the Hispano-Romans until 589 when Recared, a Visigoth ruler, accepted Catholicism, an event that cemented the alliance between the Visigothic monarchy and the Hispano-Romans that produced the Spanish nation.

The Moors' Arrival

Christian control of Spain was interrupted in 711 by an army of Muslims (Moors) from North Africa that won control over most of Spain. The victory started an occupation that lasted seven centuries until Catholics could finally drive the last of the Moors from the land. The Moorish era in Spain became known as a golden age of educational, architectural, and scientific progress. By the ninth century, the city of Cordova in southern Spain had become Europe's intellectual center where Moorish scholars translated resurrected Greek and Roman knowledge, making it available to the European Renaissance. Cordova had bookshops everywhere and more than 70 libraries (Burke in *Spain under the Moors*, 2004).

During the Moors' occupation of the country, Catholic rulers who had retained control of northern sectors of the peninsula gradually gained military strength until in 1492 armies under the Roman Catholic Spanish monarchs, Ferdinand and Isabella, vanquished the last of the Moorish rulers.

The Spanish Inquisition

In 1478, even before the Moors were routed, Ferdinand and Isabella had obtained permission from the pope in Rome to introduce a practice aimed at unifying the people of Spain under a single religion, Roman Catholicism. That practice—*inquisition*—consisted of the clergy investigating people's religious beliefs to determine which ones were true Catholics. The goal was to "purify" the citizenry by driving out Jews (the main targets), Protestants, and any others not faithful to Catholicism. The introduction of the Inquisition was the event that ushered in the era of the harshest religious control in Spanish history, an era lasting more than 350 years.

The Inquisition consisted of people in the general population accusing others of being *heretics*, meaning non-Catholics. The accused would then appear before a tribunal for the chance to confess their heresy against the Catholic Church and to identify other heretics. If they admitted their guilt and named other nonbelievers, they were released or sent to prison. If they refused to admit wrongdoing or failed to indict other heretics, they were publicly executed or imprisoned for life. After appeals from church authorities in Rome proved of little use in curtailing inquisition activities, the practice continued in various degrees of intensity until abolished in the 1830s.

In 1851, Catholicism was named Spain's state religion, with the government agreeing to pay the salaries of the clergy and to cover other church expenses—a commitment that would strengthen the influence of Catholicism in Spain over the next eight decades.

The Franco Regime

During the twentieth century, political parties sprang up to represent diverse regional and social class interests. The result was the periodic disruption of centuries of governance by pro-Catholic regimes. Of particular import was the 1931 election that gave a coalition of Socialists and Left Republicans enough seats in the Cortes (parliament) to write a constitution featuring antireligion measures that threatened the Catholic Church's place in Spanish society. The Republicans were opposed by conservative Catholics and their National Bloc allies who launched a military revolt in 1936 against the ruling leftist Popular Front. The hostilities began when an army general, Francisco Franco, led troops from Spain's Morocco protectorate against government forces and set off the three-year Spanish Civil War. During the war, the leftist Republicans received military aid from the Soviet Union while General Franco's right-wing

Nationalists were supported by Hitler's Germany, Mussolini's Italy, and the Vatican in Rome. The Nationalists won the war, and Franco assumed control of the government, ruling Spain as its dictator until his death in 1975.

During the Franco years, Roman Catholicism was the only religion to have legal status; other worship services could not be advertised, and only the Roman Catholic Church could own property or publish books. The government not only continued to pay priests' salaries and to subsidize the church, but it also assisted in the reconstruction of church buildings damaged by the war. Laws were passed abolishing divorce and banning the sale of contraceptives. Catholic religious instruction was mandatory, even in public schools. (Religion, 1986)

In a 1953 formal agreement (*concordat*) with the Vatican, Franco granted the Catholic Church wide-ranging privileges in Spain, including funds for new buildings, exemption from government taxes, the power to censor materials offensive to the church, protection from police entering church properties, and the right to establish universities, operate radio stations, and publish newspapers and magazines (Religion, 1986).

A New Constitution

Upon Franco's demise, Juan Carlos de Borbon—a member of Spain's exiled royal family—returned as the nation's monarch, assigned to head a government guided by a new 1978 constitution that declared Spain a secular state, disestablished Roman Catholicism as the state religion, and granted religious liberty to non-Catholics. However, that constitution, under which the government continued to operate in the twenty-first century, still recognized the important place of Roman Catholic tradition in Spanish society.

The following are ideals in Spain's present-day constitution (adopted in 1978, amended in 1992).

Freedom of ideology, religion, and cult of individuals and communities is guaranteed without any limitation in their demonstrations other than that which is necessary for the maintenance of public order protected by law. No one may be obliged to make a declaration on his ideology, religion, or beliefs. No religion shall have a state character. The public powers shall take into account the religious beliefs of Spanish society and maintain the appropriate relations of cooperation, with the Catholic Church and other denominations.

Everyone has the right to education. Freedom of instruction is recognized. The objective of education shall be the full development of the human personality in respect for the democratic principles of coexistence and the basic rights and liberties. The public authorities guarantee the right which will assist parents to have their children receive the religious and moral formation which is in keeping with their own convictions. Basic education is obligatory and free. (Spain—Constitution, 1978/1992)

It is useful to note that in Spain's ostensibly secular, democratic government, "Instead of divorcing church and state, the authors of the constitution opted for a handshake between the two institutions. . . . Less than a week after the constitution was put into effect in 1979, for example, the Spanish state signed a set of agreements with the Holy See in Rome that continued the Catholic Church's privileged legal and economic status—accords signed 'to resolve political problems' and ensure stability" (Pingree, 2004).

Over the last two decades of the twentieth century and into the twenty-first century, heated competition for control of the government developed between the (a) traditional Catholic-supported People's Party and (b) the Socialists and their allies. The continuing dominance of Catholicism as a religion in Spain was confirmed in a 2002 survey showing that 82.1% of the population considered themselves Catholics. However, only 19% of respondents reported that they attended church regularly, compared with 98% 50 years earlier (Tremlett, 2004). Two percent of Spaniards in 2002 followed other faiths, 10.2% were nonbelievers or agnostics, and 4.4% atheists (Spain, 2003). In addition, even though the 1979 constitution offered special privileges to the Catholic Church, a growing list of legislation sponsored by socialists had diminished the church's influence over Spaniards' lives. For example, despite fierce opposition from the Catholic leadership, a 1981 law recognized civil divorce, and 1985–1986 laws permitted abortion in special circumstances. In 1992, the government signed agreements with the Protestant, Jewish, and Muslim communities that improved those groups' official status, although the privileges they were granted fell far short of ones enjoyed by the Catholic Church. In effect, while Spanish society was still overwhelmingly Catholic in tradition, the power of the church was being whittled away.

In such a political atmosphere, José María Aznar and his conservative People's Party defeated the incumbent Socialists in the 1996 election and took command of the government. Once in office, Aznar not only intended to halt further steps toward reducing the church's role in Spanish life, but he sought to reverse the secular trend by reinstating practices that could advance the Catholic cause by providing new advantages for the church.

In the existing government/church arrangements, Aznar's regime continued to endorse the 1979 accord between Spain and the Vatican that provided the Catholic Church (a) funds from public coffers; (b) salary payments for religious teachers and for chaplains in the military, prisons, and hospitals; (c) extensive tax exemptions; and (d) the right to appoint and dismiss religious teachers in state schools. In 2003, the church received about $4.3 billion of state money to support its ecclesiastical, educational, social, and cultural activities (Pingree, 2004).

Among Aznar's new initiatives aimed at strengthening the Catholic Church's position, his late-2003 law requiring religious education in all schools drew the greatest outrage from teachers' unions, 11,500 parents' associations, and opposition political parties. The law compelled all students to

take a class each year on Roman Catholic dogma, taught by church appointees and intended for practicing Catholics, or an alternative, secular class on world religions that education officials say offers a historical approach but that opposition party leaders contend is similar to the Catholicism class. The [students'] religion grades count toward their final [grade-point] averages, which determine promotions and eligibility for competitive university programs. (Fuchs, 2003)

However, the implementation of the law, scheduled to take effect in September 2004, was shortcut when the Socialists won the March 2004 election and the new prime minister, José Luis Rodríguez Zapatero, moved to rescind the schooling legislation.

In 2005, the Socialists not only called for an end to religious instruction in schools but also convinced parliament to liberalize divorce and abortion. In addition, the new government sought to cut in half the state funds for the Catholic Church, to permit homosexuals to marry and adopt children, to honor common law marriages, to accept euthanasia, and to ban the display of such Christian symbols as crosses from public schools, prisons, and military headquarters (God and Spain, 2004).

In conclusion, during the first decade of the twenty-first century, Roman Catholicism in Spanish society suffered critical setbacks in its effort to sustain its long-held influence over the lives of the nation's citizens.

Summary

The purpose of the foregoing two-millennia review of Roman Catholic history in Spain has been to show how

- The 2004 repeal of the religious-education law was simply the most recent episode in a long series of confrontations between Roman Catholicism and other belief systems over the political control of the Spanish populace. Those earlier confrontations had begun with the conflicts between Christianity and the "pagan" faiths of Iberians, early Romans, and Germanic Visigoths during the time of the Roman Empire. The controversies had then continued with (b) Islam in the Middle Ages, (c) Judaism and Christian Protestantism during the European Renaissance, and (d) socialism, humanism, agnosticism, and atheism in modern times. Roman Catholicism, when vying with other belief systems, had scored many triumphs over the years, thus managing to remain Spain's dominant religion into the twenty-first century.
- Throughout the twentieth century, the control of public policies in Spain periodically had shuttled back and forth between pro-Catholic and pro-Socialist legislation, as conservatives and liberals alternately won the right to hold public office. That shuttling continued into the twenty-first century.
- By the first decade of the twenty-first century, the religious fervor and doctrinal fealty of Spain's Catholics had dramatically declined, paralleling a decline in the church's privileges and political influence.

As a way of summarizing the historical backgrounds of the Spanish case, Figure 8.1 displays a highly simplified pair of timelines that identify some principal critical events and belief system traditions over two millennia—0 CE

From Year 0 to 2000

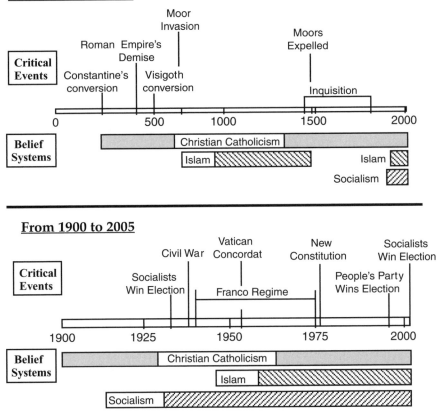

Figure 8.1 Critical events and belief systems in the Spanish case.

through 2005 CE. The timeline on the upper tier of Figure 8.1 furnishes a two-millennia view. The timeline on the lower tier focuses on events during the most recent 105 years—1900 to 2005.

Religion in the Schools

Religion has always been part of schooling in Spain. In early Roman times, prior to the adoption of Christianity as the state faith, youths from the upper social classes were instructed by tutors who introduced them to Roman gods and to Latin and Greek grammar and literature. Then, during the Roman Empire's Christian era, the study of Roman gods would be replaced by Catholic doctrine (Ancient Roman education, 2005).

Throughout the Moorish period (711–1492) almost every town and village in Spain maintained a primary school (*maktab*) in which pupils learned to read and write Arabic, master basic Islamic religious lore, memorize the Quran, and often study poetry, arithmetic, penmanship, ethics (manners), and elementary grammar (The Islamic era, 1994).

Following the expulsion of the Moors from Spain, essentially all secondary and higher education over the ensuing centuries would be provided by Catholic orders. Whatever primary schooling there was for the children who were not educated at home was also furnished by church-affiliated groups. Christian lore, as found in the Old and New Testaments of the Bible, became a central focus of a curriculum that included reading, writing, calculating, and moral precepts.

In modern times, about 70% of Spain's students have attended state schools, with the rest enrolled in private schools, mostly Catholic institutions requiring learners to include Catholicism among their studies. Over the decades, religious education in state schools has sometimes been obligatory and sometimes optional. For example, after the Socialists came into power in 1931, the study of religion became voluntary. Then, throughout the Franco era (1936–1975), classes in Catholicism were mandatory. After Franco's death, religious studies were again voluntary under the 1978 constitution. The 1999 revision of Spain's school system extended compulsory, free education through age 16 and included religious education as an optional subject at both primary and secondary levels. Finally, Prime Minister Aznar's 2003 law would have made the study of religion—principally Catholicism—mandatory if the Socialists under Zapatero had not moved in late 2004 to eliminate all religious studies from state schools.

With this brief overview of religion-in-the-schools as a background, we turn now to the constituencies involved in the controversy that accompanied the Socialists gaining control of the government in the 2004 election.

THE CONTENDING CONSTITUENCIES

The most obvious antagonists in the religious-education episode were the Socialists led by Zapatero and the People's Party headed by Aznar, but whose candidate for prime minister in the March 2004 was Mariano Rajoy. Among the Socialists' allies were left-of-center political groups and liberal Catholics. Aznar's supporters were chiefly Spain's Roman Catholic conservatives, particularly members of the church hierarchy who were bound to lose both spiritual influence and funding as a consequence of the Socialists' legislative initiatives. Although Spain had more than four dozen political parties—many of them representing regional or special-group interests—the only two of real significance in the 2004 election were the Socialists (who won 42.6% of the seats in parliament) and the People's Party (which took 37.6% of the seats) (Elections in Spain, 2004).

The nation's Muslim community favored parts of the Socialists' agenda, whereas the small Protestant and Jewish segments of the population apparently had mixed feelings about what the secularists sought to accomplish.

Socialists and Their Allies

The Spanish Socialist Workers' Party drew much of its membership from industrial workers, miners, landless laborers, and the nation's public officials. The party also maintained close ties with intellectuals and artists (PSOE, 2004).

Leading up the 2004 parliamentary election, voter surveys suggested that the People's Party would surely win. But 3 days before voters went to the polls, terrorists blew up trains in Madrid, killing 190 commuters. When the ruling People's Party unexpectedly lost the election, analysts concluded that the bombings had painfully impressed on the public the costs of the People's Party supporting an unpopular war in Iraq, so nearly 43% of the voters chose the anti-Iraq-war Socialists, enough of a margin to put that party in office (Rodríguez & de Quirós, 2004).

To bolster their strength in the election, Socialists could expect support from such left-of-center parties as the United Left (a coalition that included Communists) and from liberal Catholics who were advocates of a secular state.

Conservative Catholics

Most members of the Catholic clergy favored the People's Party and its pro-Catholic agenda. They were joined by conservative lay Catholics, and they enjoyed the blessing of the Vatican in Rome.

Muslims

By the early twenty-first century, Spain was the home of an estimated 1 million Muslims—a mixture of both legal and illegal residents. Their numbers grew rapidly, especially through immigration. Most of the Muslims came from Morocco, crossing the 9 miles of Mediterranean Sea that separates the two countries near Gibraltar. In terms of quantity, Morocco was exceeded only by Ecuador as the source of newcomers to Spain in recent times, with a large portion of the Muslim immigrants settling in Spain's southern agricultural regions as farm laborers.

As the number of Muslims increased, so did friction between the immigrants and the general public. Muslims complained of being treated as inferiors and denied the rights and privileges available to the Catholics that made up the bulk of the population. Catholics, in response, accused members of the Muslim community of criminal activity and terrorism, a charge given more credence after police investigators revealed that most of the terrorists who killed the 190 people on commuter trains in Madrid in March 2004 were Moroccans (Harrigan, 2004).

After the Socialists won the 2004 election, Zapatero's government moved to extend the same opportunities to the Islamic community as were available to other faiths—Catholics, Protestants, and Jews. To accomplish such an equity goal, the government would need to curtail the privileges traditionally enjoyed by the Catholic Church. The Socialists' plan for the Muslims touched off fears within Spain's Catholic clergy that a modern-day Moorish invasion might be in the offing. In July 2004 the government announced its intention to cancel the reintroduction of compulsory religious classes and to find ways to finance faiths other than Catholicism, with those other faiths to include Islam. In response to the announcement, Spain's leading archbishop, Cardinal Antonio María Rouco, accused the Socialists of returning the nation to medieval times when Moors ruled the country. He said, "Some people wish to place us in the year 711. It seems as if we are meant to wipe ourselves out of history" (Tremlett, 2004).

Protestants and Jews

The nation's small proportion of Protestants and Jews[1] could be expected to feel somewhat ambivalent—as would Muslims—about the Socialist proposals. On the one hand, they apparently would have liked the government to continue funding religious groups but, in doing so, bring the proportion of money for Protestant and Jewish groups up to the level traditionally available to Catholics. From such a perspective, Protestants and Jews would disagree with the Socialists' apparent long-term intention to eliminate any public funding of religious activities. At the same time, they would endorse the Socialists' policy of being evenhanded in providing whatever privilege and power the government would make available to religious groups.

Summary

An estimate of the lineup of adversaries in the conflict over mandated religious studies is displayed in Figure 8.2.

Analysis of the power potential of the main adversaries in the case shows that both the Socialists and the People's Party were organized in a hierarchical form, with local branches supporting provincial sections which, in turn, sustained a central headquarters that coordinated party policies and activities nationwide. Both parties aggressively exploited mass communication media (newspapers, radio, television, Internet) in pursuit of public endorsement. Both were headed by politically savvy, experienced politicians. Each had periodically been in office and, on those occasions, had wielded the authority to pass laws and regulations promoting the party's agenda. In effect, the two adversaries seemed about equal in resources, authority, and leadership.

The predominant force operating to conserve practices from the past was the country's long history of having Roman Catholicism provide the core of Spanish culture. In opposition to Catholic tradition, the influences encouraging social change included far greater international communication and

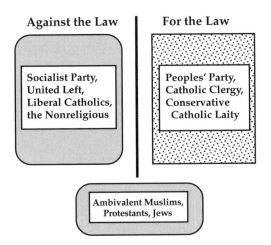

Figure 8.2 Groups' opinions of the compulsory-religious-classes law.

increased educational opportunity. The advent of radio, motion pictures, television, improved transportation (trains, autos, airplanes), and the Internet immeasurably expanded people's view of the world, and particularly of people's opportunities to learn about other cultures and belief systems. In parallel with the communication media opening more windows on the world, laws requiring universal compulsory education engaged virtually all of Spain's youths in schooling that introduced them to diverse ways of life—ways that extended beyond the perspective of one belief constituency. As a consequence, the traditional appeal of Catholicism declined as the populace became aware of newly available options.

A further influence on change was Spain's membership in the European Union, whose proposed constitution (endorsed by the Socialists) included a list of rights to which all individuals would be entitled, including the right to (a) freedom of thought, conscience, and religion; (b) have their philosophical, religious, and pedagogical convictions respected; and (c) freedom from discrimination based on any ground such as sex, race, color, ethnic or social origin, genetic features, language, political or any other opinion, membership in a national minority, age, birth, or sexual orientation (Dehousse & Coussens, 2003).

RESOLVING THE CONTROVERSY

The history of religion in Spain's state schools over the past few decades suggests that the Socialists' solution to the controversy—that of eliminating all religious instruction from schools—might be short-lived. The issue would seem to depend on which political party is in office at a particular time. We can recall that from the time Socialists took over the reins of the government in 1931 until the Civil War of 1936–1939, participation in religious classes in public schools was voluntary. Then, under Francisco Franco (1936–1975), instruction in Catholicism became obligatory. With the new 1978 constitution created following Franco's death, religious education turned voluntary once more until the People's Party passed the 2003 law requiring students to take classes on religion. Finally, when the Socialists won the 2004 election, the conflict over religious education was resolved by the Socialists moving to eliminate all religious studies in schools.

Therefore, if the pro-Catholic People's Party should win control of the government in the future—as it nearly did in 2004—we might well expect religious education in state schools to appear again, as either a required or elective subject.

CHAPTER 9

China

The China case mentioned in Chapter 1 concerned a confrontation between the Chinese government and Li Guangqiang, a member of a Christian sect who brought into Fujian Province more than 33,000 copies of a prohibited version of the Christian Bible. The "schools" involved in the case were not state schools, because no form of religion has been permitted in China's elementary or secondary schools for many decades. Instead, the learning institutions in the controversy were clandestine Sunday schools and Bible-study classes operated by an outlawed Christian group known as the Shouters.

HISTORICAL ROOTS

As a background for understanding the forbidden-Bibles controversy, the following discussion opens with (a) a brief description of religions in China, then continues with (b) the Communist government's ways of coping with religions, (c) the Shouters' place among the country's religions, and (d) recently revised government policies.

Religions in China

The religious composition of the People's Republic of China today is an accumulation of ancient indigenous religions and of foreign belief systems that were added later.

The Distant Past

Evidence from ancient records (about 2000 BCE) suggest that people worshipped many sorts of gods who they thought controlled such things as weather, crop success, health, people's decisions, and death. The ancient

Chinese also imagined that ancestors who had died became invisible spirits that continued to linger around and influence the lives of their descendents. Honoring deceased ancestors with prayer and offerings was believed to contribute to one's good fortune. However, the specific characteristics of early faiths could vary from one place to another so that diverse versions of folk religion developed, with vestiges of such beliefs still found today, particularly in remote rural regions.

The two most famous of early Chinese philosophies—and both are very much alive today—were Taoism and Confucianism, each cast in an organized manner around the sixth century BCE. The formulation of Taoism is often attributed to Lao Tzu (Lao-tse), who may have been a mythical figure. The term *Tao* means *The Way* or *Nature's Way*. According to Taoism, people's lives are most satisfactory when in harmony with a universal force that flows through all living things. Taoism teaches that observing nature's patterns and adjusting one's living to those patterns leads to contentment.

Confucius (Kung Fu-Tzu) (551?–478? BCE) is credited with assembling existing beliefs about social organization into a structured philosophy of how groups function most efficiently. He used wise sayings (analects) to explain his principles of socially effective behavior. The principles applied to groups of all sizes, beginning with the family, then on to the community, and finally to the nation. Each group should be directed by a patriarch—father, tribal leader, king—who must deal astutely and justly with the group's members. The members, in turn, are obliged to serve the leader faithfully for the common good. In the beginning, Confucianism was a philosophy of social organization without such religious elements as life after death and invisible spirits. But over the centuries, those religious features became attached to the philosophy so that by the twenty-first century certain versions of Confucianism included the worship of dead ancestors who were believed to exist in spirit form. Confucianism continues today as the official philosophical foundation of the Republic of China on the island of Taiwan. However, because the People's Republic of China on the East Asian mainland has continued at odds with the Taiwan government, Confucianism is not accepted on the mainland as a legitimate philosophy or religion, although it continues to influence many people's life perspective.

Both Taoism and Confucianism were indigenous Chinese worldviews, born and developed within Chinese culture itself. In contrast, the principal religion of foreign origin that would attract millions of Chinese over the centuries was Buddhism, imported from India. Although Buddhism appeared in China as early as 50 BCE, it did not become popular until 500 years later in the Three Kingdoms era.

During the Tang dynasty (618–907 CE), increased trade between China and the Middle East introduced additional foreign faiths—Zoroastrianism, Christianity, Judaism, Islam—that drew some converts but did not become widespread. Over the ensuing centuries until modern times, the most popular religions would continue to be Confucianism among the upper classes, Taoism and Buddhism among ordinary people, and beliefs in traditional folk gods and ancestor worship throughout much of the population.

Christianity gained a growing number of followers after the mid-nineteenth century when Britain's victory over China in the Opium Wars opened China to European powers that brought Christian missionaries to establish churches, schools, and hospitals. The most famous Chinese to attend Christian schools was Sun Yat Sen (1866–1925), today known as the "Father of Modern China," who began in a mission primary school in China, and then studied as a teenager at the Anglicans' Iolani School in Honolulu. In 1892 he became one of the first two graduates of the Hong Kong College of Medicine for Chinese.

The Imposition of Atheism

In the middle of the twentieth century, the role of religion in the lives of Chinese took a dramatic turn. At the close of World War II in 1945, the two largest political factions in China—the Nationalists and the Communists—battled each other, with Communist troops routing the Nationalists, who fled to the island of Taiwan where they established the government that rules Taiwan today under the title Republic of China. At the same time, the Communists founded the People's Republic of China that has governed the East Asian mainland ever since.

Communism in the People's Republic assumed a Marxist–Leninist–Maoist version. First, the form of dialectical materialism created by the German philosopher/social activist Karl Marx became the Soviet Union's philosophical guide, embellished by Russian Vladimir Ilyich Lenin during the Russian Revolution (1917–1921). Then Lenin's version passed from Russia to China in the early 1920s, there to be revised by Mao Zedong to suit Chinese conditions. From the viewpoint of religion, the most significant feature of Marxism–Leninism–Maoism was its rejection of all religious faiths. Lenin accepted Marx's declaration that religion was the opiate of the masses, thereby implying that religious faith was used to prevent the common people from recognizing that they were being exploited in a capitalistic economic system. Ergo, Communism needed to be atheistic, so religion should be eliminated from the envisioned perfect society of the future.

Nevertheless, in the provisional constitution devised for the fledgling People's Republic in 1949, the promise of religious freedom would need to be included so as to attract more followers to the United Front that the government sought to form in support of its programs. The constitution promised citizens "freedom of thought, speech, publication, assembly, association, correspondence, person, residence, mobility, religious belief, and demonstration" (Religious policy, 2005). Consequently, over the 15-year period following the establishment of the People's Republic, religious activities were reluctantly allowed and closely monitored until Mao Zedong launched his Cultural Revolution in 1966. Mao's aim was to transform China into an ideal classless society by forcing the elimination of all social class distinctions. He attempted this by glorifying the proletariat—laborers and peasants—and by demeaning intellectuals. Mao's Red Guards closed schools and colleges, banished teachers and their students to remote provinces to toil beside the peasants, and banned "subversive" reading materials. Missionaries were deported, pastors and their followers were persecuted, "religious activities of every kind were banned, and churches, mosques, temples, and shrines were closed, commandeered for use as factories or warehouses or in many cases willfully desecrated or destroyed" (Breen, 2002).

The Cultural Revolution soon turned into an economic, political, and social disaster. After 10 years of deep troubles, it officially ended with Mao's death in 1976. What followed was a new constitution in 1982, the one under which the People's Republic continues to operate today. According to Article 36 of that document,

No state organ, public organization, or individual may compel citizens to believe in, or not to believe in, any religion; nor may they discriminate against citizens who believe in, or do not believe in, any religion. The state protects normal religious activities. No one may make use of religion to engage in activities that disrupt public order, impair the health of citizens, or interfere with the educational system of the state. Religious bodies and religious affairs are not subject to any foreign domination. (Constitution of the People's Republic of China, 1982)

That provision has continued in effect to the present day.

What, then, was the extent of religious participation in China's population of 1.3 billion by the late twentieth century. A report issued by the Chinese government in 1997 stated that "According to incomplete statistics, there are over 100 million followers of various religious faiths, more than 85,000 sites for religious activities, some 300,000 clergy, and over 3,000 religious organizations" (Religion in China, 2004). Buddhism and Taoism were by far the most popular, with an unknown number of people still clinging to traditional folk beliefs. In addition, the government estimated that there were 18 million Moslems, 10 million Protestants, and 4 million Catholics. However, observers of the country's religious scene considered those figures extremely low, "with more accurate estimates ranging to as high as five times the official number" (Religion in China, 2004).

Religion under the People's Republic

The Republic's initial constitution in 1949 declared freedom of religion for five faiths—Buddhism, Taoism, Islam, Catholicism, and Christian Protestantism. To enable the government to maintain a measure of control over those denominations, each faith was required to operate within a government-approved national organization. The five organizations were—and are today—the Buddhist Association of China, Taoist Association of China, Islamic Association of China, Chinese Patriotic Catholic Association, and Three-Self

Patriotic Movement Committee of the Protestant Churches of China. At the same time, the government excluded from the freedom-of-religion provision all folk beliefs and fundamentalist Muslim and Christian groups that operated outside the government-defined bodies. The nature of the five official groups can be illustrated with the Three-Self Patriotic Movement Committee (TSPM), the group that the Shouters should have joined if they had wished to be recognized as a legitimate religion under the Republic's rules.

The Three-Self Patriotic Movement

The "three selves" in the organization's title are *self-governing, self-supporting,* and *self-propagating.* These selves were originally the invention of Henry Venn of the Church Missionary Society more than a century ago. Then in 1950, the selves were given a modern interpretation in *The Christian Manifesto,* written by a liberal Christian, Y. T. Wu, and approved by Zhou Enlai, the first premier of the People's Republic. The manifesto charged that during the nineteenth century and first half of the twentieth century, "Western Catholicism and Protestantism manipulated and controlled Chinese churches, turning them into the appendages of Western religious orders and mission societies" (OMF, 2004). Wu's document called upon China's Christians to become self-reliant and to cast off foreign influence in the reconstruction of modern China. In 1954 the TSPM was formally established to carry out the manifesto's mission. By the 1990s, government officials continued to characterize the TSPM as "a patriotic movement formed spontaneously by Chinese Christians who sought to defend themselves against the invasion and bullying of colonialists and imperialists in the early days" (China refutes distortions, 1995).

The five official religious bodies were outlawed during the Cultural Revolution of 1966–1976 but were subsequently revived to continue operating into the twenty-first century. The relationship between the government and the five bodies can be illustrated with passages from the TSPM constitution.

The aim of this organization is to lead Christians to love the nation and the church; to glorify God and benefit the people; to abide by the Constitution, laws, regulations, and policies of the State; to observe social mores; uphold the independence of the church; strengthen unity inside and outside the church; serve the aim of running the church well; and enable the church to adapt to socialist society . . .

The duties of the TSPM are as follows:

(1) Under the leadership of the Chinese Communist Party and the People's Government, to unite all Chinese Christians to deeply love our socialist homeland and abide by its Constitution, laws, regulations and policies;

(2) To uphold self-government, self-support, self-propagation, independence, and a self-run church as guiding principles;

(3) To actively promote theological reconstruction;

(4) To assist the government in implementing the policy of freedom of religious belief and in safeguarding the legitimate rights of the church;

(5) To contribute its efforts in safeguarding national unity and stability; building social-ist material and spiritual civilization; achieving national unification and developing friendly international relationships; and safeguarding world peace. (Constitution of the National Committee, 2002)

Such commitments in the constitutions of the five official religious organi-zations confronted members of the faiths with a difficult decision. Should they agree to have their religions subservient to the Republic's state-socialism poli-cies? Or should they avoid joining their denomination's official group in order to remain faithful to their religion's traditional authority—the Buddha's teach-ings for Buddhism, the pope in Rome for Catholics, the Prophet Muhammad for Muslims, and Jesus Christ along with church hierarchies for Protestants (Lutheran, Episcopalian, Methodist, Presbyterian, and the like)? Over the years, some adherents signed up with their faith's official group, while others refused to do so. Consequently, each religious community became divided into two camps—one that enjoyed the approval of the government and another that suffered government censure and harassment.

To belong to the TSPM gives freedom to worship and to minister legally; yet there are many restrictions. One of the main restrictions is the "three designates" policy. This means that Christian activity must take place only in designated buildings (church buildings and homes that have been registered with the TSPM), must be conducted by a designated leader (an official TSPM pastor), and must be confined to one's own area (no poaching in somebody else's "parish"). . . . Even the substance of a pastor's sermon is under scrutiny. Such subjects as the value of suffering, the return of Christ, and the life of heaven are frowned upon, as they are regarded as "escapist" themes, and thus in conflict with Marxist ideology. Such practices as praying for the sick and exorcising demons are regarded as superstitions, and should be outlawed. (Three-self, 2005)

Furthermore, religious education was to be confined to persons age 18 and over. Thus, Sunday schools for children and youths were prohibited.

Foreigners' writing about present-day Protestantism in China declare that Christianity has prospered under the TSPM.

Go to China today, and what do you find? A Protestant church officially numbering over 15 million (compared to only 700,000 in 1949 when the Communists took power), meeting in nearly 50,000 registered churches and meeting-points. Full congregations, with young men and women including many students, alongside the elderly. By the end of 2001, 28 million Bibles had been printed by the China-based Amity Press. About 20 seminaries are now open [along with] many more local Bible training classes. (The Chinese church, 2005)

Not only did China's Protestants depend on their self-support commit-ment, but they continued to welcome help from abroad, since the government permitted the officially sanctioned religious organizations to maintain international contacts that did not involve "foreign control," although what constituted "control" was not defined (China, 2003). As an example of foreign participation, the China Christian Council (action wing of the TSPM) invited the Lutheran Church in the United States to help. In response, the Lutherans provided 1.5 million audiocassettes that included Christian sermons, the Psalms, Bible stories, Christmas hymns, and other Christian instrumental and choral music. A recording studio in Shanghai distributed 250,000 New Testament reading cassettes, and 30,000 "Hymnmasters" (computerized music players with 500 hymns) were sent to churches (Today in China, 2004).

Protestantism expanded rapidly in China within the confines of the TSPM. But that movement accounted for only a portion of Chinese Protestants. Another portion was composed of believers outside the official body, members of sects not acceptable to the government—sects referred to as *house churches*, because their covert meetings were usually held in members' homes.

Although no accurate statistics exist, letters to Gospel radio stations, informed reports, and personal contacts with believers all point to a movement numbering over 20 million. Some house-church leaders put the figure as high as 70 or 80 million. (The Chinese church, 2005)

The Shouters was one such group, so we next consider the nature of outlawed sects, along with the case of the Bible smuggler.

Christian Sects—The Shouters

Over the last half of the twentieth century, a variety of Christian evangelical groups sprang up in China, much to the distress of the government. In 1995, the Communist Party's Central Committee issued a circular identifying illegal *cults*, which included not only the Shouters but also Eastern Lightning, the Society of Disciples, the Falun Gong, the Full Scope Church, the Spirit Sect, the New Testament Church, and the Guan Yin (the Way of the Goddess of Mercy). Directives in later years also banned the Lord God Sect, the Established King Church, the Unification Church, the Family of Love, the Dami Mission, and more (China, 2003).

The Local Church is the official title of the group that became popularly known as *The Shouters* because of the members' practice of stamping their feet and repeatedly yelling "O Lord Jesus" during religious services. The founder of the Shouters was Witness Lee, a Christian churchman who escaped from mainland China to Taiwan in 1949, and then moved to Southern California in 1962 where he directed the sect's international activities until his death in 1997. From the early 1980s into the twenty-first century, the Shouters became one of the fastest growing underground churches in the People's Republic, with an estimated half-million followers.

In the early eighties, large quantities of literature produced by Witness Lee began to circulate in China. The aggressive evangelism of the sect, combined with their vociferous, mantra-like shouting of Bible verses led to a head-on clash with the State-controlled "Three-Self church" and the communist authorities. By 1983, the sect had been declared counter-revolutionary and was everywhere vigorously suppressed, with its key leaders sent to prison for long periods. However, it continued its activities underground, and the death of Witness Lee appeared unlikely to dampen the ardor of its members. (Lambert, 1998)

The most prominent of Witness Lee's written works was *The Recovery Version of New Testaments*, an edition of the Christian Bible replete with Lee's commentaries. Among Lee's annotations that alienated such mainstream Christians as Baptists, Presbyterians, and Anglicans was his charge that such groups were "spiritual fornicators . . . the harlot daughters of the Whore of Babylon, and that Protestantism, Roman Catholicism, and Judaism had become organizations used by Satan as a tool to damage God's economy" (The Shouters, 2004). Such remarks caused the Protestant groups that were members of the TSPM to join the Chinese government in denouncing the Shouters as an illicit cult.

The 33,000 smuggled Bibles that led to Li Guangqiang's detention in 2002 were copies of Witness Lee's *Recovery Version*. Li was not arrested for importing Bibles as such, because Christian Bibles were not outlawed in China. In fact, more than 25 million authorized copies of the Bible had been legally distributed over the period 1997–2002 (Lev, 2002). But it was the *Recovery Version* that resulted in Li's detention. In defense of the arrest, a government spokesman explained, "It is not a case of smuggling Bibles. The Bibles were a pretext for smuggling a large amount of cult publications" (Rosenthal, 2002).

Initially Li had been charged with "using a cult to subvert the law," which could result in a death sentence. But after human rights groups and the United States government expressed strong objection to the indictment, the charge was changed to "conducting illegal business" and the penalty reduced to 2 years imprisonment (Rosenthal, 2002). Then shortly before U.S. President George W. Bush visited China in early 2002, Li was released from prison and placed under surveillance to receive treatment for hepatitis (China releases, 2002).

Revised Government Policies

In the early twenty-first century, observers of life in the People's Republic noted a change in the government's views of religion. In the past, religion had been seen as something that would need to be tolerated in the short run until state socialism had been perfected and there were no longer any social class distinctions in the populace. In effect, the Republic's leaders expected that religion would naturally die out. However, a different expectation was introduced in late 2001 by President Jiang Zemin at a National Front Work Conference when he said, "As a social phenomenon, religion has a long history and will continue to exist for a long time under socialism, perhaps outlasting both the [Communist] Party and the state," so there was good reason for Communists to live amicably with religion (Ye, 2002).

Top government officials no longer recite the Marxist saw that "religion is the opiate of the masses". . . . [When] President Jiang Zemin said religion "may outlast the party and the state," [it was] a stunning acknowledgement from a man supposedly committed to wiping out religion. (Pomfret, 2002)

Summary

By the first decade of the twenty-first century, the People's Republic of China was still officially a nonreligious state. But in reality, officials were obliged to accommodate multiple religions that attracted a growing quantity of believers. The government appeared to be in the process of adopting a new attitude toward alternative belief systems—an attitude that accepted religions as enduring forces which state socialism could willingly tolerate.

Figure 9.1 offers a much-simplified pair of timelines. The upper tier identifies major critical events and modes of governance, along with dominant belief systems, for the period 1500 BCE to 2000 CE. The lower tier provides the same variety of information for the years 1875 through 2005.

With this historical overview as a backdrop, we next consider the nature of the constituencies involved in the banned-Bibles controversy.

THE CONTENDING CONSTITUENCIES

The Bible-smuggling episode was not very significant in itself. Its real importance came from its exposing the current state of the nation's conflict over religion and from its revealing the lineup of constituencies that participated in the conflict. Those constituencies included (a) the government, (b) the Three-Self Patriotic Movement, (c) the Shouters, and (d) freedom-of-religion organizations outside the country. A further constituency that likely held ambivalent feelings about the episode consisted of mainstream Protestants and Catholics overseas.

The Communist Government

The task of coping with religious issues in the twenty-first century placed the government in a difficult bind. The Republic's leaders were caught between their atheistic Marxist ideology and the population's long history of religious belief that found a significant segment of the population yearning for religious commitment. Furthermore, policing the religious activities of 1.3 billion people who were spread across 9.57 million square kilometers was

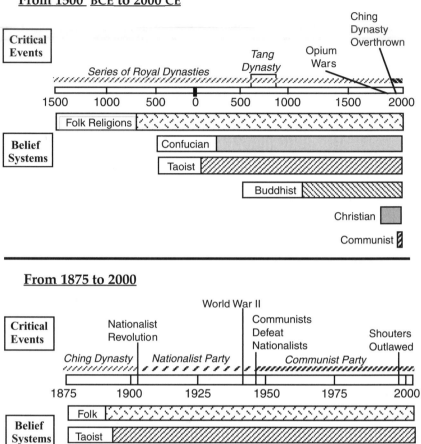

Figure 9.1 Critical events and belief systems in the Chinese case.

an extremely demanding task, so that the extent to which restrictions were imposed on illicit house churches varied greatly from one region to another. And the difference between legal and illegal religious gatherings was becoming increasingly vague.

In the past, Protestantism could be neatly divided into two categories. On one side was the official church that practiced a mainstream Protestant theology that stressed good works. . . . On the other side were unauthorized churches, meeting in houses discreetly and stressing faith-healing and individual salvation. Now the evangelical movement is taking over the mainstream church. In [the city of] Wenzhou, for example, there is no clear distinction between house and official churches. (Pomfret, 2002)

In the confrontation between the Chinese government and the Shouters, government officials obviously wielded by far the greater power by virtue of their official position of authority as supported by laws and by such resources as legislative bodies, administrative positions, the police, and the courts. Furthermore, the government's faithful supporters represented an infinitely greater number of people than did such sects as the Shouters. In that sense, the government commanded infinitely more power than did the illegal religious groups.

However, whether the government's forces were more cohesive than those of the illicit sects is a matter of doubt. Signs of disagreement within the Republic's ranks about what attitude to adopt toward religions suggested that doctrinaire old-time Communist Party members may well have been at odds with such recent leaders as President Jiang Zemin, who recommended a harmonious accommodation of religion. In agreement with Jiang's position, an article by a top official in the Republic's office for economic reform called for the Communist Party to "stop seeing religion as an opponent to be restricted and kept under control, and instead to start treating it as a force which can be of assistance to the government in such areas as politics, the building up of morality, the administration of society, cultural and educational work, and foreign affairs" (Breen, 2002). But in opposition to such a conciliatory attitude was a 2004 directive from the Republic's department of propaganda, expressing alarm over the number of Communist Party cadres and youths converting to religion. The paper urged party members to halt the "growth of religions, cultic organizations, and superstitions, and to strengthen Marxist atheism." The aim was to convince people to "voluntarily and firmly stick to the historical view of Marxist materialism" by stressing instruction in the "natural sciences" that would provide them with "knowledge of the universe, the origin of life, the rule on human evolution, and correctly deal with various natural phenomena, natural disasters, birth, aging, disease and death" (Party's secret directives, 2004).

Tony Lambert, an analyst of religious life in China, wrote that

vast areas of rural China are falling further and further behind the advanced coastal areas and the cities in the race for economic development. Ignorance and superstition are still rife and provide fertile soil for the growth of cults. In the countryside, peasants have returned largely to family-based farming and extended-clan associations. Communist Party control is often weak, and there is an ideological and spiritual vacuum [that the sects are prepared to fill]. (Lambert, 1998)

Thus, while the government could count on a much larger number of supporters than did the religious sects, those sects—and especially the forbidden house churches—were expanding rapidly and thereby growing in potential influence.

The most important ideals motivating the government's policies on religion were the tenets of international Communism as modified by certain practical considerations. Thus, the aim of the People's Republic was to eventually produce a prosperous atheistic society in which there were no social class distinctions. Such an ideal derived from the writings of Marx, Lenin, and Mao. However, in view of the deep-seated role that religion had always played in Chinese society, party leaders would be judicious in the foreseeable future to allow religious activities under government supervision. Support for this temporary toleration of religions was found in the nation's 1982 constitution and its rationale.

Some observers of China's struggle over religion suggested that "the official ideology of Communism is being fast replaced by a confused mix of hedonism, materialism, and faith. [The struggle] is also about the creation of civil society in a country where the Communist Party still fears unofficial associations. And it concerns the rights of ordinary Chinese to peacefully oppose government policies" (Pomfret, 2002).

The government's puzzlement over such matters appeared to be reflected in its handling of the forbidden-Bibles incident. The smuggler, Li Guangqiang, was first accused of a crime that could lead to the death penalty. The charge was then changed to a lesser infraction that could warrant 2 years in prison. And ultimately he was released from jail, placed under surveillance, and offered medical treatment.

The Three-Self Patriotic Movement

It seems likely that churches operating under the policies of such officially recognized religious bodies as the Three-Self Patriotic Movement would approve of the government's arresting Li for importing Witness Lee's *Recovery Version* of the Christian Bible. Not only did that version significantly alter long-honored interpretations of Christian scripture, but Lee had accused traditional Protestant denominations of being Satan's handmaidens. Perhaps the other official religious groups—Buddhists, Catholics, Taoists, and Muslims—would also approve of Li's arrest, because Li represented a sect that refused to work within the confines of the government regulations that those groups had accepted.

The Shouters

Not only would the Shouters—as one of the most successful house church movements—condemn the arrest of Li, but members of other illicit evangelical sects could also be expected to denounce the arrest because it threatened their own well-being. They could fear that their own church workers might be subject to arrest.

In contrast to the government's motives, the efforts of each of China's religious groups were inspired by a desire to extend their sect's belief system throughout the entire populace. The source of such inspiration was the sect's holy scriptures. For the Shouters, those scriptures were Witness Lee's version of the Christian Bible and his large collection of additional writings.

In the Shouters' attempt to further their cause, they sought the support of foreign governments and freedom-of-religion advocates by means of news stories sent to out-of-the-country mass communication media—newspapers, radio, television, magazines, and Internet Web sites.

Foreign Organizations

In the past—and particularly during Mao's Cultural Revolution—China had adopted an isolationist policy in foreign affairs. However, by the twenty-first century, the People's Republic was very actively engaging in economic, political, social, and educational exchanges with the rest of the world. Consequently, the government was highly sensitive to the image it conveyed internationally.

When news of Li's arrest was received overseas, alarm was voiced by a variety of international organizations that were dedicated to religious freedom. And because in 1998 China had signed the International Covenant on Civil and Political Rights, critics abroad claimed that the arrest of Li violated that 1998 commitment (Religion in China, 2004). The United States government was among those expressing concern, with U.S. interest in the Li affair particularly acute because the incident occurred shortly before U.S. President George W. Bush was scheduled to visit China.

Mainstream Churches Overseas

Traditional Christian denominations outside of China (Lutherans, Presbyterians, Baptists, Anglicans, and the like) probably had mixed reactions to the forbidden-Bible episode. They could be pleased that steps were taken by the Chinese government toward stemming the further spread of the Shouters cult, but they could also fear that members of their own sect in China might be in jeopardy.

Summary

In the China case, the forces of stability were ones that had sustained the Communist government over the past half-century. Those forces included the government's (a) insisting that religious groups operate only within the confines of the five officially designated associations and (b) punishing sects that failed to abide by official restrictions, with the punishments entailing jail sentences, beatings, the confiscation of property, and the destruction of meeting sites and religious materials.

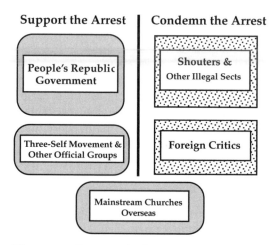

Figure 9.2 Estimated adversaries in the Bible-smuggling case.

In opposition to forces of stability, forces of change were ones that encouraged tolerance for, and the growth of, religions. Lambert, in speaking of the rapid expansion of house churches in China over the last two decades of the twentieth century, suggested that

with the vast increase of tourists and businessmen in China, China is no longer cut off from the world as was the case under Mao. Religious ideas, including cultic ones, have a much greater freedom to gain entry. It should be noted that cults strongly based in Taiwan and the Overseas Chinese community (such as the Shouters and the New Testament Church) have made far greater inroads into Mainland China than the Western-based cults such as Mormonism and the Jehovah's Witnesses whose influence appears to be negligible. (Lambert, 1998)

The estimated lineup of participants in the Bible-smuggling case is displayed graphically in Figure 9.2.

RESOLVING THE CONTROVERSY

The Li Guangqiang case was resolved by a three-stage process. First, Li was accused of "using a cult to subvert the law." Next, his crime was reduced to "conducting illegal business." Finally, he was released for medical reasons. It is unclear whether this process resulted from confusion on the part of the authorities about how best to handle the incident or, instead, the process was an intentional strategy whose purpose was to achieve two outcomes: (a) initially frighten other cult members with the "subvert-the-law" charge that could lead to a death sentence and then later (b) mollify foreign critics by showing compassion for the Bible-smuggler's health problem.

However, the disposition of the Li case probably contributed nothing toward solving the government's increasingly thorny problem of what role should be assigned to religions in the kind of society that the People's Republic was now becoming.

CHAPTER 10

Italy

The religion-and-school controversy in the Italian case was launched by a Muslim father objecting to a Christian crucifix being displayed on the wall of a public school kindergarten in which his son was enrolled. The dispute pitted the father and secularists against conservative Catholics and much of the Muslim community, with the issue finally carried to the top of the Italian court system.

HISTORICAL ROOTS

Over the centuries, Italy has been more intimately associated with Roman Catholicism than has any other nation in the world. The headquarters of the church has always been in Rome, from where the Holy Father—the pope—has directed the worldwide development of the faith. Across a span of nearly 2,000 years, there have been 263 popes, beginning with St. Peter in 32 CE and extending to Benedict XVI in 2005. More than 78% of the popes (205) have been Italians. By the early years of the twenty-first century, 98% of Italy's residents continued to identify themselves as Catholics. Throughout the world, there were more than 1 billion Catholics (Nationality of popes, 2005).

The following sketch of significant historical incidents bearing on the classroom crucifix dispute begins with (a) early church-and-government connections, then continues with (b) nineteenth-century conditions, (c) two decades of fascism, (d) the post–World War II era, and (e) the crucifix episode. This historical review features the waxing and waning of the Catholic Church's influence over civil government and schooling across the centuries.

Early Church/Government Connections

From the first century CE until the close of the third century, Christianity was a maverick sect that struggled to establish itself in communities around the Mediterranean Sea. Then the faith would spread rapidly after Roman Emperor Constantine converted to the Christian faith in the fourth century and, with the Edict of Milan (313 CE), declared Christianity the official religion for the entire Roman empire. Following the empire's dissolution around 500 CE, the Italian peninsula throughout the next millennium was never ruled as a single unit. Instead, it was divided into princedoms or states. Among those separate entities was a group of *papal states* that extended from Rome across the middle and northeastern portions of the peninsula. Papal states were governed by church authorities in Rome, thereby establishing a tradition of the Catholic Church being in direct control of political entities. For more than 1,100 years (754–1870 CE) the papal states were a unique religious enclave.

The church provided the rationale for the existence of the state, to allow the pope freedom of action without owing loyalty to any secular prince. Revenue was not considered public wealth, but income intended for charity or as support for clerics engaged in ecclesiastical work. Churchmen always held the dominant governmental offices. They legislated, judged, educated, and policed the state in such a way as to ensure that the church would have a steady base from which to operate. (Glueckert, 2004)

The papal states were at their most extensive in the eighteenth century, when they included most of Central Italy (Latium, Umbria, Marche, Ravenna, Ferrara, Bologna), two small regions in southern Italy (Benevento, Pontecorvo), and the Comtat Venaissin area around Avignon in southern France (Papal states, 2005).

Over the centuries, the small amount of formal education available in Italy was limited chiefly to the upper social classes. The tutoring and schooling of the privileged few were provided by Catholic religious orders, so church doctrine and morals formed much of the curriculum, along with reading and writing in Latin and Greek, some history, and basic mathematics.

Nineteenth-Century Conditions

The first two-thirds of the nineteenth century found the Italian peninsula in a constant state of political turmoil—a seemingly endless round of diplomatic and armed conflicts among the princely states. Some states tried to annex others' territories, would-be usurpers sought to unseat current rulers, and new alliances formed as old ones split up. France and Austria periodically seized sections of the peninsula, while Britain attempted to intervene diplomatically in states' affairs. Socialists, who proposed to put political control in the hands of voters, clashed with aristocrats, who wanted the favored elite to remain in power. Advocates of a unified government for all of the peninsula vied with defenders of the separate-states tradition.

By the early 1860s, the proponents of a nationalized Italy, through military and diplomatic victories, succeeded in forming a constitutional monarchy with King Victor Emmanuel II at its head. The entire peninsula, except for the papal states, was now ruled by the newly created Kingdom of Italy. In order to complete the unification of the country, the king in 1860 demanded that the papal states be annexed to the national government. When Pope Pius IX resisted, nationalist forces defeated the papal army, and the king deprived the pope of all his territories except Rome and its immediate vicinity. The final unification of the Kingdom of Italy was completed 10 years later when, in September 1870, the monarch's forces captured Rome. In 1871, a so-called Law of Guarantees was issued by the government, offering the pope the Vatican, the rights of a sovereign, a few palaces in Rome, and an annual stipend equal to about $650,000. Neither Pius IX nor any of his successors accepted the palaces or stipend (Pope Pius IX, 2005).

The pope, whose previous residence, the Quirinal Palace, had become the royal palace of the kings of Italy, withdrew in protest into the Vatican, where he lived as a self-proclaimed "prisoner," refusing to leave or to set foot in St. Peter's Square, and ordering Catholics on pain of excommunication not to participate in elections in the new Italian state. (Papal states, 2004)

Thus ended more than a thousand years of Roman Catholic governmental control over major areas of the Italian peninsula.

Around the same time that the fledgling monarchy was annexing the papal states (1859–1861), the new government established a national education system. Schools for the common people and ones for the ruling class were already operating, most of them conducted by Catholic orders. However, the fact that schooling was restricted to a very limited segment of the population is suggested by literacy figures—an estimated 75–80% of Italians were illiterate.

Over the next half-century, even though the church had no direct influence over civil affairs, most Italians continued to follow the Catholic faith, and Catholic orders still provided much of the nation's schooling. Then in the 1920s, events would alter church/state relations in a manner that significantly strengthened the Vatican's influence over the nation's education system.

Two Decades of Fascism

As a young man, Benito Mussolini (1883–1945) had been a socialist atheist who referred to Catholic priests as "black germs" (Mussolini, 2004). When planning to get married, Mussolini chose a civil ceremony rather than being wed in a church. But his attitude about Catholicism changed dramatically when, in 1922, he was elected head of the Italian government. Over the following years, he and his Black Shirt militia progressively forced Fascist-Party dictatorial control over the populace. As *Il Duce* (The Leader), Mussolini recognized that while he governed the political side of Italy, the Roman Catholic Church governed the spiritual side. Even as early as 1920 he had observed that the pope represented "400 million men scattered the world over . . . a colossal force" (Mussolini, 2004). Hence, he could not afford to anger the pope and the cardinals. Therefore, as the years advanced, he created ever-stronger ties with the Vatican by requiring the display of a crucifix in every school classroom (1924, 1927), by his remarriage in a church ceremony (1925), and by his arranging the Lateran Treaty of 1929. The treaty recognized the Vatican as a sovereign state, accorded the pope the privileges of a head of state, and awarded the Roman Catholic Church a large sum of money as reparation for the treatment the church had suffered in 1870 when the Vatican's control over the papal states was forcibly terminated.

A Concordat was signed by which the Catholic Church recovered all the former prominence which had been denied it by the secular State. Catholicism was proclaimed the only religion of the State; religious education was made compulsory in schools; teachers had to be approved by the Church; and only those textbooks "approved by the ecclesiastical authority" could be used. (Manhattan, 1949)

The treaty granted the Catholic Church 109 acres in Rome for its newly created state—the Vatican—and the pope was allowed to maintain a small army, police force, post office, and rail station. He was also given a country retreat, Castel Gandolfo.

The Lateran Treaty was warmly welcomed by church officials. Pope Pius XI announced that Mussolini was the man through whom "Divine Providence" had made the treaty and the concordat possible. In a reception at the Vatican, "the Papal Aristocracy and Hierarchy applauded Mussolini when he appeared in a film; and the following month all the cardinals in Rome declared in an address to the Pope that Mussolini ruled Italy 'by a decree of Divine Providence.'" In addition, Vatican authorities ordered priests, at the end of their daily mass, to pray for the salvation of "the King and Il Duce" (Manhattan, 1949).

In 1932, Cardinal Gasparri, the Italian Papal Legate, declared that

the Fascist Government of Italy is the only exception to the political anarchy of governments, parliaments, and schools the world over. . . . Mussolini is the man who saw first clearly in the present world chaos. He is now endeavoring to place the heavy Government machinery on its right track, namely to have it work in accordance with the moral laws of God. (Manhattan, 1949)

In sum, during Fascist rule in Italy (1922–1943), the Catholic Church regained influence in governmental affairs and acquired new powers over the nation's schools. But the alliance between the Church and the Fascist Party ended in 1945 with Mussolini's death and Italy's military defeat by American and British military forces.

The Post–World War II Era (1945–2005)

The governance of Italy as a constitutional monarchy ended with the close of the war, replaced by a democratic republic. The new government's commitment to religious freedom was included in the constitution of 1948, a constitution still in effect in the twenty-first century.

All citizens have equal social status and are equal before the law, without regard to their sex, race, language, religion, political opinions, and personal or social conditions. Everyone is entitled to freely profess religious beliefs in any form, individually or with others, to promote them, and to celebrate rites in public or in private, provided they are not offensive to public morality. (Italy—Constitution, 1948)

While providing everyone the same religious rights, the constitution still included features of the Lateran Treaty that granted the Catholic Church greater privileges than those available to other faiths (Ergas, 2004). Furthermore, a new concordat in 1984 would require public schools to provide religious instruction by teachers approved by the church. At the same time, the concordat repealed the earlier provision that made Catholicism the formal state religion.

Now we arrive at the crucifix incident of 2003.

The Crucifix Incident

The Muslim father who set off the crucifix controversy was 43-year-old Abel Smith, raised in Egypt as the son of an Italian father of Scottish origin and an Egyptian mother. Smith now lived in Italy, engaged in the printing trade. He was not a lifelong Muslim but, rather, had converted to Islam in 1987. In 2001 he founded the Union of Muslims in Italy, a group that claimed a membership of 5,300, most of them converts to Islam (Spillman, 2003).

In 2003, the statuette of Christ-dying-on-the-cross that upset Smith was the one on the wall of the kindergarten in which Smith's son was enrolled in the town of Ofena, east of Rome. By law, a crucifix had been displayed in every Italian classroom since 1924. Smith not only objected to the symbol of a selected religious faith being featured in his child's classroom, but he referred to crucifixes as "small cadavers . . . [so the] morphology of the crucifix is nothing but a corpse that could scare children" (Spillman, 2003). Initially, when school authorities refused to remove the statuette, Smith proposed that, in keeping the Italian constitution's guarantee of equal respect for all religions, an Islamic symbol also be displayed. The school's headmaster acceded to this request and allowed verse (*sura*) 112 from the Quran to be added to the classroom wall: "There is no God but Allah." But angry Catholic parents tore the sura down. In response, Smith took the issue to a civil affairs court in the town of

L'Aquila, where a junior district judge, Mario Montanaro, found in Smith's favor and ordered the state kindergarten in Ofena to remove crucifixes from classrooms. Judge Montanaro stated that Italy was in the process of cultural transformation and that the nation's constitution required that belief systems other than Catholicism be respected. He called the display of crucifixes in classrooms "anachronistic" (Defending the public display, 2003).

The court verdict read:

The presence of the symbol of the cross . . . shows the will of the State in the case of state-run schools to put the Catholic religion at the center of the universe as though it were an absolute truth, without the slightest respect for the role played by other religious and social phenomena in the development of humanity. (Italian court, 2003)

After the ruling, Smith said, "I have simply been granted a constitutional right that religious symbols should not be on display in the classroom where my children study" (Storm over Italy, 2003).

The court decision was greeted with dismay by a host of outspoken Italians but was applauded by others, thereby igniting a nationwide debate about church/state relationships, the nature of Italian culture, and immigration practices. The details of the controversy are reflected in the opinions of the constituencies on the two sides of the conflict.

Summary

A graphic overview of the foregoing historical sketch is offered in Figure 10.1 where the timeline on the upper tier identifies several critical events and two belief constituencies over two millennia—0 to 2000. The timeline on the lower tier focuses on events, forms of government, and dominant belief systems between 1900 and 2005.

THE CONTENDING CONSTITUENCIES

The people who engaged most actively in the controversy included (a) Catholic Church authorities, (b) government officials, (c) Muslims, (d) the Italian courts, (e) Abel Smith, and (f) secularists.

Roman Catholic Church Authorities

Leading officials in the Catholic Church strongly objected to the L'Aquila court's ruling. Pope John Paul II, in a speech to European Union ministers, said that interreligious and intercultural dialogue does "not exclude an adequate recognition, even legislative, of the specific religious traditions in which each people is rooted and with which they are often identified in a special way." He asserted that cohesion and peace are not achieved by removing a culture's characteristic religiosity. He added that "the crucifix is an eloquent symbol

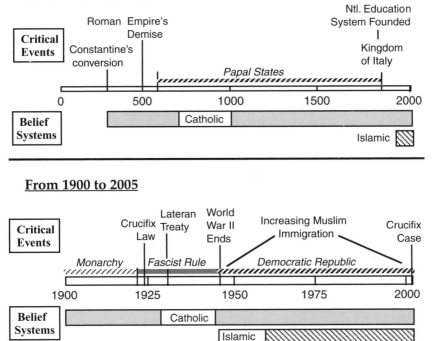

Figure 10.1 Critical events and belief systems in the Italian case.

of a civilization of love" (Defending the public display, 2003; Di Meglio, 2003).

Cardinal Ersilio Tonini said, "You cannot eliminate a symbol of a nation's religious and cultural values simply because it offends someone." Rino Fisichella, deputy chairman of the Italian bishops' conference warned that "A decision like this will encourage a form of intolerance towards symbols of Christian faith" (Defending the public display, 2003).

In the general population, traditional conservative Catholics could be expected to support the church leaders' disapproval of the ban on classroom crucifixes. The number of Italians of the faithful-conformist type might be estimated on the basis of studies showing how many of the nation's Catholics attended church regularly. A 1991 survey found that 45% of Italy's Catholics went to church at least once a week, a figure that had dwindled to an estimated 30% by the early twenty-first century (Boston, 2004; How many people, 2004). Thus, the corps of conservative Catholics was substantial in size, but apparently did not represent a majority of the nation's nominal Catholics.

Government Officials

Italian President Carlo Azeglio Ciampi assailed the court decision, arguing that "the crucifix has always been considered not only as a distinctive sign of a particular religious credo, but above all as a symbol of the values that are at the base of our Italian identity." Members of Premier Silvio Berlusconi's conservative coalition government and center-left politicians also denounced the judgment (Italy president, 2003).

Interior Minister Giuseppe Pisanu said that, as both a Christian and an Italian citizen, he was offended by the court ruling: "The crucifix is not only the symbol of my religion, but is also the highest expression of 2,000 years of civilization that belong in their entirety to the Italian people." A constitutional expert, Augusto Barbera, said the judge was mistaken in his ruling, because the 1924 provision for crucifixes in schools was still in effect, as affirmed by a 1998 Constitutional Court verdict stating that the public display of the crucifix was not a violation of religious liberty (Defending the public display, 2003). Labor Secretary Roberto Maroni said, "It is unacceptable that one judge should cancel out millennia of history."

Education Minister Letizia Moratti said the cross should remain in state schools and hospitals. She also endorsed the controversial state funding of Catholic schools (Italian court, 2003).

Muslims

The number of Muslims in Italy has been estimated at between 800,000 and 1 million. The imprecision of that estimate is due largely to the fact that the Muslim population consists of (a) Italian converts, (b) legal immigrants, and (c) a rising tide of illegal immigrants. Determining how many people are in each of these groups has been a difficult task, particularly in the case of the illegals.

As growing numbers of Muslims entered Italy from North Africa, the Middle East, and Albania in recent years, tension increased between native-born Catholic Italians and the expanding Islamic population. Many of the country's Muslims sought to minimize intercultural conflict by adjusting to Italian traditions, including the acceptance of omnipresent displays of Christian symbols in public places. This effort to adapt to the deep-seated Catholicism in Italian culture was demonstrated in the response of the Islamic leadership to the L'Aquila court ruling. Not only did the heads of Islamic organizations find crucifixes in schools acceptable, but they rejected Abel Smith as a legitimate representative of the Muslim population.

Hmza Roberto Piccardo, secretary of the Islamic Communities in Italy, said his organization represented more than 90% of the nation's Islamic associations and that, even though Italy's Muslims favored a secular state, they also felt it was improper to ignore the feelings of the great majority of citizens. Thus, "We believe that this attack against a religious symbol is an attack against all

Italian religious symbols." Piccardo said there were five school-age children in his family, and he had no problem with their attending schools in which crucifixes were displayed (Defending the public display, 2003).

The imam of a mosque at Segrate in Milan—regarded as the authority for 70,000 of the region's Muslims—agreed with Piccardo and labeled Abel Smith an "isolated provocateur." Ali Abu Shwaima, head of the Islamic Center of Milan, commented that "Smith is not considered a part of the Islamic community and does not attend any mosque." The newspaper *Corriere della Sera* reported that none of the 70 Muslims whom journalists interviewed had agreed with the removal of crucifixes (Spillman, 2003).

In short, Smith's effort to outlaw religious symbols in state schools was condemned by leaders of most of the nation's Muslims.

The Italian Courts

The young judge in the L'Aquila district court had found in Smith's favor, thereby rendering a decision contradicting the 1998 Constitutional Court ruling that exhibiting a crucifix in schools was proper, as authorized by the 1924 crucifix law that had never been repealed. Hence, the courts were divided on the issue of crucifixes in public buildings.

Abel Smith

How many members of the organization Smith headed (Union of Muslims in Italy) agreed with his attack on crucifixes in classrooms is unknown, but it seems likely that he would receive the approval of at least some of his followers.

Italy's Catholic daily newspaper, *Avvenire*, noted that, with rare exception, all major political groups disagreed with Smith's position. Even Giuseppe Vacca, a former Communist Party member of Parliament, said, "I don't know of a higher symbol in the world than Christ's cross." He added that the conflict was not about whether Italy was a secular state but, rather, was an effort to exclude a symbol that touched on "the deepest elements of cultural and national traditions" and was part of both the Italian and European cultural identity (Defending the public display, 2003).

However, the small community of Jews in Italy seemed to agree with Smith. Chief Rabbi Riccardo Di Segni said, "We appreciate the positive values that Christians attribute to the cross, like peace and life, but we have had a negative history with the cross and what it represented for us, a sign of oppression and intolerance in the name of religion" (Di Meglio, 2003).

Secularists

One of the few groups that publicly supported Smith was a teachers union, which saw Smith's lawsuit as properly reinforcing the secular status of the public education system (Storm over Italy, 2003).

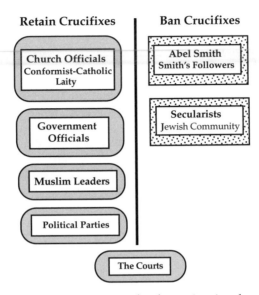

Figure 10.2 Estimated adversaries in the crucifix case.

Among the estimated 98% of Italians who were at least Catholics in name, a substantial minority—perhaps even a majority—apparently placed the state's secularism above the dictates of the Catholic faith. The *New York Times* reported that "In one recent poll, only 32 percent of Italians surveyed said it was right for religion to have an influence on the laws of the state" (Boston, 2004). Therefore, within the general population, Smith's effort to remove Christian symbols from schoolrooms may have enjoyed a substantial measure of approval, or at least an attitude of indifference.

Summary

Figure 10.2 provides an estimate of the constituencies on the opposite sides of the crucifix controversy.

The forces in favor of retaining crucifixes in schools loomed far larger than those advocating an end to such practices. Furthermore, crucifix supporters seemed to agree with each other about why crosses should continue to be exhibited in schools. That is, Catholic leaders, government officials, and Muslim leaders alike suggested that religious traditions embedded in a culture should be cherished. On the other hand, people who advocated the removal of crucifixes from schools seemed to differ in their reasons doing away with schools' crosses. Smith wanted equal treatment for religions (either display each religion's symbols or display none), the teachers union wanted strict secularization of state schools, and the Jewish community objected to the crucifix's symbolizing the inference that Jews had been responsible for Jesus's death.

Each side in the conflict drew on the nation's constitution to buttress its position. However, in doing so, each emphasized different passages of that document. Smith and his backers could cite the secular and equality provisions in support of their censure of Catholic crucifixes in schoolrooms.

Italy is a democratic republic. . . . [that] guarantees the inviolable human rights, be it as an individual or in social groups expressing their personality. All citizens have equal social status and are equal before the law, without regard to their sex, race, language, religion, political opinions, and personal or social conditions. Religious denominations are equally free before the law. (Italy—Constitution, 1948)

The anti-crucifix argument was strengthened by the 1984 concordat that had removed Catholicism as the official state religion. Although the concordat still required Catholic religious education in state schools, it no longer insisted that all pupils attend those classes. According to the concordat,

the Italian Republic, recognizing the value of religious culture, and keeping in mind that the principles of Catholicism are part of the historic patrimony of the Italian people, will continue to assure, among the broader goals of education, the teaching of the Catholic religion in all public schools below university level. Respecting the freedom of conscience and educational responsibility of parents, everyone is guaranteed the right to choose whether or not to take advantage of such teaching. (Religion in school, 2004)

In contrast to the groups that concurred with Smith's lawsuit, crucifix proponents could cite the Lateran Treaty from the Mussolini era that furnished special privileges to the Catholic Church, privileges that could be increased in the future by agreement between the government and the Church without the need to alter the constitution.

The State and the Catholic Church are, each within their own reign, independent and sovereign. Their relationship is regulated by the Lateran Pacts. Amendments to these pacts which are accepted by both parties do not require the procedure of constitutional amendments. (Italy—Constitution, 1948)

The most obvious barrier to changing the long-established Catholic dominance in Italian society was the traditional bond between the Catholic Church and the Italian government, an intimate relationship going back to the papal states and strengthened during the Fascist regime with its Lateran Treaty. That the desire to cling to the past was still pronounced in 2003 is suggested by the strong support for retaining school crucifixes expressed by the Catholic clergy and laity, government officials, and members of political parties. At the same time, secular influences that were reducing religious fervor throughout Europe were pressing for change. Italians were turning less and less to the church for guidance in their daily lives.

Abortion and divorce are legal and most Italians hold liberal views on social issues that clash sharply with conservative Catholic doctrine. When Rocco Buttiglione, a government minister, made critical comments about homosexuality, the outcry from the public was so great that Buttiglione was forced to withdraw his name from consideration for an important European Union post. . . . Italians still want a church wedding, baptism for the kids, and a church funeral—but not much else. (Boston, 2004)

Emma Bonino, a leader of Italy's Radical Party, said, "Everybody thinks that the pope is the only moral figure in my country as far as war and social justice go. But on personal behavior—meaning sex, divorce, motherhood, and pregnancy—people frankly do not care" (Boston, 2004).

RESOLVING THE CONTROVERSY

The question of whether crucifixes should be permitted in state schools was settled in December 2004 by Italy's Constitutional Court, where judges reversed the earlier district court decision by arguing that Abel Smith was not entitled to raise in court the issue of crucifixes in public places. Hence, the 1924 law mandating the display of crosses in schools continued in effect (Chan, 2004).

The Constitutional Court ruling showed that (a) even though Italy ostensibly had a secular government, the nation's dominant culture was still Catholic, and (b) Catholicism continued to wield significant influence over the state.

CHAPTER 11

Pakistan

The religion/school controversy in the Pakistan case mentioned in Chapter 1 set the Pakistan government against the supporters of thousands of private Islamic schools called madrassas. The conflict involved government officials—at the urging of the United States government—seeking to gain a measure of control over the curriculum of the madrassas, with that attempt bluntly rejected by the madrassas' headmasters. The issue at stake was not whether religion should be taught in the schools. Rather, the threefold issue concerned (a) what proportion of the curriculum should consist of religious topics, (b) who should determine the curriculum, and (c) what should religious instruction emphasize.

HISTORICAL ROOTS

Understanding the cause of the controversy and the likelihood of its being resolved is fostered by historical information about (a) the Pakistan government, (b) schooling in Pakistan, (c) the nature of madrassas, (d) effects of September 11, 2001, and (e) efforts to control madrassas.

The Pakistan Government

The Islamic Republic of Pakistan has existed hardly more than half a century. It came into being in 1947 out of warfare between Hindus and Muslims after the British relinquished political control over their former South Asia colony of India. By an agreement that ended the warfare, the major territory of the former British colony went to Hindu-dominated India and the minor portion to a newly created Muslim-dominated Islamic Republic of Pakistan that was divided into two sectors, one in the northwest region of the Indian subcontinent and the other in the northeast region. A civil war between those two sectors in 1971 was settled when the northeastern division was granted political independence and was assigned the name Bangladesh, leaving the western portion with its original title, Pakistan.

By 2004, the estimated religious affiliation within Pakistan's population of 150 million was 96% Islamic, 2.5% Christian, 1.3% Hindu, and less than 1% other belief systems (Sparks, 2004). In contrast to India's constitution that portrays India as a secular democratic republic, Pakistan's constitution commits the government to ordering life "in accordance with the teachings and requirements of Islam as set out in the Holy Quran and Sunnah" (Pakistan Constitution, 2001). Thus, in Pakistan there is no question about whether religion should be a part of learners' education. Islam is officially at the core of education, a point emphasized by the defenders of madrassas as they resisted the government's attempt to interfere with their teaching.

In regard to religion and schooling, the Pakistan Constitution states that

every citizen shall have the right to profess, practice, and propagate his religion; and every religious denomination and every sect thereof shall have the right to establish, maintain, and manage its religious institutions. No person attending any educational institution shall be required to receive religious instruction, or take part in any religious ceremony, or attend religious worship, if such instruction, ceremony, or worship relates to a religion other than his own. (Pakistan Constitution, 2001)

Therefore, Pakistan officially provides freedom of religion for individuals and religious sects. However, such freedom is "subject to any reasonable re-strictions imposed by law in the interest of the glory of Islam or the integrity, security, or defense of Pakistan or any part thereof, friendly relations with foreign States, public order, decency or morality, or in relation to contempt of court, or incitement to an offence" (Pakistan Constitution, 2001). Thus, under this proviso, laws could be issued at any time to curtail individuals' or groups' religious activities.

Schooling in Pakistan

In terms of curricula and sponsorship, Pakistan has three main kinds of schools—government, private, and Islamic-religious. Government schools have been attended chiefly by students from middle-class families, although ones from poor families may enroll if parents can afford the nominal fees. In government schools, Urdu has been the language of instruction. The curriculum has consisted primarily of secular subjects (reading, writing, mathematics, history, science) and some Islamic studies. Private schools, taught in English, are generally regarded as providing the best education. They charge substantial fees and thus are attended mainly by children from families from the higher so-cial classes. The subjects taught are those typical of the British school tradition (reading, writing, mathematics, history, geography, science). The third type of school, the *madrassa*, typically limits students' studies to Islamic religion, with the chief focus on Islam's most revered book, the Quran (Allah's revealed word), and on the Sunnah (wise sayings and acts of the Prophet Muhammad).

In the early twenty-first century, out of Pakistan's total of 182,636 public and private schools, 81% were public (government) and 19% private. Of the 142,308 primary schools, 90% were public and 10% private. Among the 25,461 middle schools, half were public and half private. Of 14,867 high schools, 58% were public and 42% private. Therefore, while most of the 5-year primary schools were government-operated, close to half of the nation's 2-year middle schools and 5-year high schools were private ventures.

A gross estimate of the success of a nation's education system can be drawn from the literacy level of the populace. For Pakistan, that level in the early twenty-first century was a matter of considerable debate. Iqbal (2001) reported that "Although the government claims that Pakistan's literacy rate is 49%, independent sources say it is not higher than 23% in reality." But whatever the actual figure might have been, it was unquestionably low in comparison to that of most nations. Furthermore, the holding power of government schools left much to be desired. Critics blamed poverty, poor quality instruction, and gender bias for a 50% primary school dropout rate, with girls leaving school in greater numbers than boys (Zia, 2003). And the level of learning in such schools has been criticized: "According to UNICEF figures, a nationwide sample of children in grade five revealed that only 33% could read with comprehension, while a mere 17% were able to write a simple letter" (Asia Child Rights, 2003).

A study by the European Commission reported that

increasing poverty, the cost of schooling, and the failure of the system to deliver quality education are the root cause of the current declining enrolment rates in Pakistan. The physical conditions in which many teachers teach and children learn are inadequate and often either non-existent or dangerous. . . . The quality of education is adversely affected by untrained or poorly trained teachers, lack of classroom resources, and the unavailability of textbooks, either due to poor distribution or the inability of parents to pay for them. (European Commission, 2002)

In summary, Pakistan's government schools have proven to be seriously inadequate in buildings, equipment, and teachers. Among the causes identified by critics has been the government's habit of drastically underfunding education. The Pakistan government's 2004–2005 budget (equal to US$15.5 billion) allocated $5.3 billion (34%) for national defense and $200 million (1%) for education (Kapisthalam, 2004).

Such a record of failure of government-sponsored schooling over recent decades produced important consequences for the nation's third type of school—the *madrassa*.

The Islamic Madrassa

The English-language term *madrassa* used throughout this chapter refers to the same sort of Islamic religious school that is identified in other publications as a *madrasah*, *madrasa*, or *madaris*. That kind of school can also be known in other societies by even different labels—*khalwa* in the Sudan, *pesantren* in Indonesia, *pondok* in Malaysia.

The madrassa is a private school established by an individual Islamic scholar or Muslim group and financed by public and private donations. Students typically live at the school, with food and lodging given to poorer youths free of charge. However, some students live at home and attend the madrassa only in the daytime. The traditional madrassa curriculum has been composed entirely of Islamic religious studies. The students' most basic learning task has been to rote-memorize the Quran, then to study the Sunnah's *hadiths*, which are verses describing sayings and acts of the Prophet Muhammad. More advanced students learn Arabic language, Islamic customs, law, history, and the operation of the worldwide Islamic movement.

As enrollment in Pakistan's government schools declined in recent times, Pakistan's madrassas experienced a remarkable growth. For families in poverty,

the madrassas offered a place where their children could get free boarding, food, and education, and it turned out to be an irresistible option when compared to crumbling or non-existent government-funded secular schools. Pakistani governments also encouraged this to avoid spending much on education. The sheer magnitude of this increase can be fathomed by this simple statistic: according to former Pakistani diplomat Hussain Haqqani, only 7,000 Pakistani children attended madrassas as early as 20 years ago. That number has grown today to closer to 2 million, by conservative estimates. (Kapisthalam, 2004)

Calculations of the number of madrassas in Pakistan differ wildly, ranging from 8,000 to 45,000 and even to 80,000, with some schools having only a few students and others thousands (Brokaw, 2004; Pakistan, 2004; Singer, 2001).

Analysts have proposed that one highly important factor behind the growth and curriculum focus of the madrassas has been money from fundamentalist Islamic foundations in oil-rich Persian Gulf states. During testimony before the United States Senate in 2003, Alex Alexiev of the Center for Security Policy said that foreign funding (mainly from Saudi Arabia, but also from Kuwait and Iran) of Pakistan's madrassas was "estimated at no less than $350 million per year" (Kapisthalam, 2004). The Gulf-states money was intended to promote the ultraconservative Saudi Arabian Wahabism version of Islam. According to Kaushik Kapisthalam, the madrassa curriculum before the 1970s focused on such traditional pillars of faith as praying five times a day, promoting charity, and joining in the pilgrimage to the holy city, Mecca. However, under the influence of Wahabism, the emphasis in the curriculum changed to teaching students that the only way to produce a pure Islamic state would be to wage "a near-perpetual war, pursued by any and all means against unbelievers as well as 'impure' sects among Muslims. The era of the *jihadi madrassas* [warrior schools] was born" (Kapisthalam, 2004). Singer (2001) has proposed that present-day madrassas combine a mix of puritanical Wahabism with "Deobandism (a strand from the Indian subcontinent that is anti-Western, claiming that the West is the source of corruption in contemporary Islamic states, and thus the laws of [secular] states are not legitimate)."

The Pakistan elite educate their children in prestigious private educational establishments in the cities, [whereas] the bulk of Pakistan's people have a choice of either a struggling public education system or *madrassas*. . . . For most Pakistanis *madrassas* function as a de facto welfare system that few non-governmental organizations, let alone the Pakistani government, can match. (Jacinto, 2004)

Pakistan's madrassas first attracted international attention when neighboring Afghanistan was invaded by Soviet Union military forces in the 1980s. In the Afghans' struggle against Soviet troops, the madrassas across the border in Pakistan became a fertile source of both leaders and foot soldiers to wage guerilla war against the invaders. The United States sided with the Afghan fighters, providing them arms and funds to support their cause, thereby strengthening the Pakistan madrassa movement without realizing that the movement would be directed against Western societies in future years. Political chaos followed the expulsion of the Soviet forces in 1989 as Afghan warlords competed for power. Order was finally restored in 1996 when a fundamentalist Islamic faction called the Taliban took control of the country and imposed a harsh version of Islamic law that banned frivolities like music and television, that introduced public executions and amputations, and that prevented girls from going to school and women from working. During the Taliban regime, Afghanistan became the training center for international terrorists under the direction of a wealthy Saudi Arabian, Osama bin Laden, as the Taliban continued to depend on Pakistan madrassas for recruits. However, analysts have suggested that after the fall of the Taliban, terrorists in Pakistan and Afghanistan were more often graduates of English-medium schools than of madrassas. Nevertheless, the anti-Western attitudes fostered in madrassas did increase popular resistance to altering the religious schools' teachings.

In summary, during the final three decades of the twentieth century and into the early years of the twenty-first century, Pakistan's madrassas (a) increased in number and enrollment at a remarkable pace and (b) emphasized *jihad*—the use of armed force to defeat proponents of other belief systems and thereby extend the dominance of Islam throughout the world.

September 11, 2001

What has become known as "The 9/11 Incident" consisted of Islamic terrorists hijacking four commercial airplanes in the United States and smashing two of them into New York skyscrapers and one into the U.S. armed services' Pentagon building in Washington, D.C. The fourth plane crashed in a field in the state of Pennsylvania. The United States government identified Afghanistan as the operating base and training center for the terrorists. When

American military forces then attacked Afghanistan to destroy the Islamic fundamentalist Taliban government that had supported the terrorists, Pakistan officials found themselves in a precarious predicament—caught between (a) their next-door neighbor, Afghanistan, with whom many Pakistanis sympathized, and (b) the military and economic strength of the world's most powerful nation, the United States, and its allies. The Americans needed Pakistan's cooperation in conducting the war in Afghanistan—permission to fly planes in Pakistan's airspace, land bases for military operations, intelligence resources, and aid in preventing Taliban leaders and fighters from fleeing across the lengthy border between Afghanistan and Pakistan. In acceding to the Americans' request, Pakistan's president, General Pervez Musharraf, was influenced not only by the U.S. economic and military might, but also by Pakistan's thorny confrontation with India over such matters as the control of the Kashmir province, which was held by India but populated chiefly by Muslims. Pakistanis had seen India being favored by the United States in the past. Now, with the United States needing Pakistan's help against the Taliban, that favoritism might be reversed, or at least moderated. Musharraf chose to help the Americans. The United States, in return, would give Pakistan massive economic aid, including funds for improving the weak and deteriorating government school system.

The Americans' efforts to influence schooling in Pakistan could be seen as both philanthropic and self-serving. The philanthropic aim was that of increasing school attendance and instructional efficiency in order to furnish a well-trained work force that would upgrade the country's economic productivity and would reduce poverty. The self-serving aim was that of changing public opinion from hatred for non-Islamic societies (particularly for those with Christian and Jewish traditions) to that of admiration for Western nations and their belief systems, including their capitalism, representative democracy, gender equality, scientific progress, and "modern" lifestyles. Accomplishing those two educational goals would require radical changes in Pakistan's madrassas by (a) altering the madrassa curriculum to include substantial amounts of secular subjects useful in modern-day economies (mathematics, science, social studies, English language, computer skills, vocational education) and (b) ridding the schools of the jihad (holy war) commitment to waging relentless battle against non-Muslims, particularly those in Western societies.

The first of those aims—adding secular subjects to the madrassa curriculum—was welcomed by Pakistan officials, particularly by the modernists among them who wished to expand the extremely limited occupational skills of madrassa graduates. Madrassa students' knowledge was confined mainly to religious matters. Even graduates with the most advanced preparation—those who had earned the title *alim*—were qualified only to carry out the religious functions of leading prayers five times a day, delivering lectures to Friday congregations, preparing marriage contracts, and performing rituals at births and burials (Iqbal, 2001). But most madrassa students left school long before becoming alims, able only to recite the Quran and passages of the Sunnah. To make a living, they were obliged to take up a traditional trade—farmer, fisherman, peddler, bicycle repairman, shoemaker, or the like. In effect, their madrassa training was of no occupational value.

The second aim of the American-promoted change in madrassas—that of diminishing students' adherence to Islamic traditions and of enticing them to embrace Western attitudes and lifestyles—proved far less appealing to Pakistanis. Although that goal was given lip service by government officials, it apparently was not enthusiastically adopted and probably not shared by the majority of the populace. Nevertheless, the government moved to implement a program of madrassa reform that would include downplaying jihad.

Efforts to Control Madrassas

The Pakistan government had never exercised control over madrassas. The creation of such schools, as well as their administration and curriculum, depended on the initiative, aims, and resources of private individuals and groups. And because 97% of the nation's 150 million people were Muslims, the madrassas' traditional teachings were esteemed by a large segment of the population, thereby making it painfully difficult for the government to expand and alter the schools' religious curriculum. Nevertheless, President Musharraf issued a *Deeni Madaris Ordinance* (Voluntary Registration and Regulation Decree) in 2002, requiring all madrassas to register with the government and to reveal who operated which schools. Furthermore, each madrassa would be obliged to follow a government-designed curriculum that would include such subjects as mathematics, science, social science, economics, and English, thereby integrating madrassas into the government-operated education system. The government would also establish model *madrassas* that provided modern, useful education and did not encourage extremism. Neither schools nor mosques would be allowed to spread politically and religiously inflammatory statements and publications. Madrassas would need to provide an audit of their funds from foreign sources and, according to the decree, no further foreign money would be permitted. The number of foreign students would be curtailed, and those that enrolled would need to register with the government (Iqbal, 2001; Madrassah schools, 2004; Peri, 2004). Such, then, was the government's plan for resolving the madrassa controversy.

Summary

A graphic overview of several critical events and belief systems in the Pakistan case is offered in Figure 11.1. The upper-tier timeline extends from 1940 to 2005. The lower-tier timeline identifies events over the 2001–2005 period. In both timelines, three belief systems are portrayed—Islamic, Christian, and Hindu. Of the three worldviews, the Islamic is by far the most significant, since 97% of the Pakistan population consists of professed Muslims, whereas only 2.5% are Christians and 1.3% Hindus.

From 1940 to 2000

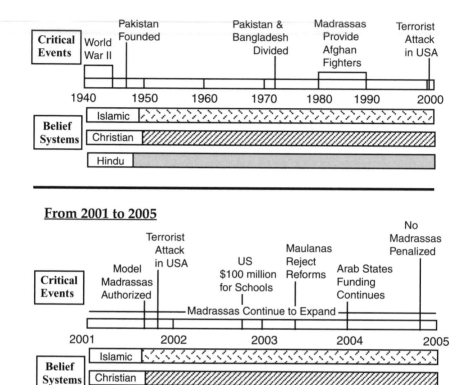

Figure 11.1 Critical events and belief systems in the Pakistan case.

THE CONTENDING CONSTITUENCIES

In the confrontation over madrassas, the constituencies supporting President Musharraf's intended reform included (a) top-level government officials, (b) Pakistani Islamic modernists, and (c) representatives of the United States government. Groups opposing the plan included (a) the sponsors and staff members of madrassas, (b) Pakistani Islamic traditionalists, and (c) Persian Gulf states that helped finance Pakistan's religious schools.

Top-Level Government Officials

Over the years 2001–2005, executives at the apex of the Pakistan government publicly voiced their enthusiasm for madrassa reform. In a public address, President Musharraf announced that "We have formulated a new strategy for the madaris [madrassas], and there is need to implement it so as to galvanize their good aspects and remove their drawbacks" (Jacinto, 2004). To implement the reform, he convinced the Pakistan parliament to vote $100 million to broaden the madrassa curriculum to include mathematics, science, and English language (Brokaw, 2004).

Pakistan's foreign minister, Khurshid Mehmood Kasuri, and the interior minister, Faisal Saleh Hayat, both promised to remodel madrassas by cutting those schools' ties to militancy. During a public appearance in Belgium in late 2003, Kasuri said the only way to "tackle such beliefs [in militancy] is by education" (Bokhari, 2003). Information Minister Shaikh Rashid announced that, when implementing the reform, "We are not looking to confront the [religious scholars]; we want a constructive engagement" (Iqbal, 2003).

Musharraf's government's ordinance of August 18, 2001, had established a Pakistan Madrassa Education Board authorized to set up model madrassas and regulate the conditions of existing madrassas, but the board was not empowered to force madrassas to register. By the end of 2004, only 449 schools had applied for affiliation with the board. By 2005 the government had established three model madrassas that enrolled a total of 300 learners. However, that number was miniscule compared to an estimated 1.6 million students in the country's private "official" 25,000 madrassas. Another 25,000–40,000 "unofficial" madrassas were said to serve nearly an equal number of Pakistani youths in remote villages (Kahn, 2004; Kapisthalam, 2004).

Other government acts designed to support the reform program included restrictions against Islamic clerics and madrassa students who staged street protests against the reforms. A few of the most vocal religious leaders were placed under house arrest; and Maulana Sufi Mohammed, who had led thousands of Pakistanis into Afghanistan to fight alongside the Taliban, was arrested on his return to Pakistan and sentenced to 3 years in prison. However, such measures had little effect on altering the madrassas. (Abraham, 2001)

Pakistani Islamic Modernists

Modernists among Pakistan's Muslims consisted chiefly of those educated in the elite English-style private schools or abroad, ones who believed the nation's economic and social progress depended on students studying subjects useful in a modern-day occupational world. At least a portion of such modernists also saw the jihad attitude of warring against non-Muslims as a self-defeating policy. They believed in tolerating other belief systems. As a consequence, they supported the idea of madrassa reform, but they recognized that such reform would not be adopted willingly by the imams who administered the schools. Such a conviction was expressed in the following fashion by an editorial writer for *The News*, a Pakistan English-language newspaper.

Any expectation that the clergy trained and groomed in a conservative education environment will understand the importance of opening up new [curricular] doors to their students is as misplaced as an effort to grow a pine tree in a desert. It is incomprehensible why the government continues to expect the [madrassa] seminaries to voluntarily comply with its wish list when similar approaches failed more than once in the past. What is needed is a law that will bind the seminaries to register as educational institutions just like all others in the private sector, follow a certain curriculum that is not divisive on sectarian lines, declare all their sources of funding, and adopt a standardized examination system. (Madrassa muddle, 2005)

Some observers warned that the reform should be gradual and not heavy-handed. Dr. Anis Ahmad, professor of social sciences at International Islamic University in Islamabad, cautioned that Musharraf should avoid a complete crackdown on madrassas. Instead, the government should gradually help expand the curriculum of the religious academies (Abraham, 2001).

The United States Government

Three steps taken by the U.S. government in support of educational reform involved (a) condemning the teaching of anti-American attitudes in madrassas, (b) urging Pakistan's leaders to revise the curriculum and focus of madrassas, and (c) providing funds toward improving government schools.

In expressing the U.S. government's perception of the religious schools, Secretary of State Colin Powell denounced madrassas as breeding grounds for "fundamentalists and terrorists," but also admitted that "We have to understand that a lot of these [religious schools] reflect . . . the desire of the community to have such places. We can't substitute for all of the feeding programs of all of these madrassas throughout the Muslim world. Nor would we know how to do it if we had the resources" (Powell, 2004).

As for funding, the U.S. Agency for International Development in August 2002 committed $100 million to rehabilitate Pakistan's public schools (Peri, 2004).

Madrassas Personnel and Sponsors

With few exceptions, the thousands of private religious schools rejected government efforts to influence the schools' administration, curriculum, or funding. Maulana Fazlur Rahman, head of the country's largest religious political alliance (Muttahid Majlis-e-Amal), protested that the government's reform plan was designed to control the madrassas, but "We will not let that happen—never" (Iqbal, 2003). Qari Hanif Jallundhari, secretary general of the Madrassa education board for the Deobandi school of thought, contended that the madrassa reform project was "not a sincere offer to help Islamic institutions" but "actually a part of a global conspiracy to deviate us from our basic purpose—to teach the Quran and Hadith" (Hussain, 2003). The leader of a prominent madrassa, Maulana Muhammad Hassan Jan, asked, "Why does the government interfere in our business? We are not preparing antigovernment people; we are preparing religious minds. Islam is the doctrine on which this country is created. We are protecting that" (Abraham, 2001).

The political power of the madrassa forces derived not only from their larger numbers but also from their cohesiveness. In effect, madrassas leaders—the *maulanas*—claimed to be united in their opposition to the proposed reforms. For instance, Pir Saifullah Khalid said that all madrassas in the *Ittehad Tanzimat Madaris-e-Deenia* alliance were of one mind in resisting government interference and were committed to abide by the alliance's decisions (Hussain, 2003).

An analyst of madrassa organizations concluded that

the administrators of religious madrassas have a well-thought out opinion that there is no need to modify or reform their syllabi or education system because it is in line with the teachings of the Quran and Hadith [Sunnah], and fulfills the basic purpose of learning Islam, i.e. to preach and promote it. (Hussain, 2003)

Hanif Jallundhari, speaking for the alliance of all madrassa boards of different schools of thought in Pakistan (Ittehad Tanzimat Madaris-e-Deenia), said that madrassas already taught such modern subjects as English language, science, mathematics, social studies, economics, and computer literacy. In support of that claim, Dr. Sarfraz Naeemi, secretary general of the madrassa board for the Barelvi school of thought, said, "All ulema [religious instructors] are equipped with modern education, since a bachelor's degree from a government university is mandatory for them in most madrassas" (Hussain, 2003). Naeemi charged that Musharraf's reform project was not initiated by the Pakistan government but, rather, by the United States in an effort to suppress the growing Islamic influence in the world: "The West has always tried to pollute the Islamic values of morality, decency, and brotherhood. And for this basic purpose it has always been keen to introduce its cultural waywardness, family planning methods, and obscenity on media into our society" (Hussain, 2003).

When an American journalist visited a 250-student madrassa in the city of Peshawar, the 81-year-old head of the school, Al-Sheikh Rahat Gul, pointed to a cartoon on the back of a pamphlet showing Afghanistan encircled by a chain with a padlock labeled "United Nations." Inside the chain were weeping, starving children who were attempting to reach food and money but were thwarted by hands labeled "U.S.A." (Bragg, 2001).

Not only did the madrassa leaders voice their objections to the government's plan, but also the religious political parties rallied crowds in opposition to the reform. As a result, the Pakistan government suspended the madrassas-registration program in 2003, although in May 2004 the minister of education asked that registration be resumed. By September 2004, no madrassas had been closed or otherwise penalized for failing to comply with the ordinance (Pakistan, 2004).

Pakistani Islamic Traditionalists

A large majority of the Pakistan population would qualify as Islamic traditionalists, in that they consider the Quran and Sunnah as the divine truth about life. They judge their own behavior and that of others by Islamic law and customs as interpreted by religious leaders who are typically graduates of madrassas. Thus, there is widespread respect for madrassas within the general populace.

Most young boys in madrassas go there because their families could not pay the costs of either secular-private or government schools. "In a country where economic opportunities for the mainstream population are showing few signs of bold recovery, it's not surprising that many Pakistanis would turn to institutions such as madrassa schools for the education of their children" (Bokhari, 2003).

Evidence of the high regard in which madrassas are held by the citizenry is found in the International Crisis Group report that madrassas received more than 90 billion rupees every year through charitable donations, an amount almost equal to the government's annual direct income tax revenue. Ninety-four percent of charitable donations made by Pakistani individuals and business corporations have gone to religious institutions. In addition, "The biggest source of financing for madrassas is external—from Muslim countries as well as private donors and Pakistani expatriates" (Hussain, 2004).

The human resources that the antireform movement could muster far outweighed those the government could command. For example, in the government's effort to quell public protests to the reform, the army's willingness to disperse crowds and detain demonstrators was questionable. "Even if ordered by senior leadership (who tend to have been trained at foreign and/or private schools), [the military's] line troops could balk at the orders to crush the protests" (Singer, 2001).

Persian Gulf States

The most potent foreign influences on Pakistan's madrassas have been the Persian Gulf states that have functioned as madrassa patrons. Not only were those states the source of funds but they also weighed heavily on decisions affecting curricula. A journalist who interviewed a group of headmasters of madrassas discovered that "when they proposed the teaching of secular subjects specifically to provide students with marketable skills, they were quickly prohibited from doing so by funders in Saudi Arabia and Kuwait" (Peri, 2004).

The Persian Gulf states enjoyed a far longer history of influence on madrassas than did the United States through its recent pressure on the Pakistan government. And the amount of funds the Gulf states furnished the madrassas far exceeded the amount the United States provided for school improvement in Pakistan.

Summary

The government, by virtue of the nation's constitution, had official authority over secular matters. But whether it had authority over the curriculum of Islamic madrassas was a matter of debate, because the core of madrassa studies was provided by the Quran and Sunnah, and the constitution identified those

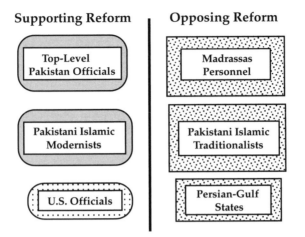

Figure 11.2 The adversaries in the madrassas-reform controversy.

two holy works as essential for equipping Muslims "to order their lives in the individual and collective spheres in accordance with the teachings and requirements of Islam" (Pakistan Constitution, 2001).

The government's main source of evidence to support the reform plan was the description of the kinds of education in the world's most prosperous nations—universal schooling that centered on studies useful in modern-day economies. The antireform group's source of evidence was chiefly the nation's constitution with its emphasis on the Quran's and Sunnah's prescription for how people's lives should be ordered.

Among the long-term forces pressing for change in the madrassas were Pakistan's high incidence of poverty, sluggish economy, and high illiteracy rate when compared with other nations'. An important immediate force was the pressure exerted on Pakistan political leaders by the U.S. government during the U.S. war against the Taliban in Afghanistan. Forces opposing madrassa change included (a) the madrassas' noteworthy ability to accommodate many thousands of youths from poor families, youths who otherwise would have no schooling at all, (b) the difficulty of retraining madrassa teachers to offer instruction in areas other than Islamic religious subjects, and (c) the continuing insistence of Gulf-states patrons that Pakistan's madrassas limit their curricula to centuries-old religious lore.

In conclusion, Figure 11.2 displays the most prominent constituencies in the madrassas-reform case.

RESOLVING THE CONTROVERSY

In view of the multiplicity of powerful forces opposing President Musharraf's madrassas-reform program, the likelihood that the controversy would be settled in favor of his plan was extremely remote. The Pakistan government lacked both the ability and the resolve needed to implement the program.

As for the government's ability to effect the reform, the task of even identifying the locations of the thousands of madrassas was overwhelming. The government had neither a system nor personnel for investigating and monitoring madrassas' operations. Furthermore, there were no viable sanctions for compelling madrassas to comply with the government plan. And a demand that madrassas submit to government control would mean political suicide for Musharraf. He could not afford to alienate the religious political parties whose support he needed to stay in office.

Musharraf's going to back away from encroaching on to the power base of the Islamic groups, which are the madrassas. That's where they train the population. That's where they are creating the next generation of voters. This is a political battle that the government has to engage in, not an educational conflict. (Hasan, 2004)

By 2005, among the half-dozen changes the government planned for the madrassas, the only one for which the government had made an effort was the establishment of the three "model" madrassas that enrolled barely 300 students. Although some madrassas had tried to add secular subjects to their religious fare, they faced obstacles in their attempt. Even when the government offered financial incentives for madrassas to hire math and physics teachers, there were none to be had. The most radical madrassas rejected the model and continued to teach from a medieval syllabus that rejected "Western science" as un-Islamic.

The Pakistani defense for slow progress is that *madrassa* reform is difficult and dangerous, so it may take a while. The problem with that is that the longer the *madrassas* operate as they do, the fewer people there will be in Pakistan who would support such change. (Kapisthalam, 2004)

In summary, the proposed madrassa reform that U.S. officials had pressed on the Musharraf government was clearly doomed. It turned out to be a plan in word only, apparently a ploy to mollify the Americans without really altering the madrassa status quo.

CHAPTER 12

United States of America

The controversy in the American case mentioned in Chapter 1 arrayed biblical creationists against evolutionists over the question of whether the word *evolution* should be permitted in the state of Georgia's public-school science curriculum. The following interpretation of the conflict views the case from the vantage points of (a) its historical background, (b) key characteristics of the conflict's adversaries, and (c) the controversy's resolution.

HISTORICAL ROOTS

In the history of America, the most dramatic and highly publicized encounter between proevolution and antievolution activists took the form of a court trial in the town of Dayton, Tennessee, during the summer of 1925. The episode has been remembered as *The Scopes Case* or *The Monkey Trial*. On that occasion the question was whether evolution should be taught in schools in violation of Tennessee's antievolution statute that made it unlawful "to teach any theory that denies the story of divine creation as taught by the Bible and to teach instead that man was descended from a lower order of animals" (State v. John Scopes, 2004). John Scopes, a substitute biology teacher, was tried in court for teaching Charles Darwin's 1859 theory that humans were not created of a sudden in the Garden of Eden but, instead, they evolved over many thousands of years from gradual changes in animal species. The upshot of the case was that Scopes was declared guilty of breaking the law. However, the nationwide publicity the case attracted was instrumental in the defeat of antievolution-teaching laws in all but 2 (Arkansas and Mississippi) of the 15 states that had such proposals before legislatures in 1925.

Over the three-quarters of a century since the Scopes trial, the debate about teaching evolution had continued to surface periodically in various parts of the nation. The U.S. Supreme Court ruled in 1968 that a 1929 Arkansas statute prohibiting the teaching of evolution was unconstitutional. A U.S. district court in 1982 rejected a newly passed "balanced treatment" law mandating that the biblical version of creation be taught in Arkansas public schools along with evolution. In 1987, the U.S. Supreme Court ruled unconstitutional a similar 1981 Louisiana law requiring the teaching of "creation science" in public schools whenever evolution was taught. In 1999, the Kansas state board of education ordered the biblical story of creation to be taught and dropped Darwin's theory from standardized tests taken by Kansas students. That policy was discarded in 2001 when procreationist members of the board were voted out of office. But the return of creationists to the board in 2005 promised a renewal of the issue when the board scheduled public hearings for comparing evolution and intelligent design as proper fare for science classes—hearings boycotted by scientists who felt that the sessions would be manipulated to accord scientific status to a religious conviction (Hanna, 2005). In 2001, the Hawaii board of education had struck down a proposal that would permit a biblical version in science classes along with Darwin's theory of evolution. In 2002, the Ohio board of education gave a form of creationism equal status with evolution in the public-school curriculum. In 2004, the Grantsburg, Wisconsin, school board issued a resolution allowing "various theories/models of origins" to be included among science studies. In effect, since the Scopes incident, confrontations between creationists and evolutionists have never ceased and will likely continue to crop up in the future. During the first years of the twenty-first century, the creationism/evolution debate became more widespread and contentious than at any time during the previous 75-year interim. The Georgia episode that involved removing the word *evolution* from the state-mandated curriculum was only one recent example of the perennial dispute.

As a foundation for understanding the creationist/evolutionist debate, we now turn to (a) the premises that advocates on each side of the controversy have used to support their claims and (b) the history of the separation of church and state in the U.S. American form of government.

Creationism

There are several versions of creationist doctrine. One is *young-earth creationism*, which proposes that (a) God produced the universe and everything within it during 6 days and (b) Earth is only a few thousand years old. Another version accepts the notion that Earth is millions of years old but holds that God originally created humans complete in their present form, distinctly different from all other forms of life. A third version rejects the notion of macroevolution (all species tracing their origins back to a common simple cell organism) but accepts microevolution (changes within a given species as the result of selective breeding or adjustments to changed environments, as with humans in intense sunlight tropical regions developing more protective dark skin pigment than humans in temperate zones).

In order to recognize more precisely the substance of typical creationist belief, consider the first chapter of the book of Genesis as found in both the Jewish Torah and the Christian Old Testament. This version of the universe's beginnings is also honored by Muslims who accept as truth much of the Judaic account of humankind's early history.

In the beginning God created the heaven and the earth. And the earth was without form and void; and the darkness was upon the face of the deep. And the Spirit of God moved upon the face of the waters. And God said, "Let there be light," and there was light. . . . And God called the light Day, and the darkness he called Night. And the evening and the morning were the first day. (Genesis 1, verses 1–4, 1611)

On the second day God created a region—a dome-like firmament—that He called Heaven. On the third day, He created dry land below Heaven which He called Earth, and He produced waters that He called Seas, along with grass and fruit trees. On the fourth day He created the sun to light the day and the moon and stars to light the night and attached stars to the heavenly firmament. On the fifth day He created all sorts of fish for the seas and fowl for the earth. On the sixth day God said, "Let the earth bring forth every living creature after his kind—cattle, and creeping thing, and beast of the earth after his kind: and it was so."

And God said, "Let us make man in our image, after our likeness: and let them have dominion over the fish of the sea, and over the fowl of the air, and over the cattle, and over all the earth, and over every creeping thing that creepeth upon the earth." So God created man in His *own* image . . . male and female created He them. And God blessed them and . . . said unto them, "Be fruitful, and multiply, and replenish the earth, and subdue it: and have dominion over . . . every living thing that moveth upon the earth." (Genesis 1, verses 1–28, 1611)

In a more detailed passage, the second chapter of Genesis explains that

the Lord God formed man of the dust of the ground, and breathed into his nostrils the breath of life; and man [named Adam] became a living soul. . . . And the Lord God caused a deep sleep to fall upon Adam . . . and took one of his ribs . . . [from which He] made a woman [Eve]. (Genesis 2, verses 7, 21–22, 1611)

Thus, the evidence on which creationists base their conviction is a holy book, respected as the source of authoritative truth. In addition, advocates of a newer variant of creationism called *intelligent design theory* buttress their belief with "logical analysis." They contend that it is only reasonable to recognize that all of the universe's contents and their complex relationships could not have "just happened" but must have been planned by a supreme intellect that people often call God.

Darwinism

Charles Darwin (1809–1882) was a British naturalist who, during a 5-year scientific exploration voyage around the world (1831–1836), carefully examined species of animal life in such varied sites as Brazilian jungles, the Andes Mountains, and the Galapagos Islands. From the detailed descriptions he compiled, Darwin extracted an explanation of how living species must have developed over time and were related to each other. His explanation was published as *The Origin of Species* in which he used observations from his voyage to support the claim that the earth's variegated forms of life—all the species—had originated from the same simple cells that evolved into multiple varieties with the passing of millions of years. Humans, he proposed, were therefore linked biologically to other kinds of animal life and thus were not a unique form created entirely separate from other living things. Darwin's proposal became known as a theory of evolution, an explanation that serves as a foundation for much of present-day biological science.

Darwin's theory was described in the following manner in the 1996 court case of *McLean versus Arkansas Board of Education* in which the judge ruled that Act 590 of the state board of education was unconstitutional because it required the teaching of *creation science* whose "purpose and effect is the advancement of religion in the public schools" (Dorman, 1996).

"Evolution-science" means the scientific evidences for evolution and inferences from those scientific evidences . . . [which] indicate: (1) Emergence by naturalistic processes of the universe from disordered matter and emergence of life from nonlife; (2) The sufficiency of mutation and natural selection in bringing about development of present living kinds from simple earlier kinds; (3) Emergence of man from a common ancestor with apes; (4) Explanation of the earth's geology and the evolutionary sequence by uniformitarianism [the belief that the geological processes which operated in the past are not different from those operating now]; and (5) An inception several billion years ago of the earth and somewhat later of life. (Dorman, 1996)

Since the time of the Scopes trial, the proportion of Americans who subscribe to Darwin's theory has increased while the proportion of creationists has declined. This change has been due in large part to the teaching of evolution in public schools' science programs. Such a trend understandably disturbs people devoted to a fundamentalist Christian, Jewish, or Islamic interpretation of human origins. However, according to an opinion survey conducted in the United States in late 2004, 55% of respondents still said they believed God created humans in their present form (Hurdle, 2005a).

Separation of Church and State

Legal battles over teaching creationism in the schools have typically involved one or both of two questions:

1. Does teaching creationism violate the U.S. American doctrine of separating religion from the conduct of government?
2. Is creationism a "scientific explanation" of human origins and thus properly belongs in science textbooks and classes?

The first of these questions is addressed in the following paragraphs. The second question is discussed in the chapter's next subsection.

Arguments about the legality of teaching a biblical account of human creation in public schools typically allude to the first amendment to the U.S. Constitution.

Congress shall make no law respecting an establishment of religion, or prohibiting the free exercise thereof.

This amendment was added in 1791 to the original 1789 constitution as part of a Bill of Rights. The first half of the provision is known as the *establishment clause* and the second half as the *free exercise clause*. From 1791 until the present day there has been continual debate about what exactly such a church/state policy entails, particularly because in practice its two provisions can be in conflict. For example, what if a public school—on the basis of the establishment clause—denies a religious leader the chance to offer, in a public-school classroom, after-school religious instruction to children whose parents are of the leader's faith? Does that denial violate the children's right to the free exercise of religion, and does it illegally prohibit the religious leader from freely exercising his or her faith?

In attempting to offer guidance to the specific intent of the establishment clause, jurists over the decades have tended to adopt a position suggested by the writings of such key framers of the Constitution as Thomas Jefferson and James Madison who urged the need to establish "a wall of separation" between church and state. Such an interpretation of the establishment clause has typically been applied in U.S. courts as they have declared unconstitutional any laws advocating the teaching of creationism in public schools. However, the vagueness of the clause as it appears in the Bill of Rights has left the door open for other interpretations of whether teaching creationism—or its recent intelligent design alternative—is illegal in publicly financed educational institutions.

The question of whether privately financed schools can legally teach creationism has always been clear—they are quite free to do as they please. But what if such schools or their students receive some special public funds? Are those private schools then still free to teach creationism? That matter has recently become a point of contention as the U.S. federal government has increasingly furnished money to private schools by including them within rules that govern the funding of school vouchers, special-education services, charter schools, textbooks, and more.

Creation Science

In the somewhat distant past, supporters of teaching creationism in public schools openly stated that their proposal was founded on religious faith—on their conviction that the Bible version of human origins was the revealed word of God. However, in more recent times, an increasing number of creationism's proponents have labeled their proposal *scientific creationism* while others have called it *intelligent design*. The following pair of examples illustrates more precisely the nature of specific versions of what has been termed *creation science*.

Scientific Creationism

This type has been promoted by the Institute for Creation Research located in Southern California. Scientific creationism is founded on nine tenets. The first two are:

1. The physical universe of space, time, matter, and energy has not always existed, but was supernaturally created by a transcendent personal Creator who alone has existed from eternity.
2. The phenomenon of biological life did not develop by natural processes from inanimate systems but was specially and supernaturally created by the Creator. (Tenets of scientific creationism, 1985, p. 12)

In a similar vein, the remaining seven principles assert that (3) all major types of plants and animals were in complete form from the time the Creator produced them; (4) humans did not evolve from animal ancestors but were complete with a moral consciousness, language, abstract thought, and religious nature from their very beginning; (5) the universe and earth were created in the rather recent past; (6) the natural laws by which the universe operates were originated and are daily maintained by their Creator; (7) imperfections (disease, catastrophe) in the way the originally perfect universe now operates show that the Creator has an ultimate purpose for the universe; (8) the world awaits the revelation of that purpose; and (9) "the human mind (if open to the possibility of creation) is able to explore the manifestations of that Creator rationally and scientifically, and to reach an intelligent decision regarding one's place in the Creator's plan" (Tenets of scientific creationism, 1985, pp. 12–13).

Two books among those offering scientific creationism versions of the Earth's and humans' beginnings are *Grand Canyon: A Different View* (2003) and *Torah Views on Science and Its Problems* (1988). Authors of such volumes use several methods of lending their schemes a scientific cast. For example, the Grand Canyon book asserts that 6,000 years ago God created the universe in 6 days, and then subsequently produced a worldwide flood to wipe out "the wickedness of man." Photographs of the canyon on the Colorado River in the state of Arizona are combined with verses from the Bible as ostensible evidence that the canyon was formed from the gigantic biblical deluge of Noah's time (Dean, 2004). The *Torah Views* volume offers a kind of timewarp explanation of how the universe and all its inhabitants were produced within 6 days. According to Rabbi Simon Schwab, author of one of the book's chapters, time was extremely condensed during biblical creation's initial week, so that work which would require millions of years by our present calculation of the length of days was accomplished in 6 days at supercosmic speed. After that first week, the passing of time immediately slowed to its current 24-hour-day rate and has continued at that deliberate pace ever since (Zindler, 1992).

Intelligent Design

Proponents of *intelligent design* have contended that the natural world is in the form of an extremely complex, integrated pattern that could not have occurred spontaneously. According to intelligent design advocates, logic dictates that the universe's intricate pattern had to be devised by an extremely wise designer who not only created the universe but also continues to supervise its operation and the conduct of its inhabitants. Most intelligent design adherents identify God as the designer and subscribe to a variation of biblical creationism, but others are unwilling, in a scientific context, to identify the source of the alleged intelligence.

Although intelligent design theory is less overtly religion-based than creation science, it is obviously sponsored by fundamentalist Christians, as illustrated in the version espoused by the Seattle-based Discovery Institute. Rather than offering specific explanations of how the universe and humans began, proponents of the scheme (a) state that life arose through a purposeful plan by a divine being and (b) seek to expose flaws in specific applications of Darwinian theory. Thus, the Discovery Institute's position on teaching about human beginnings is that

examination of evidence and critical thinking are the hallmarks of good science education. . . . It follows that students should learn about the scientific data that supports Darwin's theory of evolution, as well as the data that goes against the theory and which continues to puzzle scientists. . . . Our recommendation is that students receive a full and fair disclosure of the facts surrounding Darwin's theory and that the leading scientific criticisms of the theory not be censored from classroom discussion. (Cooper, 2004)

In summary, rather than denouncing scientific approaches to questions about the origin of the universe and humans, critics of Darwin's theory have increasingly furnished their own versions of *science*—versions they believe should be in public-school science curricula. The emphasis in promoting comparisons between Darwin's views and alternative versions of human beginnings has been on "the data that goes [*sic*] against the theory" as featured in such books as Sarfati's *Refuting Evolution* (1999).

Evolutionists' Responses

Three reactions of Darwin's supporters to the claims of creation science advocates have concerned how to define *science*, *theory*, and *alternative explanations*.

Science Defined

The word *science*, in its commonly accepted version, refers to (a) collecting empirical observations of events, (b) organizing those observations, and (c) logically interpreting how the observations (facts) relate to each other. This three-step process is often referred to as *scientific method*. Actually, there is no single scientific method. Instead, scientific method consists of applying several operating principles that scientists share, such as the following trio.

- Science is concerned with understanding perceptible things—things seen, heard, touched, smelled. Increasingly, scientists depend on aids for extending and refining the impressions from their own senses, such aids as microscopes, telescopes, computers, radar, sonar, x-rays, magnetic resonance imaging, radiocarbon dating, cyclotrons, and more. Nonmaterial conceptions—invisible spirits, angels, jinns, gods, heaven, and the like—are thus outside the realm of science, although people's *reports* of believing in such things are within the purvey of scientists who study characteristics of people's beliefs.
- All observations (facts) and their interpretation are tentative, subject to revision and refinement on the basis of additional empirical observations. No observation or explanation is final.
- Interpreting cause-and-effect relationships among observations involves proposing hypotheses that can be tested to determine how likely they are true.

Evolutionists, who subscribe to such principles, claim that creationists are not being scientific when they accept an ancient holy book's rendition of human origins that fails to yield testable hypotheses. Ergo, creationism does not qualify as *science*.

Theory Defined

A typical charge that creationists aim at Darwinism is that it is "merely theory, not fact." In response, scientists argue that such critics misunderstand the meaning of *theory* in science. The board of directors of the

Genetics Society of America wrote that

in common usage "theory" means "conjecture" or "speculation," whereas in scientific usage it means a systematically organized body of knowledge that explains a large set of observations and makes testable predictions. Science operates first by observation and then by developing a hypothesis as a preliminary explanation of the data. A theory is a hypothesis that has been subsequently confirmed by abundant, consistent data obtained from tests of the hypothesis. (Genetics Society of America, 2003)

Alternative Explanations

As noted earlier, in recent times efforts to teach creationism in public schools have focused on including alternative versions of human beginnings that students can compare with Darwin's theory. Such a proposal provides for teaching biblical creationism while avoiding the appearance of privileging Jews and Christians over other religious groups. However useful such an approach might be for fostering students' critical thinking, scientists have raised several questions about how practical the approach would be. Most, if not all, of the world's multitude of cultures have their own creation stories— Hindus, Shintoists, South African Zulus, Samoans, America's Navajos and Sioux, Haiti's Voodoo adherents, and on and on. So, which of these alternatives would students study? And how much time should be devoted to each version compared to the time dedicated to all of the other topics found in the science curriculum? In answering such queries, a University of Wisconsin botanist, Don Waller, has argued that "insisting that teachers teach alternative theories of origin in biology classes takes time away from real learning, confuses some students, and is a misuse of limited class time and public funds" (Wisconsin district, 2004).

Summary

Across the eight decades since the 1925 "monkey trial," the controversy between creationists and evolutionists has gone through times of greater and lesser attention but has never entirely abated. The conflict continues to be active in the twenty-first century in the form of *creation science* and *intelligent design* jousting against neo-Darwinism in an atmosphere of dilemmas over the separation of church and state.

Figure 12.1 depicts the historical development of the creationism/evolution debate in the form of two timelines. The one on the upper tier identifies critical events from the time of Darwin to 2005. The timeline on the lower tier displays several events from 1980 to 2005. The three belief systems in Figure 12.1 distinguish among fundamentalist-Christian, moderate-Christian, and empirical science worldviews.

With the foregoing historical overview as a background, we turn now to the nature of constituencies involved in present-day versions of the creationism/Darwinism confrontation.

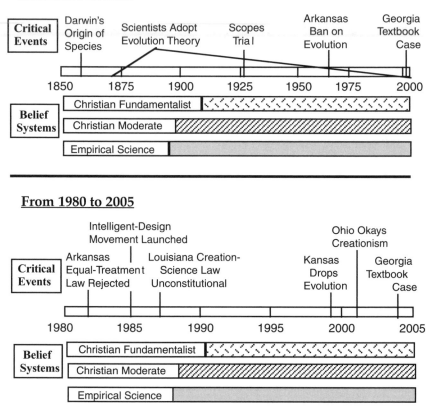

Figure 12.1 Critical events and belief systems in the United States case.

THE CONTENDING CONSTITUENCIES

For convenience of analysis, people involved in the creationism/Darwinism controversy can be classified under four categories: (a) fundamentalist Christians, (b) nondoctrinaire Christians, (c) secularists, and (d) professional scientists and science teachers. These classes are not mutually exclusive, since scientists can be either Christians or secularists, and nondoctrinaire Christians can vary from those who almost qualify as fundamentalists to ones who are nearly secularists. However, even though the categories are not entirely separate, they are still useful for analyzing people's attitudes toward creationism and evolution.

Fundamentalist Christians Versus Moderate Christians

The U.S. American population of 290 million at the end of the twentieth century—when divided into gross religious categories—was Christian 85.3% (Protestant 57.9%, Roman Catholic 21%, other Christian 6.4%), nonreligious

8.7%, Jewish 2.1%, Muslim 1.9%, and other beliefs 2% (Sparks, 2004, p. 723). In a 1998 survey, 53% of Americans considered religion very important in their lives, a figure far higher than the 16% reported in Britain, 14% in France, and 13% in Germany. However, only about 20% of Americans actually went to church one or more times a week (How many people, 2004).

For present purposes, the people designated as Christians can be divided into fundamentalist and moderate categories. Fundamentalists—often also identified as *conservatives, evangelicals,* or *pentacostals*—accept the words of the Bible as literal truth. They subscribe unquestionably to the account of creation offered in the first two chapters of Genesis. Jews and Muslims who also accept that account as the revealed truth belong with the group of fundamentalist Christians.

In contrast, moderate or nondoctrinaire Christians—along with nondoctrinaire Jews and Muslims—subscribe to certain beliefs of their religious tradition but not to the Genesis depiction of human beginnings. Instead, they accept a Darwinian explanation of species evolution.

Three characteristics that tend to distinguish fundamentalists from nondoctrinaire Christians are (a) the source of the evidence on which they base their beliefs, (b) their geographic location, and (c) their denominational affiliation.

Sources of Evidence

As explained earlier, creationists base their convictions on holy writings from the ancient past, writings they regard as infallible. They also support their beliefs by identifying ostensible inconsistencies in Darwinian theory, thereby using a negative form of argument to bolster their own version of human beginnings. That is, if errors in Darwin's proposal render it unacceptable, then the other alternative—biblical creationism—must be right.

Nondoctrinaire Christians, Jews, and Muslims reject the biblical creation story by agreeing that the accumulation of empirical observations in support of Darwin's line of logic is highly persuasive. In effect, they can believe in an all-powerful God, heaven, hell, and life after death without having to accept the Bible's creation tale. They often interpret the Darwinian view as evidence that God's plan is marvelously more complex and awe-inspiring than (what they regard as) the simplistic tale in Genesis.

Geographic Location

A geographic pattern appears to be formed by the states and communities most prominent in attempts to mandate the teaching of creationism and/or to block the teaching of Darwin's theory. Most evident in that pattern has been the sweep of states across the U.S. South—Georgia, Alabama, Kentucky, Tennessee, Mississippi, Louisiana, Arkansas, Oklahoma, and Texas—a region often referred to as *The Bible Belt*. Of secondary importance have been states and communities in the Midwest. Ohio on the east and Kansas on the west have provided the most publicized recent statewide examples, with earlier individual-community cases appearing in Indiana, Illinois, Michigan, Pennsylvania, and Nebraska. Far less often and with less public attention, creationism/evolution controversies have appeared in New England, the mid-Atlantic States, and the Far West.

Creationist/evolutionist confrontations reported in the public press also suggest that creationist efforts appear more frequently in rural than in urban communities, as illustrated in the 2004 case of the school board in Grantsburg, Wisconsin (population 4,494), authorizing the teaching of creationism in public schools. A similar case involved a school board in Dover, Pennsylvania (school population 3,600), mandating teaching about intelligent design beginning in 2005, a decision that resulted in a lawsuit being filed against the board by the American Civil Liberties Union. A Union representative called intelligent design "a Trojan horse for bringing religious creationism back into the public school science classroom" (Worden, 2004). Dover school authorities later retreated a step from their original mandate by deciding that science teachers who objected to presenting their students the board's intelligent design statement would not be required to do so. Instead, an administrator would read the statement to classes. Furthermore, students could be excused from having to listen if their parents objected (Morello, 2005; Teachers get choice, 2005).

Denominational Affiliation

Some Christian denominations are more prone than others to advocate teaching creationism in public schools. The most prominent creationist efforts have come from the Southern Baptist Convention, which is a coalition of thousands of individual Baptist congregations that boast a total of 16 million church members, making the Convention the largest organization of Baptist churches in the world and the largest Protestant denomination in America. Although there are both fundamentalist and moderate members of the organization, the fundamentalists—past and present—have dominated the group's policies (Cline, 2004a). Numerous other types of pentecostal and evangelical churches also subscribe to creationism. So do Mormons, with the result that a biblical account of beginnings is informally included in both public and private schools in Utah, where the majority of students are from Mormon families. The following assessment of Darwinism is from a Jehovah's Witnesses book titled *Life: How Did It Get Here? By Evolution or by Creation?*

We need to face the fact that the theory of evolution serves the purposes of Satan. He wants people to imitate his course, and that of Adam and Eve, in rebelling against God. . . . Thus, believing in evolution would mean promoting [Satan's] interests and blinding oneself to the wonderful purposes of the Creator. (Quoted in Cline, 2004b)

While polls find that only 18% of Americans interpret the Bible as literal truth, about 45% reject evolution because they do not like the implication that humans are genetically related to animals (Filiatreau, 2000).

In contrast to the efforts of evangelical denominations to teach biblical creationism is the position expressed by other Christian bodies that represents a nondoctrinaire viewpoint. An example of that position is the 1982 resolution adopted by the general assembly of the United Presbyterian Church of North America, a resolution that closed in the following manner:

[The General Assembly] affirms that, required teaching of a [biblical creationist] view constitutes an establishment of religion and a violation of the separation of church and state, as provided in the First Amendment to the Constitution and laws of the United States;

Affirms that, exposure to the Genesis account is best sought through the teaching about religion, history, social studies, and literature, provinces other than the discipline of natural science, and

Calls upon Presbyterians, and upon legislators and school board members, to resist all efforts to establish any requirements upon teachers and schools to teach "creationism" or "creation science." (Evolution and creationism, 1982)

In issuing similar statements, representatives of Methodist, Episcopalian, Roman Catholic, Lutheran, Christian Science, and Unitarian churches have accepted the theory of evolution and have denounced the teaching of creationism in science classes.

Secularists

The secularist category includes humanists, agnostics, atheists, realists, and people who simply consider themselves nonreligious. They typically support the teaching of evolution and either condemn or merely disregard proposals to teach creationism.

Scientists

The term *scientists* in the present context does not identify a group that is entirely separate from the religious and secularist categories but, rather, is a subgroup derived from portions of those categories. Scientists are people whose professional life consists of teaching science and/or conducting scientific research. They form a separate class in the creationism/evolution debate because they command detailed knowledge of the empirical evidence and logic supporting Darwin's theory and thus are specially equipped to marshal arguments in favor of the theory. With rare exceptions, scientists urge the teaching of evolution in the schools and reject the teaching of creationism in science classes. In support of such a position, a wide range of scientific societies have issued statements similar to the following declaration of the National Science Teachers Association.

Science curricula, state science standards, and teachers should emphasize evolution in a manner commensurate with its importance as a unifying concept in science and its overall explanatory power.

Science teachers should not advocate any religious interpretations of nature and should be nonjudgmental about the personal beliefs of students.

Policy makers and administrators should not mandate policies requiring the teaching of "creation science" or related concepts, such as so-called "intelligent design," "abrupt appearance," and "arguments against evolution." Administrators also should support teachers against pressure to promote nonscientific views or to diminish or eliminate the study of evolution. (The teaching of evolution, 2004)

Summary

An estimate in graphic form of the opposing constituencies in the creationism/evolution debate is shown in Figure 12.2.

Both creationists and evolutionists have employed a variety of resources for promoting their beliefs. Creationists have (a) urged state legislators to pass laws that block the teaching of evolution and encourage the teaching of creationism, (b) strongly supported the election of creationists to state and district school boards, (c) pasted disclaimer statements in science textbooks, warning pupils that the material about evolution in the books was "only theory, not fact," (d) published articles and books identifying what allegedly were fatal flaws in Darwin's proposal, (e) in church sermons and at religious conferences condemned the teaching of evolution, (f) written letters-to-the-editor in newspapers, and (g) placed criticisms of Darwinism on Internet Web sites.

Evolutionists have (a) published books and articles in support of evolution and critical of creationism, (b) under the imprimatur of scientific societies,

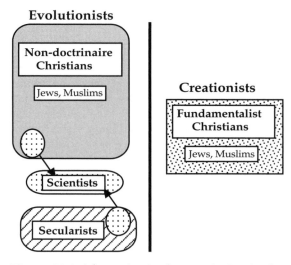

Figure 12.2 Adversaries in the creationism/evolution controversy.

issued proevolution and anticreationist declarations, (c) urged state legisla-tors, school board members, and school personnel to support the teaching of evolution and prevent the teaching of creationism in science classes, and (d) argued their case on Internet Web sites.

Both creationists and evolutionists have sought to acquire positions of au-thority that enable them to determine the versions of human origins taught in school. This competition has been most obvious in state and local school board elections. Somewhat less apparent have been the attempts of school ad-ministrators and teachers to promote their own beliefs through their choice of teaching materials and curriculum content.

Creationists and evolutionists are separated in terms of what they believe is convincing evidence. Creationists have been persuaded by assertions in ancient holy books. Evolutionists, on the other hand, have been persuaded by a line of logic built from a collection of empirical observations of nature. So long as the two sides in the debate trust such contrasting sources of evidence, they will continue to disagree over the question of human beginnings.

One of the great appeals of established religions is that they offer believ-ers unquestionable, lasting truths. As such, religions contribute stability to people's lives. They offer something to count on in times of change. On the other hand, science, as a method of investigation, intentionally contributes to change; its facts and theories are always subject to revision and refinement on the basis of more accurate observations and more persuasive logic. Cer-tainly the concept of evolution by its very nature features change. Hence, in the creationism/evolution controversy, the conservative force of established religious doctrine has been set against a key foundational belief about change in present-day biological science.

RESOLVING THE CONTROVERSY

With the foregoing review of the creationism/evolution debate as a back-ground, we return now to the original case of (a) the superintendent of ed-ucation in Georgia, Kathy Cox, announcing that the word *evolution* would be eliminated from the state curriculum and (b) her announcement being greeted with strong objection on the part of the scientific community and of such formidable political figures as former Georgia Governor and U.S. Presi-dent Jimmy Carter. The clamor that followed Ms. Cox's proposal caused her, within 6 days, to abandon her plan, explaining that

I made the decision to remove the word evolution from the draft of the proposed biology curriculum in an effort to avoid controversy that would prevent people from reading the substance of the document itself. Instead, a greater controversy ensued. I am here to tell you that I misjudged the situation and I want to apologize for that. I want you to know today that I will recommend . . . that the word evolution be put back in the curriculum. (The evolution of Kathy Cox, 2004)[1]

Whereas Ms. Cox's change of mind settled the immediate confrontation over the word *evolution* in the state curriculum, it did not resolve the underlying conflict over creationism versus evolution. That conflict was bound to continue, as it has since the 1925 Scopes trial. Even in Georgia the issue rose again within 6 months of the Cox episode, when Cobb County school officials put a warning sticker in a suburban Atlanta school system's biology textbooks saying that evolution was "a theory, not a fact." The stickers were added after 2,300 parents complained that the texts presented evolution as fact without mentioning rival ideas about the origin of life, namely creationism. The matter ended up in court when critics charged that the stickers violated the principle of separation of church and state (Wyatt, 2004). In mid-January 2005, a federal district court judge ruled that the stickers had to be removed because they conveyed "a message of endorsement of religion" and thereby conflicted with the U.S. Constitution's separation of church and state and "the Georgia Constitution's prohibition against using public money to aid religion" (Hart, 2005). The Cobb County school board, in a 5–2 vote, responded by appealing the judgment. At the same time, ninth-grade science teachers at Pennsylvania's Dover Area High School refused to read to their students a statement promoting intelligent design. Thus, the statement had to be read to classes by the district's assistant superintendent (Two school boards, 2005).

In the twenty-first century, proponents of Darwinism continued to face formidable opposition. As noted earlier, an opinion survey in late 2004 reported that 55% of respondents said they believed God created humans in their present form. An additional 27% believed humans evolved but, in keeping with intelligent design theory, thought that God had guided the process (Hurdle, 2005a).

According to the National Council for Science Education, a pro-evolution group in Oakland, California, other states considering legislation on the issue [in 2005 were] Georgia, South Carolina, Mississippi, Montana, Oklahoma, Alabama and Texas. Other state or local school boards debating the teaching of intelligent design included those in Ohio, Arkansas, Wisconsin, Kansas, Maryland, Michigan, Tennessee, and Alaska. (Hurdle, 2005a)

Proponents of intelligent design were pleased when U.S. President George W. Bush in August 2005 recommended the teaching of intelligent design as a reasonable alternative to Darwinian theory (Hurdle, 2005b). Thus, the creationism/evolution controversy in the early years of the twenty-first century was still very much alive. There now remained the question of whether the continued teaching of Darwinian theory in public schools' science programs, along with the mounting evidence supporting that viewpoint, would significantly alter most Americans' beliefs about the process by which humans first appeared on earth.

CHAPTER 13

Thailand

In the Thai case mentioned in Chapter 1, the confrontation was between Thailand's Buddhist government and the Muslims who administered private Islamic schools in the southern section of the country. The controversy was over the issue of who should determine what was taught in the Islamic schools—the Thai government or the *imams* (Muslim leaders) who operated the schools.

HISTORICAL ROOTS

Geographically, the Kingdom of Thailand consists of a broad body of land in the center of Southeast Asia plus a long, narrow peninsula extending south from the main body. The peninsula connects Thailand with the northern boundary of Malaysia.

In religious affiliation, Thailand's 60 million people at the outset of the twenty-first century were Buddhist 94.2%, Muslim 4.6%, and Christian and other faiths 1.2%. Most Thais subscribed to the Theravada variety of Buddhist belief. In ethnic composition, the Thai population was 81.4% Thai, 10.6% Han Chinese, 3.7% Malay, and 4.4% other origins (Sparks, 2004, p. 710). The Islamic Malays were concentrated in Thailand's southernmost provinces adjacent to Malaysia, the neighbor whose population was chiefly of Malay heritage and whose official state religion was Islam.

Two sorts of background information useful for understanding the Islamic schools case are (a) the history of Thailand's troubled southern provinces and (b) the nature of the province's religious schools—the *pondoks*.

A Troubled Region

Thailand's five far-south provinces (Satun, Songkhla, Pattani, Yala, Narathiwat) were originally part of the ancient Kingdom of Pattani, a semiautonomous Malay sultanate that had adopted Islam in the mid-thirteenth century CE. Prior to the twentieth century, the remaining segments of the Pattani kingdom occupied the portion of the peninsula that separated Thailand from the British-controlled Malay States—the states that eventually would become the nation of Malaysia. In 1902, Siam (the name of Thailand until 1939) annexed the Pattani territory, a move defended by the Siamese as a legitimate peace-keeping act but criticized by outsiders as an imperialist takeover. Past centuries had witnessed frequent armed clashes between Siamese and Pattani forces. For more than 500 years, Muslim ethnic Malays had battled Siamese security troops with hit-and-run attacks in an effort to end what they perceived as Thailand's "racist" Buddhist domination. And Siamese Buddhists had crushed major Pattani Muslim uprisings in both 1564 and 1776 (Ehrlich, 2004).

After Siam took control of the area in 1902, the newly acquired provinces continued in turmoil, divided by both religion and ethnicity from the main Siamese population. Throughout the twentieth century, the five provinces were plagued by a variety of problems—banditry, vandalism, drug trafficking, arms smuggling, general lawlessness, high unemployment, a lower standard of living than in the rest of the nation, and fewer government services. The passing decades witnessed the rise of a militant Muslim separatist movement aimed at winning political independence from Thailand. All the while, Thai authorities found it very difficult "to differentiate between criminal lawlessness and terrorist acts commissioned by domestic Thai terrorists or Muslim Separatist groups" (Thailand Islamic insurgency, 2004). The territory's unruly condition continued throughout the 1900s and grew even more alarming by 2004, when at least 550 people died in clashes involving separatists, government troops, bandits, and ordinary civilians (Thailand's restive south, 2004). Observers noted that the separatist "quest for an autonomous homeland [was] rekindled partly because of the Iraq war and Israel's violent suppression of the Palestinian intifada" (Islamist schools, 2004).

The brutal nature of the confrontations is illustrated by the following incidents in 2004.

- In January, 30 Muslim raiders stole more than 100 assault rifles and killed four Thai soldiers in an attack on an army depot. In response, Thai Prime Minister Thaksin Shinawatra declared martial law in the provinces of Narathiwat, Pattani, and Yala (Thailand Islamic insurgency, 2004).

- Government security forces seriously crippled a Muslim separatist group— the New Pattani United Liberation Organization—by killing its leader, Saarli Taloh-Meyaw. Authorities claimed that Taloh-Meyaw had been responsible for 90% of terrorist activities in Narathiwat province (Thailand Islamic insurgency, 2004).

- During the year, radical Muslims burned down nearly 100 public schools (Islamist schools, 2004).

- Scores of separatists were killed in April when more than 100 Muslims on motorbikes were gunned down by Thai soldiers who had been tipped off about a plan to ransack army posts throughout the region (Islamist schools, 2004).

- In May, a Bangkok court issued an arrest warrant for a Muslim teacher accused of organizing the worst of the separatist attacks. Critics of Muslim separatist forces said that many of the southern provinces' Muslim-Thai teachers had studied overseas at Islamic schools that were operated by hard-line Muslim fundamentalists bent on making war against non-Muslims (Bradley, 2004).

- Members of the Buddhist minority in the south circulated pamphlets citing examples of Muslim extremism that they felt threatened both the Buddhist religion and the Thai government. A high-level Thai official criticized Muslim attempts at "ethnic cleansing" in Narathiwat province. He said, "Some Thai Buddhist families have been told to leave under the threat of violence" (Islamist schools, 2004).

- In October, police in the Tak Bai district of Narathiwat province arrested six youths suspected of stealing army weapons and giving them to Islamic militants. When 3,000 protestors collected outside the police station, security forces opened fire on the crowd and arrested more than 1,300 protestors. During the melee, six demonstrators were shot dead. Another 85 of the arrested ones suffocated to death when they were bound together, forced into trucks, stacked on top of each other, and covered with tarpaulins during a six-hour journey. Authorities claimed that the protestors had weapons and hand grenades, and so the violent police response had been warranted (Lintner, 2004).

- Informants reported that the Pattani United Liberation Organization had several hundred fighters deployed on both sides of the Thai-Malaysian border (Ehrlich, 2004).

- In late December, nearly 60% of Pattani province's 400 state schools closed down indefinitely after two teachers were shot to death by suspected separatists. Officials said that more of the province's public schools were likely to close in Pattani as well as in Narathiwat and Yala. Religious schools continued to operate. Teachers in state schools demanded bulletproof vests and greater police protection (Hundreds of schools, 2004).

It was against such a background of social turmoil that the Thai government announced its intention to take supervisory control over the curriculum content and teaching methods in the southern provinces' Muslim schools.

The Pondok Tradition

Before the middle of the nineteenth century, Siamese children's education was provided mainly within the family. For male adolescents and adults who sought training as Buddhist monks, family education was followed by studies at a Buddhist temple (*wat*). Then, during the reign of King Chulalongkorn (1868 to 1910), formal schooling was introduced, initially as wat schools associated with temples. At the time that Chulalongkorn founded the nation's department of education in 1887, there were 34 schools under the department with 81 teachers and 1,994 pupils (Buripakdi & Mahakhan, 1980). Over the next century, state schools and private schools expanded rapidly, with the private schools obligated to register with the government and submit to some state supervision. Prominent among the nation's private schools during the twentieth century were the Islamic *pondoks*, most of them located in the southern provinces. The politically active pondoks were at the center of the 2004 conflict between the Thai government and the Muslim schools' administrators.

As explained in Chapter 11, the type of Islamic school known as a *madrassa* in Pakistan and a *pesantren* in Indonesia is called a *pondok* in Malaysia and Thailand. The precise number of pondoks in Thailand's southern provinces is unknown because by 2004, out of an estimated 500, only about 300 had registered with state authorities. Government officials suspected that at least 30 of the 500 preached violence in the name of Islam (Liow, 2004).

Before the Siamese government annexed the Pattani sultanate in 1902, Pattani had been a regional center for Islamic learning, with students from across Southeast Asia spending time at a Pattani pondok before traveling to the Middle East for advanced Islamic education. Pattani scholars and religious teachers (*tok gurus*) had translated Islamic religious works from Arabic into both Malay and the local Yawi language. Thus, when the Siamese seized the Pattani territory, pondoks were already a powerful force for transmitting the region's Muslim culture from one generation to the next—a culture significantly different from that of the nation's Buddhist majority.

In the pondok tradition, teaching was in the Malay and Arabic languages, with emphasis on religious learning—prayer, memorizing the Quran, and accepting a tok guru's interpretations of scripture. Because pondoks had no system for assessing students' learning, the schools were not accredited by the government.

The 2004 confrontation was not the first instance of the Buddhist government trying to influence what was taught in pondoks. In the 1930s and 1940s, the government had attempted to assimilate the Malay-Muslim community into Thai society by changing the language used in pondoks from Malay-Arabic to Thai. That effort was bluntly rejected by the Muslims and served, instead, to mobilize the pondoks' efforts to

disseminate ideas of pan-Malay nationalism and Islamic revivalism. Similarly, policies of later Thai governments to transform pondok schools to private institutions eligible for state funding but subject to government regulation were met with resistance. Such policies of the [Thai government's] Sarit Thanarat administration toward pondok schools in the early 1960s laid the ground for two decades of separatist violence, with pondok schools choosing to disband themselves and move underground rather than be absorbed into the Thai education system. (Liow, 2004)

Therefore, the 2004 conflict was not a unique event. It followed others from the past. But the 2004 incident was perhaps the most alarming of the series, since it was related to the heightened violence in the southern provinces that government officials linked to worldwide terrorist attacks attributed to radical Islamic factions. Thai authorities recognized that many Muslim-Thai activists had attended Islamic schools in the Middle East, where they were tutored by hard-line advocates of *jihad* holy war against all non-Muslims. During 2004, an estimated 160 Thai-Muslim students were enrolled in Islamic institutions in Saudi Arabia and 1,500 in Egypt. Some were alleged to have fought against the Soviet Army in Afghanistan in the 1990s, and then returned to Thailand as jihad extremists, often operating through pondoks (Thailand Islamic insurgency, 2004).

The Thai government's concern was not only with radicalism in pondoks but also in Yala Islamic College, founded in 1998 by a Wahabi cleric, Ismail Lutfi, and staffed by Arab teachers from the Middle East. In 2004, Yala's student enrollment was estimated at between 1,300 and 1,500.

[The college has received] a seemingly endless flow of funds from Saudi Arabia, Qatar, and Kuwait. Yala has become the most obvious manifestation of what critics say is an "Arab threat" to the traditionally moderate and tolerant local Islamic tradition. [The threat] was first brought home in 2002 when two dozen Middle Eastern suspects were arrested in the south for forging travel documents, visas, and passports for al-Qaeda [terrorist] operatives. (Islamist schools, 2004)

Joseph Liow (2004) has noted that some people harbor mistaken notions about Thailand's pondoks. One such notion is that pondoks teach only Muslim religious subjects, when, in actuality, many include secular and vocational subjects as well. A second mistaken impression has been

that Muslim parents prefer to send their children to pondoks rather than state schools. This is not entirely so. Recent research conducted by the Prince of Songkhla University (in Pattani) has found that up to 64% of the people desire general education for their children. Nevertheless, they also want secular education to be balanced with religious instruction from the pondok. (Liow, 2004)

Whatever the true nature of pondoks and their patrons might have been, it is clear that Thai authorities' intention to establish state-sponsored pondoks was a response to the authorities' conviction that the recent public disorder in the southern provinces had been fostered by radical Malay-Muslim activists from the region's private Islamic schools. Throughout 2004, the conduct of education in both state schools and pondoks was seriously disrupted as

militants targeted state schools in repeated arson attacks; security forces searching for an elusive enemy have raided Islamic schools; and teachers, both Muslim and Buddhist, have become prime targets for assassination, prompting hundreds in the state sector to apply for transfers out of the border provinces. Punctuated by closures of schools and conducted frequently under armed guard, education has become an arena of suspicion, fear, and violence. (Davis, 2004)

Summary

Significant events and the dominant belief systems in the Thai case are depicted in Figure 13.1 as a timeline extending from 1875 to 2000.

From 1875 to 2000

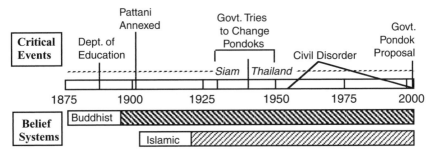

Figure 13.1 Critical events and belief systems in the Thai case.

THE CONTENDING CONSTITUENCIES

The two most obvious constituencies involved in the pondok controversy were Thailand's Buddhist-dominated government and the supporters of the southern provinces' Malay-Islamic private schools. The contrasting positions that the two groups held are revealed in (a) the accusations that each made about its opponents and (b) the arguments that each adduced in support of its own actions.

Thai Buddhist Government

The Thai government was reluctant to admit publicly that much of the disorder in the southern provinces was the work of separatist groups rather than of bandits. This reluctance was apparently due to officials' unwillingness to acknowledge that a significant portion of the Malay-Muslim inhabitants of those provinces were not satisfied to be citizens of Thailand and wanted to be politically independent or, at least, to be attached to Malaysia where the majority of citizens were Malay and Muslim.

Eventually, Thai authorities were obliged to recognize that religious extremists were behind much of the disorder and that at least some of the pondoks were heavily involved in urging the attacks on army posts, state schools, and Buddhist residents of the region. Part of the evidence leading to the government's admission was the large number of pondok teachers charged with terrorist activities. For example, out of eight Malay-Muslims accused in court of killing four soldiers in an attack on an army camp, seven were pondok teachers who, according to prosecutors, had recruited students to carry out the attack (Eight Thai Muslims, 2005).

[Officials' concern about] "distorted" Islamic teaching as an ideological catalyst for unrest has been exacerbated by the realization that some young Islamic teachers (*ustaz*) are now serving as the recruiting sergeants and field commanders of jihad. The role of such teachers in the radicalization of large numbers of the region's Muslim youth has been such that the Royal Thai Army's Southern 4th Army command now refers to the unrest as the "Ustaz rebellion." (Davis, 2004)

Thai officials blamed Islamic activists for crippling the government's efforts to achieve national unity, charging that the Muslims (a) refused to use the Thai language as the medium of instruction in Islamic schools, (b) attacked Buddhist citizens and state schools, (c) failed to register pondoks, and (d) rejected government supervision of the content of instruction in pondoks.

Given the important role that pondok schools play in reinforcing Malay-Muslim identity through religious and language training, these institutions have posed a major challenge to the Thai government, which views education as the central instrument for assimilating and integrating minorities into the nation-state. (Liow, 2004)

After the Thai army was accused of employing excessive force in dealing with Islamic protestors and lawbreakers, the government denied "allegations of intentional mistreatment of Thailand's Muslims" and insisted that separatist guerrillas were "bandits enriching themselves while spewing religious and political rhetoric" (Ehrlich, 2004).

The government's attitude about "the troubles in the south" was likely shared by a large proportion of the country's Buddhist majority.

Pondok Supporters

The constituency that opposed the government's plan to gain control of pondoks included the tok gurus who administered the schools, a variety of separatist organizations, and Middle-East Arab states that sent teachers and funds to Thailand's pondoks.

The government's claim that raids in the southern provinces were the work of bandits rather than of separatists conflicted with reports that formally organized separatist groups were operating on both sides of the Thai-Malaysian border—groups bearing such names as Bersatu, Barison Revolusi Nasional (BRN), Gerakan Mujahideen Islam Pattani (GMIP), Pattani United Liberation Organization (PULO), and Kumpulan Mujahiden Malaysia (KMM) (Thailand Islamic insurgency, 2004).

The pondok supporters constituency accused the Thai government of both brutality and sociopolitical neglect. The brutality charge included the claim that the government pursued a policy of abducting and murdering tok gurus who were suspected of advocating separatism and violence. "This perception, fueled by the fact that several pondok teachers have gone missing [since the April massacre at the Krisek Mosque where security forces shot dead 32 lightly armed separatists] only serves to feed further the climate of suspicion and distrust [among Muslims] in the south" (Liow, 2004).

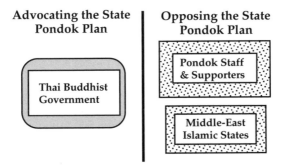

Figure 13.2 Adversaries in the case of the government plan to supervise Islamic schools.

The claim of neglect was based on a well-documented impression that the southern provinces traditionally served as a "dumping ground for corrupt and/or incompetent civilian and military officials." The alleged dumping practice was accompanied by a lack of attention to economic development, job opportunities, and education (Thailand Islamic insurgency, 2004).

Separatists defended their raids on army posts and schools as necessary instruments for maintaining their traditional cultural and religious identity in the face of government strong-arm attempts to impose Buddhist culture on Muslims.

Overseas allies of Thailand's Malay-Muslims helped undermine the Thai government's pondok plan. Most important were the advice, funds, teachers, and learning materials furnished to pondoks by Arab states. In addition, such international bodies as The Organization of the Islamic Conference (OIC) publicly appealed to the government of Thailand to stop "persistent bloody acts of violence" against Muslims in southern Thailand (Shaikh, 2005). This objection to brutality was buttressed by an investigation by Thailand's own human rights commission that led Commissioner Saneh Jamarik to report that "the use of force [at the Krisek Mosque] was excessive, and someone should be held responsible. We found that the key problem is government policy. We have proposed advice in previous letters, but the government was not interested in our opinions" (Thailand: Rights groups, 2004).

Summary

Figure 13.2 offers a graphic display of the principal participants in the controversy over the Thai government's proposed establishment of state-operated pondoks.

If we can assume that the majority of Thailand's Buddhists would support the government position in the controversy, and that most Muslims would be sympathetic with the separatists' stance, then it is obvious that the Buddhists' constituency was far larger than the Muslims'. However, if we add the Muslims' overseas allies, then the Islamic constituency is the larger group.

As for cohesiveness, there was some division of opinion within each of the two groups. The operators of some pondoks were adamantly opposed to any government meddling in their affairs, and they urged students to engage in acts of violence. However, other tok gurus registered their schools with the government and limited their curricula to the study of Islam, free from the jihad theme. Likewise, among Buddhists, some would endorse violent treatment of Muslim separatists and others—such as members of the human rights commission—would condemn such acts. In effect, neither the Buddhists nor the Muslims appeared entirely unified in their attitudes toward the controversy.

Within Thailand, the government had greater resources (troops, funds, access to mass communication media) and more official authority (elected officials with the legal right to hire and assign members of the workforce, including those in the armed services) than did the Malay-Muslims. For example, when the raids on army posts and schools escalated in 2004, the government could promptly assign 3,000 more well-equipped soldiers to the southern provinces. The separatists could not assemble a similar number to oppose the troops but had to depend on fewer fighters who could not confront the army directly but were obliged to limit their efforts to sneak attacks. However, the separatists were able to profit from resources (funds, teachers) and leadership from the Arab states.

The Malay-Muslim community could cite passages from two respected documents in support of their actions—Thailand's constitution and the Islamic Quran. First, they could claim that the government's attempt to determine what was taught in pondoks violated Muslims' religious rights provided in the nation's constitutional provision that

Every person shall enjoy full liberty to profess a religion, a religious sect or creed, and to exercise a form of worship in accordance with his belief; provided that it is not contrary to his civic duties and to public order or good morals. . . . [and] every person is protected from any act of the State, which is derogatory to his rights or detrimental to his due benefits, on the grounds of professing a religion, a religious sect or creed, or of exercising a form of worship in accordance with his belief different from that of others. (Constitution of Thailand, 1991)

Second, radical Muslims could claim that the Quran superceded any government's laws and that there were passages in that holy book which preached jihad—violence against infidels, which included Buddhists.

On the other hand, the Thai government could also draw on the nation's constitution to support police and army efforts to quell lawlessness in the southern provinces. In effect, the authorities could charge Malay-Muslim guerillas with destroying "public order" and violating "good morals."

Each side in the controversy was attempting to conserve one aspect of the status quo and trying to change another aspect. The Malay-Muslims sought to keep their cultural identity intact by resisting government efforts to change their language, religion, and customs. To achieve this aim, they were trying to change their political and economic condition by forcing the Thai government to grant them independence. On the other hand, the Thai government was seeking to maintain its political/economic domination of the southern provinces, partly by changing the pondoks' traditional control over their schools' curriculum content.

RESOLVING THE CONTROVERSY

The likelihood that the controversy over pondoks' instructional content and methods would be resolved in the government's favor was extremely remote. Similar plans in the past had failed, and the social climate surrounding this most recent proposal was so filled with violence and vindictiveness that it is difficult to imagine the Malay-Muslim community accepting the government's interfering with the pondoks' curricula.

Observers have suggested that the Thai government could profitably attempt a different mode of action in the southern provinces than it had used in the past. According to Ehrlich (2004), unless such a fresh approach was adopted, the region would continue to be "relatively poor, alienated, and misunderstood by Bangkok's government and military officials" (Ehrlich, 2004). Such a new departure would need to address Muslims' complaints about a shortage of job opportunities, education, and economic development in their region.

Critics claimed that the government erred in considering all pondoks a threat to the nation rather than distinguishing among pondoks. Following the heightened level of hostility in early 2004, government security forces launched raids without warning on pondoks and revived efforts to register the schools in order to regulate Islamic education. But the Muslim community considered the raids a violation of their religious and cultural rights. As a result, pondoks increasingly went underground, operating in secret to avoid registration that they feared would lead to further government intrusions into Malay-Muslim society. In Joseph Liow's opinion (Liow, 2004), only a small percentage of Thailand's pondoks preached jihad radicalism. The vast majority were far less a danger to the government, since they only encouraged students to acquire a deeper knowledge of Islamic holy scripture and a measure of secular skills. That traditional type of pondok, with its stress on Islamic doctrine as taught in Malay and Arabic languages rather than on jihad, has continued to be a key force in perpetuating the Malay-Muslim identity and lifestyle, and, as critics advised, that kind of pondok deserved to be respected by the Thai government.

The error of considering all pondoks the enemies of Thailand's Buddhist majority served, in the opinion of Islamic writers, to exacerbate the conflict. Yusria, a Thai Muslim living in Malaysia, warned that

as long as [government forces] are targeting good Muslims, the war against terrorism will fail and the authorities will never be able to contain the young generation of Muslims from making demands and from being involved in acts of desperation against the authorities. (Mahmood, 2003)

Mansor Saleh, a Muslim writer and social worker, said that

not all Muslims are fighters, some are members of a new group called the Mujahideen, and they are ready to die for the cause of separatism. We cannot stop [the separatism movement] as long as there is no development that allows Muslims to progress in the South. (Mahmood, 2003)

On the other hand, observers of recent events noted that even with the Thai government assuming a new approach in the southern provinces, the troubles would not cease as long as radical Islamic forces outside of Thailand continued to finance terrorist groups and to preach separatism. Changes would be needed on both sides of the conflict if peace and amity were to prevail. In any event, the issue of the government attempting to influence the content to instruction in pondoks was not likely to be settled in the foreseeable future.

CHAPTER 14

Australia

The Australian case mentioned in Chapter 1 concerned a controversy over whether religious explanations of natural phenomena—including Australian Aboriginal explanations—should be accorded the same status in the teaching of science as explanations based on internationally accepted scientific standards. Therefore, the issue in the case was not whether religion should be taught in schools, because there is clearly a provision in Australia that permits the teaching of religion in both state and private schools. Instead, the controversy was over whether religious beliefs should be taught in science classes.

HISTORICAL ROOTS

Before the British began to colonize Australia in 1788, the country was inhabited by Aborigines who composed a population that exceeded 350,000. The first British settlers in 1788 consisted of 730 convicts (570 men, 160 women) and their guards, as Britain sought to relieve the pressure on its prisons by shipping lawbreakers to Australia. Over the following decades the British population grew steadily as more convicts arrived, worked out their sentences, and stayed to establish new lives in farming, herding, crafts, or commerce. For three decades such newcomers were the principal immigrants from Britain, along with a growing number of ordinary citizens who hoped for a better life abroad than they had led in Europe. By 1825 the number of Europeans had grown to 50,000. Then, in a great surge of immigration, their ranks swelled to 450,000 by 1851 and 1,150,000 by 1861 (Roe, 1994).

The largest areas of fertile land and good harbors were in Australia's southeastern and southwestern coastal regions, which were the territories in which the newcomers settled. The incursion of so many Europeans forced the Aboriginal peoples into the wild and often barren central areas of the country—the outback. Early confrontations between Europeans and Aborigines were often bloody, with the immigrants' superior weapons and technology enabling them to prevail. As a result, the Aborigines were gradually diminished in numbers, partly by diseases brought by the foreigners. Ultimately they became a socially and economically disadvantaged minority, denigrated and despised as "primitive and uncivilized" by the foreigners who occupied the indigenous tribes' homeland.

The Aborigines and Europeans were separated not only by appearance and technology but, more importantly, by a great chasm that divided their worldviews. The two groups' basic belief systems rendered each incapable of understanding and appreciating the other's way of interpreting life. In the current controversy over religion in science classes, those disparate belief systems became a key issue, as explained in the following section titled "Three Contrasting Worldviews." In addition, changes in the Aborigines' rights and social status over recent decades were also significant in the case, as explained in the later section titled "Multiculturalism and Postmodernism."

Three Contrasting Worldviews

The three perspectives of consequence in the Australian case were those of Aborigines' Dreamtime, of Christianity, and of Western science.

Aboriginal Dreamtime

The belief system known as *Dreamtime* or *Dreaming* is a worldview common to all indigenous Australians, with the system assuming different variations in different tribal groups. Although not everyone assigns the two terms precisely the same meanings, *Dreamtime* most often refers to the "time before time" or "the time of the creation of all things," whereas *Dreaming* more frequently means an individual's or group's particular beliefs (Australian Dreamtime, 2005).

The Dreamtime contains many parts: It is the story of things that have happened, how the universe came to be, how human beings were created, and how the Creator intended for humans to function within the cosmos. . . . In the Aboriginal worldview, every meaningful activity, event, or life process that occurs at a particular place leaves behind a vibrational residue in the earth, as plants leave an image of themselves as seeds. The shape of the land—its mountains, rocks, riverbeds, and waterholes—and its unseen vibrations echo the events that brought that place into creation. Everything in the natural world is a symbolic footprint of the metaphysical beings whose actions created our world. As with a seed, the potency of an earthly location is wedded to the memory of its origin. The Aborigines called this potency the "Dreaming" of a place. . . . Only in extraordinary states of consciousness can one be aware of, or attuned to, the inner dreaming of the Earth. (Lawlor, 1991)

The following story about how the sun was created illustrates the narrative form in which Dreamtime accounts have been passed from one generation to the next over the centuries.

For a long time there was no sun, only a moon and stars. That was before there were men on the earth, only birds and beasts, all of which were many sizes larger than they are now. One day Dinewan the emu and Brolga the native companion were . . . fighting. Brolga, in her rage, rushed to the nest of Dinewan and seized from it one of the huge eggs, which she threw with all her force up to the sky. There it broke on a heap of firewood, which burst into flame as the yellow yolk spilled all over it, and lit up the world below to the astonishment of every creature on it. They had been used to the semi-darkness and were dazzled by such brightness. A good spirit who lived in the sky saw how bright and beautiful the earth looked when lit up by this blaze. He thought it would be a good thing to make a fire every day, and from that time he has done so. All night he and his attendant spirits collect wood and heap it up. When the heap is nearly big enough they send out the morning star to warn those on earth that the fire will soon be lit. (Australian Dreamtime, 2005)

As shown in this tale, *personification* is involved in Dreamtime explanations of how the world's happenings occur. Personification, in the present context, means the conviction that all of the world's objects and events are caused by "persons" (invisible spirits or earthly creatures) whose actions result from such human attributes as intention, intelligence, anger, joy, fear, shame, amazement, greed, vengeance, and more. The evidence supporting Dreamtime narratives includes (a) the authority of tradition (believing that an explanation must be true if it has been so long-lasting and if virtually everyone believes it), (b) respect for the elders who tell the Dreamtime tales, and (c) a form of logic that imagines all phenomena must be the result of human-like intent.

In contrast to Dreamtime's visions of the causes of the universe's contents, two other features of Aboriginal culture are more akin to Western science. Those features are the indigenous peoples' (a) methods of classifying objects and events and (b) observations of correlations between objects and/or events.

Classification Schemes.   One major scientific activity in Western civilization is that of categorizing phenomena on the basis of how many characteristics those phenomena share. In a Western tree-like diagram or mapping of animal life, humans and chimpanzees are located closer to each other—both on the same branch—than are humans and garden slugs, because humans and chimpanzees have more components in common than do humans and slugs. In Western science, such classification systems are called *typologies* or *taxonomies*. Observant Aborigines have also classified many aspects of their environments—plant life, animal life, tools, kinds of weather, objects in the night sky, ethnic groups (tribes and races), and more. But rarely if ever have Aborigines cast their classification schemes as formal graphic displays. Instead, their systems have been "kept in mind" and transmitted orally from one generation to the next.

Causal Correlations.   Another Aboriginal activity much like a principal activity of Western scientists is that of observing correlations between events—correlations suggesting that one of the events is the result of the other. For instance, when a person who has touched a particular plant in the forest will subsequently break out in a skin rash—and that same pairing of events occurs with other people as well—then an observer may well conclude that touching the plant was responsible for (the *cause* of) the rash (the *effect*). Or, if folks with stomach pains drink a potion offered by a medical healer, and in each of those folks the pain subsides, then observers are likely to assume a causal relation between the potion and the pain—the potion cured the pain. In effect, the activity of interpreting correlations is common to both Aborigines and Western scientists, although modern science has more sophisticated methods than does traditional Aboriginal culture for determining which correlations are *causal* and which are merely coincidental. Among the most useful of the Aboriginal collections of correlations have been those in the field of folk medicine, particularly in the curative use of herbs (Pennacchio, 2005).

Summary.   At the center of the Australian science curricula controversy was the question of which, if any, of the Aboriginal beliefs and practices deserved a place in Australian schools' science classes.

Christian

Two belief systems that European immigrants brought to Australia were those of Christianity and of Western civilization science.

Christianity, like Aboriginal Dreamtime, included beliefs about how the universe was created and how events in the world continue to be affected by invisible spirits. However, the Christian and Aboriginal versions differed significantly, so that Christians disparaged Aboriginal beliefs as "primitive" and "naive," and then sought to replace such convictions in Aborigines' minds with a Christian worldview. Those missionary efforts were often successful, and so a growing number of indigenous Australians adopted a biblical version of life's events.

Over the decades, and continuing today, that Christian worldview has been taught both in private religious schools and in state schools' religious-education classes, which usually have consisted of a representative from a given denomination offering instruction to pupils of that faith during time provided in the school week. Therefore, in the Australian science controversy there was not a question of whether a religious interpretation of creation should be taught in public schools. Rather, the question was only whether such beliefs should be taught as "science."

Scientific

The second life-perspective imported by Europeans—that of Western civilization's science—focused on two matters: (a) methods of gathering and interpreting information about the universe and (b) the body of knowledge compiled by using those methods.

As proposed in Chapter 3, there is no single scientific method to which all scientists subscribe. However, there are principles that proponents of Western science hold in common. One is that conclusions about reality should be founded on empirical evidence derived from the direct study of objects and events—from observations of the universe that are collected and summarized. Then logical interpretations are drawn about what the collected information means. Interpretations may be cast in the form of scientific theories that suggest (a) which features of the universe are the focus of attention at the moment and (b) how those features seem related to each other.

A second principle of science is that all interpretations are subject to revision on the basis of additional empirical evidence and its analysis. Each answer about reality is presumed to be no more than an approximation of the truth, an approximation that requires more data, further testing, critical review, and refinement.

Frequently there is no conflict between scientific and religious (either Aboriginal or Christian) descriptions of the universe or of causes of events, because the phenomena in question are not matters that religious systems address. For example, the question of how and why a gasoline engine operates or how a humming bird manages to fly is not a source of disagreement between scientific and religious worldviews, because religious lore has little or nothing to say about such matters. But in other realms of belief, conflicts can be quite intense, such as in proposals about the creation, contents, and general operation of the universe. That conflict was illustrated in Chapter 12 with the confrontation between Christian fundamentalists and supporters of Darwin's theory of evolution. A similar confrontation in Australia has obtained between Aboriginal and scientific versions of the universe's creation. In addition, there are also differences between Aboriginal and Western scientific ways of classifying such things as animals, plants, time, weather, geographic locations, ethnic groups, occupations, and more.

Summary

Three worldviews in present-day Australian society are the Aboriginal, Christian, and scientific, with the three apparently incompatible, at least in some important instances. The question of whether Aboriginal interpretations of events should be included in science instruction is an instance of assumed incompatibility.

Multiculturalism and Postmodernism

The final three decades of the twentieth century witnessed the development and expansion of two, often-related, philosophical movements referred to as *multiculturalism* and *postmodernism*.

Multiculturalism

The expression *multiculturalism*, as intended here, means (a) the existence within a community or nation of diverse cultures (ways of life) that are related to people's ethnicity, religious affiliation, and/or national origin and (b) a public commitment to accord those cultures proper respect and the opportunity to promote their beneficial attributes. Such multiculturalism has expanded worldwide at a great rate in recent decades, stimulated particularly by (a) the decline of colonialism, (b) rapidly increasing migration, (c) international organizations' declarations, and (d) guilt and compassion.

Colonialism's Decline.   World War II was a watershed for colonialism. Until the war, a variety of European nations, the United States, and Japan controlled territories beyond their own borders. Most of Africa and much of Asia and the Pacific Islands were those nations' colonies, dominated politically, economically, and culturally by the colonizing masters. But after the war, from the late 1940s well into the 1970s, most colonized territories won their political independence, either through violent conflict or peaceful negotiation. Although colonialism was not entirely killed off, it did suffer irreparable damage. The freed peoples then demanded respect for their indigenous cultures, a new regard that their former masters would be obliged to recognize.

Increased Migration.   The postwar era also witnessed rapidly growing migration, primarily of people attempting to escape poverty or political oppression in their homelands by traveling to more prosperous and safer countries. For example, the number of international migrants worldwide rose from 75 million in 1965 to 120 million in 1990 (International migration, 1997). By 2004, more than 175 million people were living outside their home country (International migration, 2004). The resulting dramatic increase of foreigners settling in such nations as Australia and countries of Western Europe and North America significantly increased cultural diversity in those places. And as the proportion of newcomers in the society rose, so did their political activism and significance. Their demands to have their cultures shown proper regard forced the recipient nations to provide a growing array of rights and privileges to such peoples.

International Declarations.   A third force encouraging multiculturalism was the growing number of international organizations issuing worldwide commitments to human welfare. For example, the United Nations Charter (1945) required member nations to show "due respect for . . . peoples, their political, economic, social, and educational advancement, their just treatment, and their protection against abuses" (Tarrow, 1987, p. 237). The Universal Declaration of Human Rights obligated United Nations member states to provide education for all of their inhabitants—education "directed to the full development of the human personality and to the strengthening of respect for human rights and fundamental freedoms. [That education] shall promote understanding, tolerance, and friendship among all nations [and] racial or religious groups" (Tarrow, 1987, pp. 237–238).

Guilt and Compassion.   Anticolonialism, migration, and international commitments were accompanied by an increased sense of shame among descendents of colonialists for the way native populations had been treated. Driven by guilt and compassion, governments and sensitive citizens now sought to compensate formerly exploited peoples for past wrongs, such wrongs as unsatisfactory educational provisions in the past.

Attention to the education of indigenous peoples in various countries has, in recent years, stressed the importance of encouraging them to embrace their own cultural and spiritual traditions. To help heal the social and psychological damage that has resulted from the clash between their cultures and the dominant western culture and lifestyle, they have been encouraged to deepen their familiarity with their spiritual heritage and to repair the links between the land, culture, and personal/social identity. . . . In Australia, the study of Aboriginal culture is now presumed to be important not only for the Aborigines, but also for white Australians. (Rossiter, 1999)

In keeping with this new spirit of multiculturalism, curriculum plans in present-day Australia have focused special attention on the needs of the nation's indigenous peoples.

Science courses have not always taken into account the experiences and knowledge of Torres Strait Islander students and Aboriginal students. This has limited their participation. Science curricula which include the experiences, contributions, and achievements of Aboriginal people and Torres Strait Islander people, supported by culturally sensitive teaching practices, have the potential to enhance equitable participation and outcomes. (A statement on science, 1994, p. 12)

Postmodernism

What is referred to as "the postmodernism movement" of the past three decades has been a reaction against "a positivist worldview." Thus, the nature of postmodernism is perhaps most easily explained in its relation to positivism.

Positivism/Modernism.   The words *modernism* and *positivism* are so closely linked in recent discussions that the two terms can be considered synonymous. Positivism has functioned over the past two centuries as the principal paradigm guiding the conduct of modern science. Here are three typical assumptions on which a positivist or modernist world perspective is founded.

First, "What is the nature of reality?" Positivists assert that there is an objective real world beyond the individual's body, and that world can be known and described. All conclusions about reality—about the "truth" of what exists—must be based on empirical observations and measurements, that is, on real-life experiences and not on speculation about things that cannot be publicly verified (seen, heard, touched, smelled, measured) or that cannot be reduced by logical operations to public observations. Logical positivists reject "statements of only emotional significance, as judged by an inability to be verified against a formal analysis involving the facts of experience" (Moore, 1995, p. 53).

Second, "What is the purpose of collecting empirical evidence and interpreting it?" The aim of a positivist approach is to discover principles or natural laws that can be organized in the form of theories or models of reality. Models of reality are always tentative, subject to revision on the basis of better methods of data collection, more complete sampling of contexts, convincing statistical analysis, and the application of more adequate logic for drawing interpretations.

Third, "What about validity?" Decisions about whether an account about events is "valid" or "true" (accurately reflects the real world) are guided by (a) criteria of objectivity (the methods of research are free from the researcher's personal biases), (b) representativeness (a study's conclusions are based on a convincing sample of observations), and (c) replicability (the conclusions of a study can be tested or verified by other researchers using similar methods of investigation).

Such positivism principles continue today to guide most scientific research. And—in the opinion of influential participants in the Australian school science controversy—those principles provide the proper foundation for teaching science in Australia's schools.

Postmodernism.   During the 1960s, unconventional perspectives in the arts, literature, philosophy, and the sciences were emerging in Europe under the label *postmodernism*, a movement that appealed to a body of writers (a) who sought to correct what they considered social wrongs from the past, and (b) who also objected to traditional positivist tenets of Western science that concerned matters of objectivity, the nature of acceptable evidence, the value of controlled experiments, and the discovery of general laws of nature purporting to explain cause-and-effect relationships in nature and human affairs. The social wrongs that advocates of postmodernism hoped to fix included the social status and life conditions of colonized and oppressed persons, especially of (a) persons on the lowest rungs of the socioeconomic ladder (the poor), (b) disadvantaged ethnic groups, (c) females, and (d) individuals whose preferences for sexual partners traditionally had been viewed as unconventional (homosexuals and bisexuals). Postmodernism (sometimes called *poststructuralism*) has linked such vaguely allied groups as avant-garde artists and architects, literati, critical social scientists, feminists, representatives of disadvantaged ethnic minorities, postcolonialists, anti-imperialists, neo-Marxists, and gay and lesbian liberationists. Thus, postmodernism is not a unified, coherent movement but, rather, is what Clark (1993, p. 22) characterized as an "ill-defined melange of attitudes, theories, and cultural criticism." A principal inspiration behind postmodernism since 1970 has been a collection of French philosophers, including Michel Foucault, Jacques Derrida, Jacques Lacan, Julia Kristeva, and Jean Baudrillard.

Because there are far more variations of postmodern belief than can be explained in a few paragraphs, in the following account I try to convey the general sense of postmodernism by reducing the varieties to one moderate version. Here, then, are typical assumptions on which a postmodernist worldview is founded.

First, "What is reality?" In postmodernists' opinion, the conviction that there is an objective "real world out there" beyond a person's own mind can be questioned. Although there apparently is such a real world, people can never know it objectively because each investigator's own needs, cultural traditions, training, and biases filter her or his experiences. Consequently, any account of "reality" is a combination "of the ways of life of the writer and those [things that are] written about" (Denzin, 1997, p. 3). Hence, there is no such thing as true "objectivity." Every "fact" about the world has been "constructed" in some person's mind. Reported "facts," therefore, are *interpretations* or *mental constructions* of what people have observed.

Second, "What are postmodern investigative techniques?" Postmodern research involves collecting, organizing, and reporting people's linguistic reactions to experiences in "the world out there." These written or spoken accounts are narratives, tales, or stories—certainly not objective descriptions of the world. They are subjective "glimpses and slices of the [world] in action" (Denzin, 1997, p. 8). Each glimpse or slice is unique, such as an observation of animals in a forest. No generalizations extracted from those particular animals' behavior can legitimately be applied to explaining other animals' actions. Each narrative stands on its own. The narrative serves as its own validation, requiring no sampling techniques, statistical analyses, replication, or the like.

Any given practice [or event] that is studied is significant because it is an instance of a cultural practice that happened in a particular time and place. This practice cannot be generalized to other practices; its importance lies in the fact that it instantiates a cultural practice, a cultural performance (story telling), and a set of shifting, conflicting cultural meanings. (Denzin, 1997, pp. 8–9)

In contrast to the positivists' goal of describing how the physical/social world "out there" operates, the purpose of postmodernists is frankly political—to expose and remedy injustices suffered by people in situations of unfair social disadvantage. In other words, the goal of postmodernists is to correct society's wrongs (Giroux, 1992).

[A] critical social science project seeks its external grounding not in science . . . but rather in a commitment to post-Marxism. . . . It seeks to understand how power and ideology operate through systems of discourse. . . . A good text exposes how race, class, and gender work their ways into the concrete lives of interacting individuals. (Denzin, 1997, p. 10)

From 1750 to 2005

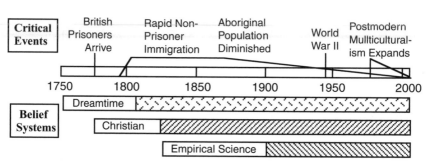

Figure 14.1 Critical events and belief systems in the Australian case.

As for the validity of postmodern narratives, Hammersley (1992, p. 58) proposed that the character of such studies "implies that there can be no criteria for judging its products," so that each speaker's voice deserves equal regard. "This position doubts all criteria and privileges none, although those who work within it [may] favor criteria such as [respect for] subjectivity and feeling" (Denzin, 1997, pp. 8–9). Each person's narrative is "truth" from that person's perspective and must be respected as such.

As will be shown in the following section, the contents of national curriculum guidebooks for teaching science (introduced in the 1990s and still in effect by 2005) suggest that adherents of multiculturalism and postmodernism influenced the nature of the books.

Summary

Several critical events and relevant belief systems affecting the Australian case over the period 1750–2005 are shown on the timeline in Figure 14.1.

THE CONTENDING CONSTITUENCIES

For convenience of discussion, the three main constituencies participating in the Australian science-education controversy can be labeled (a) postmodern multiculturalists, (b) positivists or scientific traditionalists, and (c) gradual-adaptation advocates. At the same time, it should be recognized that there are variants of each of these groups in which one group often shares some of the others' beliefs.

Postmodern Multiculturalists

Doctrinaire postmodern multiculturalists contend that each culture's explanation of phenomena is as valid as every other culture's, because no explanation is truly "objective," in the sense of being free from the bias necessarily imposed on explanations by a culture's worldview. All descriptions and explanations of events are "mental constructions" founded on assumptions embedded in cultural tradition. To be fair, all viewpoints in a multicultural society deserve an equal chance to be heard in school. To suggest that one culture's explanations are superior to another's is *cultural imperialism*—the unfair imposition of one culture's life perspective on another's. In the past, such imperialism has appeared in Australian schools in the form of limiting science instruction to Western perspectives, completely disregarding Aboriginal beliefs.

The influence of multicultural/postmodern convictions appears to be reflected in such passages as the following from the national curriculum guidebook *A Statement on Science for Australian Schools* (1994, pp. 9–10).

Aboriginal traditions and Torres Strait Islander traditions of knowledge production have some similarities with western scientific tradition and some differences from it. Among other things, they share a commitment to explaining and understanding the world, they both create models to explain natural phenomena, and they both use complex classification systems. There are important cultural differences, however. For instance, Aboriginal traditions . . . of knowledge production are less likely to be quantitatively based and less likely to separate the empirical from the aesthetic, spiritual, and social. . . . Content and contexts relevant to Aboriginal cultures . . . should be included in a science curriculum so that the curriculum is more relevant and accessible for Aboriginal students and Torres Strait Islander students, and increase all students' appreciation of these cultures.

Positivists-Scientific Traditionalists

In opposition to dedicated multiculturalists, most members of the nation's scientific community and like-minded educators have argued that

(a) there are, indeed, both a universal scientific mode of investigation and resulting knowledge that are not simply a particular culture's viewpoint, and

(b) it is clearly not true that conclusions reached by other methodologies (uncritical faith in ancient lore, a seer's inspired insights, revelations of invisible beings' pronouncements) are equally valid descriptions of the universe as those derived from traditional scientific principles and procedures.

John Maratos called the 1994 *Statement on Science*

fatally flawed, as it attempts to treat science education as a vehicle for dealing with myriad social and moral concerns that are unrelated to science. This ideological approach presents a serious obstacle to good science teaching and creates a confused and distorted image of science. . . . Goal 8 [in the *Statement's* list of science-teaching objectives] makes plain that we are witnessing the birth of a new tradition in science education. It demands that we produce "students with an understanding of and respect for our cultural heritage, including the particular cultural background of Aboriginal and ethnic groups, and for other cultures." All of this distorts science education. (Maratos, 1995, pp. 357–358)

In a similar spirit, the Australian Academy of Science issued a statement condemning the practice of including in science classes any religious versions of the beginnings of the universe, such versions as Judeo-Christian-Islamic biblical creationism and or Australian Aboriginal creation tales.

The creationist account of the origin of life has been and remains an important idea in human culture. However it is not a *scientific* idea. That is, it is not open to empirical test. It is an article of religious faith. [It] is not therefore appropriate to a course in the science of biology; and the claim that it is a viable scientific explanation of the diversity of life does not warrant support. The Academy sees no objection to the teaching of creationism in schools as part of a course in dogmatic or comparative religion, or in some other non-scientific context. There are no grounds, however, for requiring that creationism be taught as part of a science course. (Statement on creationism, 2005)

The opinion of Colin Groves, a professor of biological anthropology at the Australian National University, is typical of Australian scientists' views about including anti-Darwinian versions of human beginnings in science courses.

I have more and more felt it necessary to counter the anti-evolutionary nonsense put out by creationists—some of it simplistic and ill-informed, some of it actually malicious. It is necessary to combat this and other pseudosciences, not merely because it is wrong, but especially because, if taught in schools or widely promoted to the general public, it gives the impression that science is not a method of finding out, but a way to bolster up one's prejudices. (Groves, 2005)

Gradual-Adaptation Advocates

A third position in the science-and-culture debate is that of using Aboriginal explanations of events as vehicles for converting indigenous students' cultural beliefs into scientific modes of thought. This position is implied in the *Statement's* "principles for effective learning experiences in science."

Learning starts from and values the beliefs, concepts, and skills of students. Even the youngest students have ideas and theories they use to explain natural phenomena—ideas gleaned from their own imaginations, from myths and legends, from religious beliefs and the Dreaming. . . . Their ideas may be inconsistent with each other and with conventional science, but they are often strongly held and preferred to scientific explanations taught in classrooms. These personal ideas and theories are the student's starting point for science lessons. (A statement on science, 1994, pp. 5–6)

Thus, proponents of a gradual-adaptation approach to science instruction try to wean learners away from the Aborigines explanations of events by starting with those explanations and then illustrating how the events might be interpreted more adequately from the vantage point of Western science.

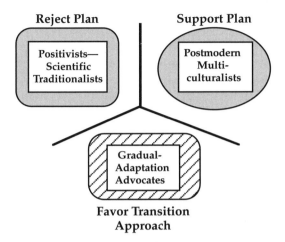

Figure 14.2 Constituencies' response to including Aboriginal lore in the study of science.

Summary

The assumed relationship among the three constituencies is cast in graphic form in Figure 14.2.

I suspect that the three constituencies might be similar in size, with the traditional science group possibly more cohesive than the other two. That is, the scientists and science teachers—steeped in Western science's methods and content—were perhaps more of one mind in the debate than were members of the other two groups. It appears that the positivists enjoyed the support of the Australian Academy of Science while the multiculturalists' position was strongly endorsed by teacher unions. Maratos observed that, at least in the early stages of the *Statement's* implementation, Australian science teachers did not "display a unity of opinion."

Individual science teachers affiliated with such bodies as the AIP [Australian Physics Institute] have certainly shown dissatisfaction. But most have allowed powerful teacher unions to speak for them. (Maratos, 1995, p. 367)

Proponents of both the multicultural and the gradual-adaptation approaches apparently influenced the preparation of the curriculum *Statement*, because proposals in that document would support either the multicultural or adaptation viewpoints.

Science courses have not always taken into account the experiences and achievements of Torres Strait Islander students and Aboriginal students. This has limited [such students'] participation. Science curricula which include the experiences, contributions, and achievements of Aboriginal people and Torres Strait Islander people, supported by culturally sensitive teaching practices, have the potential to enhance equitable participation and outcomes. (A statement on science, 1994, p. 12)

The science-teaching *Statement* was identified as "a joint project of the States, Territories, and the Commonwealth of Australia initiated by the Australian Education Council." Consequently, the *Statement's* view of proper science education appeared to enjoy the backing of government officials, including politicians sensitive to demands for reparations and fair treatment from the more than 400,000 Australians who identified themselves as Aborigines and Torres Strait Islanders (with a large proportion of that group being of mixed Aboriginal/European ancestry). To defend the inclusion of Aboriginal beliefs in *A Statement on Science*, multiculturalists could turn to such sources of societal ideals as (a) the *United Nations Declaration of Human Rights* (1945) to which Australia was a signatory and (b) the Australian task-force-on-human-rights' publication *Achieving Educational Equality for Australia's Aboriginal and Torres Strait Islander Peoples* (2000), which urged educators "to promote, maintain, and support the teaching of Aboriginal and Torres Strait Islander studies, cultures, and languages to all Indigenous and non-Indigenous students."

Objections to the *Statement* by advocates of traditional science were supported by (a) the prestige (academic degrees, publications, university positions) of the scientists who voiced objections and (b) the public status of such bodies as the Australian Academy of Science and the Australian Institute of Physics (Maratos, 1995). Proponents of traditional science could buttress their position with a multitude of publications chronicling Western science's success in explaining so much about the universe and in fostering technological progress without depending on religious lore.

RESOLVING THE CONTROVERSY

As it turned out, the controversy could be resolved in a fashion that fulfilled each constituency's desires. Ultimately, which of the three sorts of science instruction students received (positivist, multicultural, adaptive) would depend on each classroom teacher's preference. Why this was so can be explained by our considering the nature of the *Statement on Science* and the conditions governing its application.

The *Statement* was not intended to serve as a syllabus describing the content of specific science lessons. Instead, it was to "provide a foundation for courses which will meet students' needs and reflect advances in our knowledge" by means of encouraging instructional "innovation and experimentation so that students have a positive learning experience" (A statement on science, 1994, p. iii). Then, to provide more specific guidance for teachers, the *Statement's* companion book—*Science: A Curriculum Profile for Australian Schools* (1994)— offered brief examples of over 630 activities considered suitable at different grade levels. However, only two of the activities bore any relation to cultural content. As the following quotations demonstrate, both of those examples were limited to the field of astronomy. And neither of them specifically mentioned Aboriginal or Torres Strait Islanders' beliefs.

At level 4, a student locates and describes features of our universe. For example, [students] report on ways different cultures have explained and used astronomical phenomena. (p. 58)

At level 8, a student analyzes ways in which theories of astronomy have contributed to different cultures and societies. For example, [students] investigate ways various cultures have described and interpreted objects in the sky and their movements. (p. 110)

In effect, the *Statement* urged teachers to include Aboriginal and Torres Strait Islanders' views in science lessons, but when and how this might be done was not described. Furthermore, schools were not required to adopt the *Statement's* plan. Whether science would be taught according to the plan depended on the judgment of provincial departments of education, school districts, and—ultimately—individual classroom teachers.

Therefore, teachers who were devoted multiculturalists could accord indigenous explanations of events equal attention to that given to Western science explanations. But to implement that approach, teachers would need to search libraries and the Internet for Aboriginal beliefs about each science topic the class was studying at the time. Or, if the class enrolled students from Aboriginal cultural backgrounds, those students might serve as a source of indigenous knowledge.

Advocates of a gradual-adaptation approach to the study of science might also use libraries, the Internet, and Aboriginal student informants as the source of native beliefs about natural phenomena.

Finally, in contrast to multiculturalists and gradual-adaptation advocates, teachers dedicated to a positivist view of science education would have an easier time preparing lessons, because they would not feel obligated to include any religious lore in their instruction.

CHAPTER 15

Saudi Arabia

The controversy in the Saudi Arabian case was not over the issue of whether religion would be taught in government-sponsored schools, because Islamic doctrine was, without question, accepted as a required part of the curriculum. Instead, the disagreement was over the matter of whether teaching any religion other than Islam would be permitted at all in the country. The term *schools* has been expanded for the purpose of this chapter to include Sunday schools and religious-study classes. Thus, the conflict was between the Saudi Arabian government and resident foreigners—Christians—who were arrested on the charge of illegally conducting clandestine Bible-study sessions.

HISTORICAL ROOTS

Four kinds of information useful for understanding the Saudi Arabian case concern (a) important characteristics of the nation, (b) religious tolerance, (c) educational provisions, and (d) the Jeddah incident.

Important Characteristics of the Nation

Geographically, Saudi Arabia is about one-fifth the size of the United States and consists chiefly of uninhabited, sandy desert and a harsh climate of temperature extremes. The country's natural resources of greatest value are its vast petroleum deposits (one-quarter of the world's proven oil reserves), natural gas, iron ore, gold, and copper.

Prior to the twentieth century, the Arabian Peninsula was not a unified political entity but, rather, consisted of individual princedoms. In 1902, the enterprising Arab leader of the Saud family—ABD AL-AZIZ bin Abd al-Rahman Al Saud—launched a 30-year campaign to unify four-fifths of the peninsula and form the Kingdom of Saudi Arabia, a task completed in 1932.

The government was an absolute monarchy until 1992, when the royal family introduced the country's first constitution that defined the kingdom as

a sovereign Arab Islamic state with Islam as its religion; God's Book [the Quran] and the Sunnah [sayings and acts] of His Prophet [Muhammad] . . . are its constitution and Arabic is its language. . . . The state protects Islam; it implements its Shari'ah [Islamic law]; it orders people to do right and shun evil; it fulfills the duty regarding God's call. (Saudi Arabia—Constitution, 1993)

By 2005, the country's population had grown to nearly 26 million, with 22% of the total consisting of noncitizens, most of them foreigners employed in the petroleum and service sectors (Saudi Arabia, 2004). Only Muslims have been permitted to be citizens.

Saudi Arabia is revered as the most important site in the history of the Islamic faith, because it was there that Muhammad (570–632 CE) founded the Muslim religion. The two Saudi Arabian cities most intimately related to Muhammad's ministry—Mecca and Medina—continue to be visited each year by millions of Muslim pilgrims from around the world.

Religious Tolerance

More than 95% of Saudi citizens have followed the Sunni version of Islam rather than the Shi'a version (Sparks, 2005b). The variety of Sunni belief that serves as the official state religion is one introduced in the eighteenth century by an Islamic scholar, Sheikh Muhammad Ibn Abd Al-Wahhab (1703–1792). Today's Wahabist Islam (also known as Salafi Sunni) is a fundamentalist faith that limits religious doctrine to the original version of Muhammad's day and rejects interpretations and additions since that time. Wahabism is strictly enforced by the government's religious police, the Mutawwa'in (the Committee to Promote Virtue and Prevent Vice), and is aggressively exported to other countries.

Proselytizing by non-Muslims, including the distribution of non-Muslim religious materials such as Bibles, is illegal. Proselytizing by non-Sunni Muslims also is not permitted, and the promotion of non-Salafi Sunni Islam is restricted. Muslims or non-Muslims wearing religious symbols of any kind in public risk confrontation with the Mutawwa'in. The Ministry of Islamic Affairs sponsors approximately 50 so-called "Call and Guidance" centers employing approximately 500 persons to convert foreigners to Islam. Some non-Muslim foreigners convert to Islam during their stay in the country. The press often carries articles about such conversions, including testimonials. (Saudi Arabia—International, 2004)

Although the government has prohibited the public practice of non-Muslim religions, it has given informal recognition to the right of non-Muslims to worship in private. However, the right to conduct religious services at home has not been defined in law nor consistently respected in practice (Moore, 2001).

Foreigners living in the country have been required to carry legal-resident identity cards—*Iqamas*—that list a person's religious affiliation as either Muslim or non-Muslim. Apparently some Mutawwa'in officers have urged employers not to renew Iqamas as an effort to reduce the number of the nation's non-Muslim residents (Saudi Arabia—International, 2004).

Saudi leaders have used a variety of methods for protecting citizens from exposure to non-Islamic faiths and criticisms of Islam. For example, a team of researchers at Harvard University found that the Saudi government's Internet Services Unit blocked citizens' access to a large number of Internet Web sites that focused on religion, politics, women, health, or pop culture. At least 250 of 2,038 barred Web addresses were of a religious nature, such as *Answering-Islam.org*, *ReligiousTolerance.org*, *Family Bible Hour*, and *Arabic Bible Outreach* (Hertz, 2002).

Customs officials have routinely opened mail and shipments to search for contraband, including Sunni printed material deemed incompatible with the Salafi tradition of Islam, Shi'a religious materials, and non-Muslim materials, such as Bibles and religious videotapes. Banned materials are subject to confiscation, although rules appear to be applied arbitrarily (Saudi Arabia—International, 2004).

Both atheism and apostasy (conversion to another religion) are punishable by death in Saudi Arabia. The possession of non-Islamic religious objects, including Bibles, rosary beads, and crosses is strictly prohibited.

The government forbids public non-Muslim religious activity. Non-Muslim worshippers risk arrest, imprisonment, lashing, deportation, and sometimes torture for engaging in religious displays that attract official attention. The government has stated publicly, including before the U.N. Commission on Human Rights in Geneva, that its policy is to allow non-Muslim foreigners to worship privately. However, no explicit guidelines have been issued—such as acceptable locations or the number of persons permitted to attend—for determining what constitutes private worship, so the distinctions between public and private worship have remained vague. This lack of clarity and instances of inconsistent enforcement have led many non-Muslims to fear harassment and to worship in a way that minimizes discovery. The government has usually deported people for visible non-Muslim worship, sometimes after extended periods of arrest during investigation. In some cases, detainees have been sentenced to suffer a lashing before being sent from the country (Saudi Arabia—International, 2004).

In recent times, strong pressure from international religious-rights organizations and from Western democracies have motivated the Saudi government to adopt a more tolerant view of non-Wahabist faiths, at least more tolerant in word if not always in practice. As an instance of international pressure, the United States Secretary of State in 2004 cited Saudi Arabia as a "Country of Particular Concern" under the International Religious Freedom Act for the

Saudi "severe violations of religious freedom" (Saudi Arabia—International, 2004).

Among the conciliatory measures adopted by the Saudi government has been its series of "National Dialogue" conferences that have included members of different Muslim traditions. The conferees have published reports condemning violence and offering recommendations for greater tolerance and moderation in education. In addition, journalists have been allowed to publish criticisms of abuses by the religious police. However, denunciations of non-Muslim religions have continued from government-approved pulpits. Although Saudi officials have publicly stated that non-Muslims may worship in private, leaders of home-study groups have often been arrested and deported (Saudi Arabia—International, 2004).

As an example of intolerance cited by international religious-rights organizations, Saudi authorities in 2004 charged Brian O'Connor, a Christian from India, with drug use, selling alcohol, and possession of pornography. Officials also accused him of distributing Bibles and preaching Christianity. When a court sentenced him to 10 months in jail and 300 lashes for selling liquor, there was no mention of the preaching charges. Foreign critics said the court's omission of the proselytizing claim was an attempt on the part of the government to cover up its religious intolerance. According to one human-rights group—Middle East Concern—O'Connor's videos were not pornographic but were biblical excerpts, documentaries, and movies about the Bible (Sellers, 2005).

In summary, by the early years of the twenty-first century, the Saudi Arabian government appeared to maintain its traditional strict ban on non-Wahabist religions while, at the same time, offering a semiofficial facade of religious tolerance in order not to (a) alienate the thousands of foreign workers whose services the nation needed or (b) incur excessive criticism from other nations whose economic and political support were important to the country's welfare.

Educational Provisions

Until the middle of the twentieth century, education in Saudi Arabia was limited to the study of Islam—particularly to memorization of the Quran. Following World War II, the present-day education system was established, featuring Western-style schools (separate ones for boys and girls) in which secular subjects were studied in addition to a continuing emphasis on the interpretation (*tafsir*) of the Quran and Sunnah and the application of Islamic tradition in daily life. Today the Ministry of Education, which was established in 1952, supervises general education for boys, whereas girls' schooling is under the jurisdiction of the General Presidency for Girls' Education. Both sexes follow the same curriculum and take the same annual examinations.

Although public education at all schooling levels is free and liberally supported by the government, the country has no compulsory-education provision. Thus, decisions about whether children will go to school are left to parents. As a result, the literacy rate is lower than would be true if all children were required to attend school. In the early twenty-first century, literacy within the population over age 15 was reported as 62.8% (71.5% for males and an estimated 50.2% for females) (Sedgwick, 2001).

Sunni Islamic religious education is mandatory in public schools at all levels. Regardless of which Islamic tradition their families follow, all public-school children receive religious instruction that conforms to the Salafi tradition of Islam. Non-Muslim students in private schools are not required to study Islam; however, no private religious schools are permitted for non-Muslims or for Muslims adhering to non-Salafi varieties of Islam. Adherents of Shi'a Islam are banned from teaching religion in schools (Saudi Arabia—International, 2004).

Private schools are obligated to use the same textbooks and curricula as the public schools, with the government supplying the textbooks to private schools free of charge. According to Stalinsky (2002), a key feature of the religious textbooks is their interpreting Muhammad's directives to mean that the most important duty of Muslims is to wage war (*jihad*) against other religions in order to establish Allah's dominion throughout the world.

A stream of criticisms from other nations about attacks on non-Wahabist faiths in Saudi Arabian textbooks motivated the government in recent years to remove some of the books' disparaging references to other religious traditions. An example of denigrating passages is this excerpt from a ninth-grade text: "The Jews and the Christians are the enemies of the believers. They will not be favorably disposed toward Muslims and it is necessary to be cautious [in dealing with them]" (Stalinsky, 2002).

The American Jewish Committee and Center for Monitoring the Impact of Peace reported that Saudi Arabian schoolbooks portrayed Western societies as decadent and on their

way to extinction, the symptoms of which are the absence of spirituality, adultery, and sodomy that increase the number of AIDS cases in the West, and the large number of suicides in Western society, [with Israel] a wicked nation, characterized by bribery, slyness, deception, betrayal, aggressiveness and haughtiness. Peace between Muslims and non-Muslims is not advocated. Instead, the Saudi Arabian textbooks, even grammar books, are full of phrases exalting war, Jihad, and martyrdom. (American Jewish Community, 2003)

In summary, noncompulsory schooling of Saudi Arabia's children and youths is provided free of charge to all citizens. The curriculum consists of secular subjects (reading, writing, mathematics, science, social studies) plus a Wahabist version of Islam. Although religious textbooks have traditionally denigrated religious persuasions other than Wahabism, in recent times the government has eliminated some text passages that directly criticize other faiths, with this change prompted by criticism from international religious-rights groups and Western governments.

The Jeddah Incident

The Saudi Arabian case mentioned in Chapter 1 has been cited by foreign critics as typifying the Saudi government's treatment of foreign residents who engaged in Bible-study sessions in their homes—that is, in *house churches*. Christian house church worshippers throughout Saudi Arabia have been estimated to exceed 15,000 (Moore, 2001). The affair referred to as the *Jeddah incident* started in June 2001, with the government's religious police investigating a citizen's complaint about the presence of a Saudi national at a farewell party held at a public hall in the city of Jeddah. The party was attended by expatriate Christians honoring an Indian colleague, Prabhu Isaac, who had worked in a Saudi Arabian hospital for 17 years and was generally recognized as a leader among the city's network of about 250 clandestine house churches whose members were mostly foreign Protestants and Catholics. One month after the party, Saudi religious police arrested Isaac. Six days later they arrested Iskander Menghis, a Christian from Eritrea whose name the police had found on Isaac's computer.

The two men reportedly succumbed to harsh interrogation and revealed the names of church leaders in Jeddah, leading to more arrests in August and September. The arrests appear to be part of a campaign to eliminate house churches in Jeddah, according to a spokesperson for the United Churches of Saudi Arabia, an underground [house-church] network. . . . According to Isaac's wife, the Indian leader was tortured into revealing at least six names of underground leaders in Jeddah. (Two Christian leaders, 2001)

As a result, a total of 14 Christians were jailed on charges of playing key roles in Jeddah's house church network.

After the Jeddah episode, other arrests of foreign nationals occasionally occurred, with the disposition of the cases tending to be less punitive than in the more distant past. Detained church leaders were usually released from jail after a few weeks or months and then deported. In 2002, 10 Christians (six women, four men) were arrested when authorities raided a home in which foreign workers were privately holding a worship service. An account of the event by International Christian Concern said, "It is unusual for the Saudi authorities to detain women, indicating that the government is intensifying its hard-line-intolerance against Christians. Prisoners are commonly denied legal representation and visits from their embassy" (Saudi Arabia still, 2002).

In 2003, two Egyptian Christians were arrested by the Mutawwa'in for religious activities; both were freed a month later, and neither was deported. Two Catholics arrested in Riyadh in 2003 by regular police were set free the same day without charge. In 2004, an expatriate Christian was deported after giving an Arabic version of the Christian Bible to a Saudi citizen (Saudi Arabia—International, 2004).

So it was that tolerance for teaching about non-Wahabist religious beliefs in Saudi Arabia shuttled between (a) allowing house churches to operate and

From 1750 to 2000

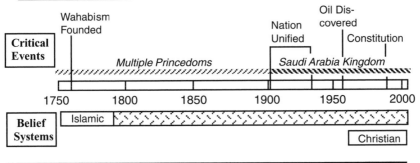

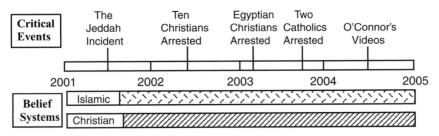

Figure 15.1 Critical events and belief systems in the Saudi case.

(b) periodically arresting expatriate leaders, especially when complaints were lodged about Christians' attempts to proselytize among Saudi citizens.

Summary

Significant events and belief systems in the Saudi Arabian case are charted on a pair of timelines in Figure 15.1. The upper-tier timeline traces events from the eighteenth-century founding of Wahabism until 2000. The lower-tier timeline identifies a series of episodes in the conflict over the practice of non-Sunni religions in the country.

THE CONTENDING CONSTITUENCIES

The direct conflict in the Jeddah incident was between two constituencies within Saudi Arabia—the Saudi Arabian government and members of house churches. But the power struggle also involved important forces outside the country—(a) other Islamic populations whose leaders agreed with the Saudi government's position and (b) other non-Wahabist religious groups, international religious-rights organizations, and foreign governments that believed individuals should be free to teach and study whatever belief systems they wished.

The Saudi Arabian Government

In the exercise of power, Saudi Arabian officials held by far the dominant position in the Jeddah confrontation with house church leaders. Not only did the officials represent a sovereign nation entitled to set the rules for behavior within its borders, but they also bore the authority to act as they chose. Their decisions about what sorts of religious study would be permitted in the country were supported by the nation's constitution—the holy Quran—that portrayed Islam as the only acceptable religion. And the fact that 78% of the country's residents were Saudi Arabian citizens, who necessarily were Wahabist Muslims, contributed further to the government's power in the Jeddah incident. Finally, the government's ability to enforce the ban on non-Islamic teaching was furthered by the continuing vigilance and tactics of a permanent official organization—the Mutawwa'in religious police.

Other Islamic Populations

The Saudi government's actions in the Jeddah affair could be expected to enjoy the approval of Muslim populations in other parts of the world, that is, the endorsement of overseas Muslims who also subscribed to the Quran's dictum that Islam is the only true religion and that it should be protected from the intrusion of false faiths. Saudi officials, aware of such support, could be expected to act with more confidence in restricting religious behavior than if they thought theirs was the only nation promoting the Muslim cause.

House Church Members

Although in terms of organization the Saudi government was far superior to the expatriates who conducted Bible-study classes, the house churches did not function as entirely separate units. Instead, their operation was coordinated through an underground network known as the United Churches of Saudi Arabia, a coalition that enhanced the ability of non-Islamic worshippers to deal with the government. A further source of house church power was the dependence of Saudi society on foreign workers. Without the services of foreigners—and particularly without ones who commanded high-level technical skills—the conduct of life on the Arabian Peninsula would be seriously crippled. Thus, the government was obliged to be cautious in applying punitive sanctions to non-Sunni expatriates.

International Religious-Rights Groups

The label *international religious-rights groups* is a title covering diverse kinds of foreign critics of Saudi Arabia's policy governing the study of religions other than the Wahabist version of Islam. Those kinds included specific human-rights or religious-rights organizations (such as Middle East Concern, International Christian Concern), international political alliances (such as the United Nations), non-Islamic religious denominations (such as Protestants, Catholics, Hindus, Jews), and individual governments (such as Canada, Germany, Great Britain, Sweden, United States).

The influence of societies outside of Saudi Arabia on that government's treatment of non-Islamic residents has been, to a great extent, the result of *globalization*, a term referring to the process of each part of the world coming into increasingly intimate contact with other parts. Throughout the twentieth century, globalization advanced at an accelerating pace because of (a) improvements in communication (radio, television, the Internet) and transportation (airplane, auto, ship, rail), (b) population movements that often resulted from wars and their aftermath, (c) political coalitions (United Nations, European Union), (d) the development of transnational corporations, and (e) increased trade among nations. Consequently, each nation's fate became increasingly dependent on the behavior of other nations. This meant that the welfare of the Saudi Arabian government became crucially affected by (a) the rest of the world's sources and quantities of petroleum, (b) non-Saudi sources of higher education, technical expertise, and industrial supplies, and (c) other nations' military strength and friendship (as during the Gulf War of 1990–1991). Consequently, political pressure exerted by other nations—particularly the Western democracies—affected how the Saudi government's religious policies were implemented. The much-publicized criticism of those policies in recent years has undoubtedly been a factor in reducing the severity of government sanctions in such cases as the Jeddah incident (Saudi Arabia—International, 2004).

We might now speculate about the motivations of the organizations that appear under our label *international religious-rights groups*. Some have censured Saudi religious intolerance out of a true spirit of giving everyone an equal opportunity to practice any belief system of one's choice. But other groups have likely operated mainly out of self-interest rather than pure philanthropy. Such could be the case with doctrinaire Christians who resented the Saudi restrictions on both (a) expatriates openly practicing their religion in Saudi Arabia and (b) Christians doing missionary work among Saudi citizens, that is, conducting classes designed to woo Muslims away from Islam. Devout Christians unlikely thought that all belief systems were equally worthy, so that everyone should choose his or her own preferred worldview. Instead, like fervent Muslims, fervent Christians would regard their own worldview as the true faith that everyone should adopt. They would be expected to carry out Jesus's directive in the Bible's New Testament to "Go ye into all the world and preach the gospel to every creature" (St. Mark, 1611, p. 56). Thus, they would seek to attract non-Christians into the fold. As a result, when faithful Christians endorsed a freedom-of-religion policy, they apparently acted out of prudence rather than a conviction that such freedom was desirable. In effect, they allowed others to follow faiths of their choice so that those others would afford them the same privilege.

The expressed attitudes of Western governments toward Saudi religious policies have consisted of censure mitigated by political and economic considerations. For example, in 2002 representatives of International Christian Concern reported that the United States government's human-rights policy as applied to Saudi Arabia was

muted because of other "more pressing" U.S. interests. Recently at a Washington, D.C. conference on Islamic Sharia Law, an unidentified White House representative said that not much action could be expected against Saudi Arabia because the U.S. needs Saudi support for "plans that President Bush has to attack Iraq early next year." (Saudi Arabia still, 2002)

Summary

The principal constituencies participating in the Saudi Arabian case are displayed graphically in Figure 15.2.

RESOLVING THE CONTROVERSY

The Jeddah incident was resolved near the end of December 2001, when 9 of the 14 arrested Christians were freed on Christmas Eve and the remaining 5 on Christmas Day. Most were immediately deported (Moore, 2001). Although the release of the 14 detainees settled the immediate problem of the Jeddah affair, it likely did nothing to solve the basic controversy over Saudi Arabia's ban on people openly teaching about religions other than Wahabism. Thus, the conflict over Saudi Arabia's religious policies seemed bound to continue into the future, significantly affected by groups beyond the nation's borders: (a) other Islamic states that supported Saudi Arabia's practices and (b) international religious-freedom organizations, non-Islamic religious denominations,

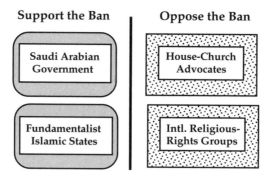

Figure 15.2 Attitudes toward the ban on teaching non-Wahabist religions.

and nations with secular governments that objected to restrictions on religious classes.

In 2002, Daniel Hoofman, director of the human-rights organization Middle East Concern, said that because the United States was an ally of Saudi Arabia in the effort to establish political stability in the region, Saudi Arabia was "sensitive to U.S. pressure and has improved its treatment of Christians in the past few years" (Sellers, 2002).

This improvement is due mainly to the fact that the Saudi authorities "burned their fingers" each time they acted against Christians—they were put under a lot of pressure. Now they often feel it is not worth the hassle. (Sellers, 2002)

PART III

In Retrospect

This final part, consisting of a single chapter, offers a review of the previous chapters in the form of a comparative analysis of the 12 country cases, drawing chiefly on the interpretation framework from Chapter 3—the framework focusing on *belief constituencies, traditions, critical events,* and *the exercise of power.*

CHAPTER 16

Answers and Trends

This closing chapter offers two approaches to summarizing key features of Chapters 4 through 15. The first approach proposes answers to a pair of questions the book was designed to analyze. The second approach compares the 12 country cases in terms of six trends.

ANSWERS

As noted in the book's preface, two questions to be addressed in subsequent chapters were:

- In what ways are the controversies in one nation similar to, and different from, the controversies in other nations?
- How might we explain why there are such similarities and differences?

One perspective from which these questions can be answered is that of the interpretation scheme introduced in Chapter 3. From such a vantage point, the religion/school cases can be seen as similar to each other to the extent that they share the same belief constituencies, traditions, critical events, and power relationships in their developmental histories. Thus, I propose that understanding the way those four variables are patterned can help account for why religion/school controversies in recent years have assumed their particular forms. The expression *help account* is used here to mean that I am not proposing that Chapter 3's simple form of interpretation completely explains the nature of religion/school controversies. Rather, I am suggesting that the scheme outlined in Chapter 3 is one useful device for casting light on the nature of religion/school conflicts.

When viewed from the perspective of the four variables (belief constituencies, traditions, critical events, and power), the religion/school relationships in nations can be seen as forming patterns that contribute to understanding the likenesses and differences among those societies. The following examples illustrate a mode of reasoning that can reveal such patterns. The task of investigating each pattern begins with adopting positions from which to view religion/school relationships. The positions assumed in the four examples are those of (a) similar traditions and varied events, (b) religious versus nonreligious traditions, (c) degrees of power, and (d) authority.

Similar Tradition, Varied Critical Events

One pattern of belief system development is that of different societies starting from a common tradition and then diverging over time as the result of differences among the societies' critical events. An example of such a pattern is that observed in France, England, Spain, and Italy. All four regions, as components of the early Roman empire, were obliged to accept Roman Catholicism as their official religion. But over the centuries each region experienced its own particular events that significantly influenced its inhabitants' dominant belief systems. In France, the revolution of the late eighteenth century was one such event. In England, Henry VIII's break with the Roman Catholic Church and his founding the Anglican Church was another. In Spain, the Moors' invasion in the Middle Ages and the Socialists' election success in 2004 were two more instances. In Italy, the establishment of the papal states and the resulting tradition of a religious order—Roman Catholicism—in control of the states' political fate was yet another.

Thus, I suggest that the four nations' recent religion/school controversies mentioned in Chapter 1 were the product of how a common original tradition—Roman Catholicism—combined with each society's own critical events over the centuries. In three of the nations—France, Spain, and Italy— the present-day religion/school confrontations were similar in that they focused on the issue of religious symbols in state schools. Two important factors accounting for such similarity were apparently (a) the three nations' ages-old commitment to Catholicism and (b) the Catholic tradition being threatened by a competing worldview imported by growing numbers of Muslim immigrants. However, the resolution of the conflict differed among the three societies because of their past differences in critical events—such events as (a) the French Revolution's commitment to a secular state, (b) the success of the Socialist Party in Spain's 2004 election, and (c) Italy's history of papal states and of the Catholic Church's headquarters being located in Rome. Consequently, the French settled the religious-symbols controversy by outlawing all ostentatious symbols, the Spanish banned both religious classes and religious symbols, and the Italians allowed the continued display of such Christian symbols as the crucifix.

In England, the matter of religious symbols was not a significant public issue, perhaps because the dominance of Catholicism in England had faded into the distant past, and subsequent events—such as immigrants bringing many different belief traditions—had now made religious tolerance a matter of greater concern.

Religious Versus Nonreligious Traditions

Another pattern of religion/school controversies is found when societies are viewed in terms of religious-versus-nonreligious constituencies. Consider, for example, how such a perspective can illuminate a comparison among the ' French, Chinese, United States, and Australian examples. In each of those cases, one of the principal adversaries was dedicated to a religious faith and the other to a nonreligious belief system: (a) Islam versus the secular state (*laïcité*) in France, (b) Christianity versus the atheistic state in China, (c) Christian Fundamentalism versus empirical science in the United States, and (d) Dreamtime versus empirical science in Australia.

In all four cases, the religious tradition was the older belief system, with the secular viewpoint a disruptive newcomer. The pair of cases that were most alike were those of the United States and Australia, where empirical science confronted an age-old religious persuasion in a debate over which beliefs deserved a place in the schools' science curricula. The two cases differed mainly in the kind of religion involved in the controversy—Evangelical Christianity in the United States and Dreamtime in Australia.

The French and Chinese cases were similar in that both concerned a government's commitment to secularity being challenged by a recently imported religious tradition—the Islamic faith in France and Evangelical Christianity in China.

Degrees of Power

A third pattern of religion/school relationships appears when societies are compared from a degrees-of-power perspective. The expression *degrees of power* refers to how strongly the presence of one belief constituency influences the behavior of another constituency. Degrees of power can range from (a) one constituency completely dominating its rival to (b) the power of one constituency equaling that of its rival, thereby producing a stalemate in their relationship. I would speculate that such a range of power was represented in the cases of Saudi Arabia, Japan, Pakistan, France, and Thailand.

The most dominant exercise of power was demonstrated in Saudi Arabia where the Islamic government exerted great control over the behavior of expatriate Christians as a result of the government's policies and the tactics of the religious police.

I estimate that slightly less power dominance obtained in the Japanese case. The nation's constitution, imposed by U.S. military forces after World War II, obligated the government and populace to behave more in accordance with a secular, democratic belief system than with the State-Shinto spirit of Meiji times. However, the recent confrontation over the national anthem suggested that the dominance of the secular-democratic position might well be declining.

The Pakistan case appears to represent another step down on the degrees-of-power scale. In the struggle to control the nation's thousands of madrassas, the government—at the behest of U.S. military forces—vied with the madrassas' leaders. Although the government sought to effect changes in madrassas' practices, very little change occurred. With only a few exceptions, the madrassas managed to retain their traditional dominant power.

The French case illustrated another degree of power relationships. Prior to the marked increase of Muslims in France over recent decades, the nation's tradition of Catholicism within a secular state continued to exist in religious symbols, classes in Catholicism, and religious holidays in state schools. However, this power dominance was increasingly challenged by the nation's Muslims as they gained in numbers and in political activism. The headscarf incident symbolized a challenge to the state's power, and particularly to the remaining vestiges of Catholicism in state schools. The fact that the incident marked a reduction in the traditional power of the state's Catholic tradition was shown by the government's being forced to eliminate all evident religious symbols from state schools.

The Thailand case appeared to reflect an equal-power standoff. The Buddhist government sought to gain control of pondoks in the Islamic southern provinces in order to reduce separatism movements in the region. In response, separatist military units continued to frustrate the government's control efforts by attacking police posts, burning state schools, and refusing to register pondoks with the government.

Authority

As defined in Chapter 3, *authority* refers to the official power held by an individual or a group. In each chapter, 4 through 15, matters of authority played an important role. Ways that issues of authority affect religion/school controversies can be illustrated with four aspects of authority: (a) mode of introducing authority, (b) an authority's domain, (c) implementation devices, and (d) extent of acceptance.

Mode of Introducing Authority

There are various ways by which authority—in the sense of the official right to govern people's behavior—can be introduced into, or imposed on, a society:

- Military conquest (Moors' invasion of Spain in the Middle Ages, eighteenth-century revolution in France, post–World War II U.S. occupation of Japan)
- Public choice (2004 national elections in Spain and India)

- Rational persuasion, proselytizing, evangelizing (State Shinto in Japan, Buddhism in Thailand, Christianity in Europe, Islam in Pakistan)
- A monarch's decree (Christianity under Roman Emperor Constantine, Anglicanism under Henry VIII)
- Immigration (a competing authority—the Quran—brought by Muslim immigrants to Catholic France, Italy, and Spain)

Authority's Domain

The term *domain* refers to the matters over which the authority wields power. For example, does a secular government have the authority to determine what is studied in private religious schools—as in Thailand's pondoks, U.S. parochial schools, or Pakistan's madrassas? Does the Vatican in Rome have the authority to decide what religious symbols can be displayed in French, Spanish, or Italian classrooms?

Implementation Devices

Individuals and groups in positions of authority employ various techniques for trying to ensure that their directives are obeyed. Such techniques include depending on

- The governed people's respect for the society's political system (accepting election results in Spain, honoring the emperor in Japan, deferring to a fascist government in pre–World War II Italy)
- Formal laws that result in punitive sanctions if they are broken (Christians arrested in China and Saudi Arabia)
- Watchdog agencies that monitor how well religion/school regulations are obeyed (religious police in China, Japan, and Saudi Arabia)
- Publicity, as in newspaper articles and television programs that condemn deviations from the authority's policies (such policies as the separation of church and state in the U.S. evolution controversy and in the French confrontation over Muslim headscarves)

Extent of Acceptance

A further factor crucial to an authority's effectiveness is the degree to which the populace accepts the authority as legitimate and worthy of obedience. Each of our 12 religion/school cases involved a conflict between at least two proclaimed authorities. In Thailand the two were the Buddhist-dominated government and international Islam. In Italy the two were the Catholic-influenced government and Islam. In the United States the confrontation was between supporters of church/state separation and Evangelical Christian denominations. In India the authority of the secular government confronted the authority of Hindu tradition.

Conflicts over authority occur whenever

- A new authority challenges a traditional one (the Pakistan government challenged the madrassas' leadership, the secular Congress Party in India challenged the Hindu People's Party)
- Competing authorities disagree over what sorts of matters legitimately belong in their domains (Should Australia's national curriculum planners rather than scientists decide if Dreamtime belongs in science courses? Should the Thai government rather than Islamic tok gurus decide what is taught in pondoks? Should England's government curriculum planners rather than religious denominations determine which belief systems are included in religious-education classes?)
- Competing authorities disagree over methods of implementing policies (Christian authorities outside of Saudi Arabia condemned the Saudi government's banning public Christian worship and physically punishing Christians who failed to obey the ban. Madrassa leaders in Pakistan criticized U.S. military forces for ostensibly intimidating the Pakistan government into trying to control the madrassas. The Congress Party in India censured the People's Party for "Hinduizing" school textbooks.)

Two rather obvious propositions that can be drawn about the acceptance of authority are as follows:

- The larger the proportion of the population and its leadership that respect and defer to a particular authority, the greater the likelihood that the religion/school policies of that authority will prevail.
- The more divided the population and its leadership are over which authority to obey, the greater the conflict that can be expected over religion/school policies and practices.

Summary

The above discussion has illustrated ways that the analysis of four perspectives toward religion/school controversies may enrich one's understanding of the controversies' complexities. But it should be recognized that those four represent only a few of the viewpoints from which controversies can be studied. Other perspectives include:

- *Evidence and reasoning.* What kinds of evidence and lines of reasoning have the belief constituencies in different cases used in supporting their positions on religion/school relationships?
- *Critical events.* What events in recent decades significantly contributed to the controversies over religion/school relationships?
- *Resolution.* How were the 12 controversies resolved and to what degree of satisfaction on the part of the contending constituencies?

TRENDS

The purpose of the following section is to illustrate ways that adopting different perspectives for comparing nations' religion/school linkages can reveal diverse national and international trends. The trends inspected in the following section concern (a) church and state-school relationships, (b) religiosity, (c) sources of evidence, (d) tolerance for diversity, (e) outside influences, and (f) the resolution of controversies.

Church and State-School Relationships

Among the 12 controversies featured in this book, four trends could be identified in the relationship between religion and schools. The four can be labeled secular, religious, alternating, and unchanging.

A *secular trend* is marked by a decreasing involvement of religion in state-financed schools. Such a decrease can range from strong to weak. A secular trend was observed in 4 of the 12 societies—France, England, Thailand, and Italy. Across the centuries, the trend in all four was toward greater secularity. In recent times, the strongest trend appeared in the French case, where secularity took precedence over all religions in the resolution of the headscarf episode. England might qualify as next in secularity strength because, even though religious education continued to be part of state-schools' curriculum, nonreligious belief systems (atheism, agnosticism, humanism) were to be included in the national framework. A weak strain of secularity could be found in Thailand, where religion continued to be taught in government-supported schools in the form of Buddhist tenets and morals (except in pondoks), but the nation's constitution required respect for all belief systems. In Italy, the secularity trend also appeared weak, because the constitution's dedication to secularity was diminished by the Catholic Church continuing to be accorded special privileges.

A *religious trend* consists of a move toward greater involvement of religion in schooling. One form of such involvement appeared in China where the government recently tolerated more religious teaching—not in public schools, but in religious-study groups of both authorized faiths and banned faiths.

An *alternating trend* involves a government periodically shifting between more secular and more religious policies. Such shuttling was seen in the Indian, Spanish, and U.S. American controversies. In all three societies, the vacillation resulted from election results. The Indian People's Party added Hindu doctrine to textbooks after unseating the Congress Party in the mid-1990s. Subsequently, the Congress Party removed such doctrine after ousting the People's Party in the 2004 election. In a similar pattern, Spain's Catholic-linked People's Party removed the Socialists from power in the 1996 election and then passed legislation requiring classes in Catholicism in public schools—with that legislation rescinded by the Socialists after they won the 2004 election. In the

United States, religion's involvement in public schools had been decreasing until the Republican Party gained control of the presidency and Congress in 2001. Then, during President George W. Bush's two 4-year terms in office, the government increased (a) public funding of schools operated by Christian groups (money for special services and vouchers), (b) the defense of prayer and posting of religious doctrines in schools (Ten Commandments), (c) acceptance of Christian studies in schools (Bible classes), and (d) support for proposals that creationism be taught alongside evolution in science classes.

An *unchanging* trend results when a society—or at least government authorities—hold fast to a traditional position on religion/school relations. Such a static stance was being maintained in the Pakistan and Saudi Arabian cases. The controversy in Pakistan was not over whether religion should be taught in schools; indeed, religion was expected to be a core subject in the curriculum. Instead, the controversy was over the contents of Islamic religious instruction. The Saudi Arabian case was not about teaching religion in either legal schools or illegal study groups. Rather, the conflict was about which religion should be permitted to offer any instruction at all within the nation's boundaries. In effect, there was no sign in either nation that secularism would likely be increased in schools.

Religiosity

The extent of religious dedication or fervor in a society is reflected in the number of people who identify themselves as members of a faith and who frequently perform the faith's rituals—attend church services, pray, give alms, study the scriptures, and the like. When these indicators of religious zeal are inspected in nations with a Western civilization tradition, it is clear that religiosity in those societies has markedly declined in recent decades. Not only has there been an increase in the percentage of people in Western nations identifying themselves as nonreligious (atheists, agnostics, humanists, realists, free thinkers, nonbelievers), but the religious dedication of those who do identify themselves with a faith has dropped dramatically. As described in earlier chapters,

- 17.3% of avowed Christians in England in 1990 were church members, with two-thirds of them (4.4 million) actually attending church services. By 2000, those figures had dropped to 15.6% members and 3.8 million attenders.
- 67% of the French declared themselves Catholics in the early twenty-first century, but only 10% attended mass regularly and only 6% went to confession at least once a year.
- 82.1% of Spaniards considered themselves Catholics in 2002, but only 19% reported attending church regularly, compared with 98% 50 years earlier.
- 45% of Italy's Catholics said they went to church at least once a week in 1991, a figure that slipped to an estimated 30% by the early twenty-first century.

- 53% of U.S. Americans in 1998 considered religion very important in their lives, a number far higher than the 16% reported in Britain, 14% in France, and 13% in Germany. However, only 20% of Americans were in church at least once a week.
- 86.5% of Swedes identified themselves with the Church of Sweden, but 30% were "nonpracticing" and only 4% attended church regularly.
- 77.1% of Canadians declared they were Christians, but only 10% went to church once a week.
- Eunice Or (2004) reported that "While Europe's churches, including those in Russia, still have 531 million worshippers, only about 10% regularly attend services, and in Britain the figure falls to a shocking 7%."

While Christian membership and zeal in Europe and North America was declining, such was not the case with Islam. Although the task of determining the total membership of a faith is very imprecise (ranging from 1.2 billion to 2 billion worldwide for Muslims), it is still apparent that Islam is the second most popular religion in the world behind Christianity, which has an estimated 2.1 billion members. By 2005, the proportion of the world's 6.5 billion people who were listed as Christians was 32% and declining, whereas the proportion of Muslims was 19% and growing (Number of adherents, 2005).

Although the numbers of nonreligious people in Western nations have increased over the past century, that trend apparently has not been true throughout the world. According to the *Religious Tolerance* Web site, the number of the world's nonreligious persons by 2005 was approximately 775 million, or 12% of the total population, and was on the decline (Number of adherents, 2005).

What, then, might such trends portend for the future of religion/school controversies? I imagine that as Islam continues to make incursions into societies that have traditionally been dominated by other faiths—such as Christianity in Europe and Buddhism in Thailand—the intensity of controversies over religion in schools may well increase. And in societies outside of Europe and North America, the influence of nonreligious people on religion/school decisions may decrease.

Sources of Evidence

In religion/school controversies, constituencies seek to bolster their positions by drawing on sources of evidence that they consider persuasive. Seven such sources are (a) religious doctrine, (b) nonreligious doctrine, (c) tradition, (d) consensus, (e) secular agreements, (f) empirical science, and (g) international human-rights declarations.

Religious doctrine consists of the beliefs and rules of a faith as expressed in holy writings (Bible, Torah, Quran, Hindu Vedas, Confucian Analects) and pronouncements of religious leaders. A belief is considered true if it is in accord with an honored religion's doctrine.

Nonreligious doctrine consists of beliefs founded on rationales that do not include invisible personified powers (gods, spirits) or life after death. The truth of a belief depends on how well it fits a line of logic about the nature of the world and people's lives. Humanism, atheism, realism, and Marxist dialectical materialism are nonreligious doctrines.

Tradition refers to the dominant beliefs of the past. A traditional belief must be true because it has stood the test of time.

Consensus refers to a substantial body of adherents subscribing to a particular belief. The greater the proportion of people who hold a belief, the greater one's confidence that the belief is true and should guide people's actions.

Secular agreements are principles and rules-of-action that members of a constituency have formulated, or at least have willingly accepted. Examples of such agreements are nations' constitutions and laws. If a principle or practice has been agreed upon by the constituents, then people are obligated to abide by it.

Empirical science involves collecting and organizing observations of worldly phenomena. Beliefs are true to the extent that they are founded on a sufficient quantity of careful observations and on convincing logic about how those observations are related to each other.

International human-rights agreements (including religious rights) are declarations of people's rights and responsibilities that enjoy the support of the groups and individuals that have been signatories to those commitments. Examples of international pledges are the United Nation's *Universal Declaration of Human Rights* and *Declaration of the Rights of the Child* (Tarrow, 1987, pp. 237–239). A religion/school relationship is proper to the extent that it accords with a widely endorsed international declaration.

This seven-item typology can now be used for comparing the 12 religion/school cases in terms of the sources of evidence on which constituents apparently depended for bolstering their arguments. Table 16.1 displays my speculation about which sources of evidence figured prominently in the positions that constituencies assumed in the religion/school conflicts. As shown in the table, two or more sources of evidence my be combined to buttress a belief constituency's stance.

During the twentieth century, a growing number of constituencies depended on secular agreements (particularly constitutions), international human-rights declarations, and empirical science to support their beliefs about religion in schools. However, traditional religious doctrine still continued to figure prominently in the sources to which conservative constituencies appealed for bolstering their arguments.

Tolerance for Diversity

In each of this book's 12 societies, tolerance of belief system diversity increased with the passing of time, urged on by relentless worldwide societal forces rather than by the desire of the belief systems' adherents. In the main,

Table 16.1
An Estimate of Constituencies' Sources of Evidence

Belief Constituencies	Sources of Evidence
France	
Government	Secular agreement (constitution)
Muslims	Religious doctrine (Quran)
Japan	
Nationalists	Religious tradition (State Shinto)
Individualists	Secular agreement (constitution)
England	
Fundamentalist Christians	Tradition (accept Bible literally)
Religious-education-framework supporters	International religious-rights agreements
India	
Congress Party's alliance	Secular agreement (constitution)
Hindu People's Party	Religious doctrine (Vedas)
Spain	
People's Party	Religious tradition (Catholicism)
Socialists' alliance	Secular agreement (constitution)
China	
Communist government	Nonreligious doctrine (Marxism)
House church activists	International religious-rights agreements
Italy	
Government	Tradition (Catholic role in Italy)
Smith and Muslim supporters	International religious-rights agreements
Pakistan	
Government (U.S.-influenced)	International religious-rights agreements
Madrassas	Religious doctrine (Islamic) and constitution (Quran)
United States of America	
Creationists	Religious doctrine (Bible)
Evolutionists	Empirical science, secular agreement (constitution)
Thailand	
Buddhist government	Buddhist tradition of governance (maintaining national unity)
Pondok operators	Religious doctrine (Quran), international human-rights agreements
Australia	
Multiculturalists	Religious doctrine (Dreamtime), nonreligious doctrine (postmodernism)
Scientists	Empirical science
Saudi Arabia	
Government	Religious doctrine (Quran)
Christian expatriates	International religious-rights agreements

belief constituencies neither initiated nor welcomed greater tolerance of other constituencies. Instead, greater acceptance of competing belief systems was imposed on traditional constituencies by critical events, particularly since the middle of the twentieth century when World War II served as a social-change watershed. Those events included remarkable advances in (a) transportation and communication, (b) rapidly increasing international migration, (c) anti-colonialism efforts, and (d) the formation of altruistic alliances among nations.

Transportation and Communication

The convenience and popularity of international travel in the nineteenth century was greatly enhanced by advances in railroad and steamship technology. Then the twentieth century's innovations in auto and aircraft technology led to an even more dramatic increase in travel, particularly following World War II. In the United States alone, the number of passengers on airlines grew from 205 million in 1975 to 297 million in 1980 and 638 million in 1990. By 2004, the number of passengers on flights worldwide reached 1.8 billion. A substantial number of those passengers were migrants and tourists.

Even more striking than improved transportation's contribution to people learning of others' worldviews were the developments in communication media over the past half-century. Prior to World War II, motion pictures, the radio, and improved methods of producing and distributing books and magazines served to expand people's experiences with belief systems other than their own. But the influence of those media paled in comparison to the postwar advent of television and computers.

Television. The television era began mainly in the 1950s and grew swiftly over the next half-century. In the case of the telephone, it took 75 years after that technology's commercial introduction before there were 50 million phones worldwide. For television, only 13 years were required before 50 million television receivers were in use. The growth rate in television viewing is reflected in the worldwide numbers of receivers in use over a 27-year period (UNESCO Institute for Statistics, 2003): 1970, 229 million; 1980, 563 million; 1990, 1.1 billion; 1997, 1.4 billion.

The availability of television receivers varied significantly from one country to another. Therefore, the opportunity for people to view programs showing diverse belief systems and the effects of different degrees of tolerance was not the same everywhere. For example, by the opening of the twenty-first century, the numbers of television sets per 1,000 people for the nations featured in this book were as follows (Sparks, 2005a):

France, 628	Italy, 494	India, 78
China, 293	Saudi Arabia, 264	USA, 854
Australia, 738	Britain, 652	Spain, 591
Japan, 725	Pakistan, 131	Thailand, 284

Computers.   The 1980s introduced the era of personal electronic computers, enabling individuals at home, at school, or in the office to find information on the Internet and to correspond personally with people around the globe via e-mail and chat groups. By 2004, there were an estimated 934 million computer users worldwide. That number was expected to grow to 1.07 billion by 2005, 1.12 billion by 2006, and 1.35 billion by 2007. The quantity of users in different countries varied significantly, as suggested by a sampling of nations in 2004 (ClickZ, 2004). (Each number in the following list refers to millions of users.)

Argentina, 5	Egypt, 2	India, 37	Pakistan, 1
China, 100	Hungary, 3	Norway, 3	Thailand, 7.5
Hong Kong, 4.5	Mexico, 14	Spain, 13	South Africa, 5
Japan, 78	Saudi Arabia, 2.5	Briton, 33	USA, 185.5
Russia, 21	Brazil, 22	Germany, 41	
Australia, 13	France, 25	Italy, 56	

Whereas it took 13 years to reach 50 million television sets worldwide, it required only 4 years to achieve 50 million computer Internet hookups after the Internet was available to the general public.

In summary, as the result of the mass adoption of television receivers and personal computers, the twenty-first century offered unprecedented access to diverse belief systems around the world. Such access opened the possibility—but did not guarantee—that more people would acquire a greater understanding of, and tolerance for, varied worldviews than had existed at any earlier time.

Immigration

The accelerating pace of worldwide migration over the past half-century not only expanded the variety of belief systems within recipient nations but also increased the size of immigrants' belief constituencies and their political power. The resulting social pressure compelled nations' traditional constituencies to display greater tolerance for the newcomers' worldviews.

The trend of people moving beyond their home borders in recent decades is suggested by Marta Vila's report that during the quarter century between 1965 and 1990 the annual number of international migrants increased from 75 million to 120 million, a 1.9% yearly growth rate. Over the 1960–1990 period, the annual number of tourists rose from 69 million to 454 million, a 6.3% yearly pace (Vila, 2002).

About 145 million people lived outside their native countries in the mid-1990s, and the number was increasing by anywhere from 2 million to 4 million each year. In the mid-1990s, the largest immigration flows were from Latin America and Asia into North America, and from Eastern Europe, the countries of the former Soviet Union, and

North Africa into Northern and Western Europe. The Middle East drew migrants from Africa and Asia and hosts millions of refugees from within the region [and there was] considerable migration within Asia, Africa, and Latin America. (Human population, 2005)

The Australian case is an example of immigration's potential impact on belief system diversity in a single country. Over the last half of the twentieth century, 5.9 million migrants settled in Australia and so by 2004 nearly 25% of the nation's 19 million people had been born overseas. The number of immigrants arriving between July 2001 and June 2002 totaled 88,900. They came from more than 150 countries. Most had been born in New Zealand (17.6%), the United Kingdom (9.8%), China (7.5%), South Africa (6.4%), India (5.7%), and Indonesia (4.7%) (Australian Department of Immigration, 2004).

Anticolonialism

A further force that hastened the spread of tolerance was the anticolonialism spirit that broke out after World War II. Prior to the 1940s, widespread territories throughout the world were held as colonies by several European nations (Britain, France, Belgium, Italy, Spain, Portugal, the Netherlands), the United States, Japan, and—to a limited extent—Australia and New Zealand. In the decades before the war, cracks had already begun to appear in the structure of colonialism as a result of increasing unrest among the colonies' indigenous peoples who wanted control over their homelands. Yet despite the annoying cracks, the edifice of colonialism managed to stand. But after the war, that changed. *Colonialism* became a bad word and its continued practice was widely condemned. As a result, through a combination of peaceful negotiations and armed conflict, most of the previously colonized regions won their independence. Freedom came to the Philippines in 1946, to India/Pakistan in 1947, Burma in 1948, Indonesia in 1950, the Sudan in 1956, Malaysia/Singapore in 1957, Ghana in 1957, Guinea in 1958, Chad and the Congo in 1960, Tanzania in 1962, Kenya in 1963, and Zambia in 1964. Others, such as Angola, did not win independence until the 1970s.

The newly created independent nations, upon the departure of their colonial masters, could now make their own decisions about which belief systems to encourage or at least to tolerate. As a result, local church leaders often took over the direction of Christian religions that had been imported and managed by the colonial powers. Furthermore, indigenous folk religions and tribal beliefs that had been discouraged or suppressed by colonial authorities were now frequently accepted and revived by the newly installed native authorities. Thus, in at least some new nations, tolerance for diverse belief constituencies increased.

A further opportunity provided by postcolonial independence was the chance for native peoples themselves to decide what role religion would play in the schools.

Altruistic Alliances

The end of World War II opened a new period of cooperation among governments to improve the lives of the world's peoples through the efforts of international associations. The most notable of these coalitions was the United Nations, along with its subsidiaries—UNESCO (United Nations Educational, Scientific, and Cultural Organization) and UNICEF (United Nations Children's Fund). Among the outcomes of such groups' activities were commitments by governments to promote the welfare of peoples everywhere. Examples of such pledges are the *United Nations Charter* (1945), *U.N. Universal Declaration of Human Rights* (1946), *Declaration of the Rights of the Child* (1959), *Convention Against Discrimination in Education* (1960), and *Declaration on the Elimination of All Forms of Intolerance and Discrimination Based on Religion and Belief* (1981) (Tarrow, 1987, pp. 237–246).

Governments came under great international pressure to affirm their support of such declarations by becoming signatories to the agreements. As a result, when incidents of intolerance within a country were publicly exposed, that nation's government was open to censure by members of an alliance and by the world's press for not enforcing its commitment. Thus, over the past half-century, more international pressure than ever before was being imposed on governments to tolerate varied belief systems.

Outside Influences

The introduction of belief systems into a society and the stimulus of a particular system's growth can come either from within the society or from outside. In past centuries, highly influential outside sources included military invasions (usually producing colonial control), missionary efforts, and trade across national boundaries. Frequently these three were combined. In Spain's conquest of Central and South America, Catholic padres accompanied the invading conquistadors. In Britain's colonization of Asian, African, and North American territories, Protestant missionaries arrived in the wake of British armed forces. In France's Southeast Asian and Pacific-island colonies, Catholic priests appeared both before and after French sailors and soldiers. Arab traders from the Middle East not only followed Muslim armies into Central Asia, but traders also carried the faith as they pursued their commercial ventures throughout Southeast Asia.

During recent decades, foreign mission efforts have continued to affect belief systems around the world, with the success of traditional Catholic and mainline Protestant missions markedly declining, while Muslim immigration and proselytizing in Europe and North America grew. At the same time, Evangelical Christian sects scored dramatic victories in Africa, Latin America, and Asia. Andrew Rice (2004), in assessing the impact of Evangelicals in Africa, concluded that

the continent today is in the throes of its own Great Awakening. From the thatch-roofed churches of desolate central Mozambique to densely urban Nigeria (another country with evangelical leaders), where hundreds of thousands flee Lagos every weekend to attend outdoor church revivals, to the war-torn Democratic Republic of the Congo, where Congolese crowd storefront congregations, Africans who used to attend mainline Protestant and Catholic churches—and even mosques—are flocking to hear evangelical preachers. Back in 1970, 17 million Africans attended Pentecostal churches, according to the World Christian Encyclopedia. Today, more than 125 million do—roughly 19% of the continent's population. Add the many millions more who profess other varieties of evangelical Christianity, or who still attend mainline churches but nonetheless call themselves "born again," and you have perhaps the most important social movement to hit Africa since postcolonial independence [in the 1950s through the 1970s].

John Mason (1996) reported that over the last three decades of the twentieth century, Protestantism—mainly of a fundamentalist variety—grew rapidly while Catholicism declined. Between 1916 and 1990, the number of Protestant adherents in Latin America increased from 200,000 to 48 million. Observers predicted that by the early years of the twenty-first century the number of active Protestants in Central and South America would exceed the number of practicing Catholics (Mason, 1996).

Other types of outside forces that exerted a rapidly increasing influence on the introduction and growth of belief systems were those described earlier—increases in air travel, radio, print media, television, the Internet, immigration, tourism, and international altruistic alliances. Each of those forces contributed to opening societies to belief systems that compete for the minds and hearts of the populace with those societies' long-standing traditions.

The Resolution of Controversies

While I was pondering the way the 12 religion/school cases turned out, I recognized that I could not identify any trends in the ways cases were resolved. Instead, I found a two-phase pattern that may well be a permanent feature of attempts to settle religion/school controversies. The pattern is one that existed in the past, is evident in the present, and probably will continue in the future.

Phase 1

The pattern's first phase concerns only the specific controversy at hand, as illustrated by each of the 12 cases described in Chapter 1. The attempt to resolve that particular conflict can result in either of two outcomes—an immediate solution or a stalemate. Out of our 12 cases, 10 were settled with an immediate solution, whereas the remaining two suffered an impasse.

Here are the 10 immediate solutions:

France—The government banned the ostentatious display of any religious symbols.

Japan—The government punished teachers who failed to stand and sing the national anthem or who failed to sing with sufficient gusto.

England—The plan to include nonreligious belief systems in state schools' religious-education classes was not mandatory, so individual schools and teachers could do as they wished.

India—After winning the 2004 election, the Congress Party ordered the removal of Hindu doctrine from textbooks that the People's Party had inserted.

Spain—The victorious Socialists repealed the compulsory religious-classes law that the Spanish People's Party had passed.

China—The government arrested the importer of forbidden Bibles, but then released him, ostensibly because of his ill health.

Italy—The high court ruled that the display of crucifixes in state-school classrooms was legal, so the crucifixes could remain.

United States of America—The superintendent of public education in the state of Georgia removed her ban on the term *evolution* in science curricula and textbooks.

Australia—The curriculum planners' proposal to include Dreamtime explanations in science classes was not obligatory, so individual schools and teachers could decide whether to accept the proposal.

Saudi Arabia—Expatriates accused of publicly teaching a non-Islamic religion were arrested and usually expelled from the country.

Consider, now, the pair of stalemates:

Pakistan—With few exceptions, the madrassas refused to comply with the government's revisions of the schools' instructional content, and the government failed to do anything substantial to effect compliance.

Thailand—In a large number of the nation's pondoks, the government failed to achieve any control at all over pondoks' curricula, instructional methods, or teachers' pro-Muslim, separatist political activism.

Phase 2

The pattern's second phase consists of a long-term—perhaps permanent—condition of disagreement and antagonism. Even after the apparent resolution of a specific religion/school controversy, the belief system differences between the adversaries remain, ready to produce other religion/school confrontations in other settings. Such was the case of the creationism/evolution conflict in America, where numerous other creationism/evolution confrontations arose in other places than Georgia. In China the government periodically contended with house church incidents other than the Shouters' banned-Bibles episode. Such was also true of the religious-relics incidents in France and Italy, the state-schools' textbook debate in India, and the Dreamtime issue in Australia.

In summary, none of the apparent resolutions of any immediate case permanently averted future religion/school conflicts, because the underlying incompatibility among competing belief systems continued to affect constituencies' attitudes and behavior.

CONCLUSION

The intent of this chapter was to achieve two aims. The first was to show how a four-component interpretation scheme (belief constituencies, tradition, critical events, the exercise of power) might help explain the likenesses and differences among controversies over religion in schools. I sought to illustrate the scheme's application by demonstrating how it might be applied from four perspectives, those of (a) similar traditions and varied events, (b) religious versus nonreligious traditions, (c) degrees of power, and (d) authority.

The second aim of the chapter was to demonstrate how adopting various viewpoints toward religion/school controversies might reveal trends over time. The six perspectives chosen for that purpose were (a) church and state-school relationships, (b) religiosity, (c) sources of evidence, (d) tolerance for diversity, (e) outside influences, and (f) the resolution of controversies.

Notes

CHAPTER 2

1. In keeping with modern usage, throughout this book the symbol BCE (*before the common era* or *before the Christian era*) replaces the traditional BC (*before Christ*) to identify dates more than two millennia in the past. Dates within the past 2,000 years are either cited with no appended letters or are accompanied by the symbol CE (*common era*) instead of the traditional AD (Latin *anno Domini* that stands for *year of our Lord*).

CHAPTER 3

1. "The true figures show that only about . . . 10% of Canadians actually go to church one or more times a week. Many . . . Canadians tell pollsters that they have gone to church even though they have not. Whether this happens in other countries, with different cultures, is difficult to predict" (Robinson, 2001).

CHAPTER 8

1. In 2002, out of a total population of 40 million, there were 350,000 churchgoing Protestants and 50,000 practicing Jews living permanently in Spain (Backgrounds, 2004).

CHAPTER 12

1. By curious coincidence, around the same time that Cox was eliminating evolution from the Georgia state curriculum, Italy's minister of education, Letizia Moratti, removed any mention of evolution from the nation's middle-school science curriculum. Moratti's act was met with such a vociferous outcry from the public and the scientific community that she quickly recanted and announced that "The discussion of Darwin's theories will be included in the education of all students from 6 to 18 years" (Lorenzi, 2004).

References

Abdussalam, R. (2003, September 24). French secularism: A problem, not a solution. *Dar Al-Hayat.* Available online: http://english.daralhayat.com/opinion/09–2003/Article-20030924-d4e1baef-c0a8–01ed-0015cd9a7a97babb/story.html.

Abraham, Y. (2001, November 29). Pakistan set to try again to curb schools run by clerics. *Boston Globe*, A1. Available online: http://bridget.jatol.com/pipermail/sacw_insaf.net/2001/001180.html.

Achieving educational equality for Australia's Aboriginal and Torres Strait Islander peoples. (2000). MCEETYA Taskforce on Indigenous Education. Available online: http://216.239.63.104/search?q=cache:L1xJsV4WkGAJ:www.mceetya.edu.au/pdf/reporta.pdf+Australia+Aboriginal+educational+rights&hl=en&ie=UTF-8#5.

Adelore, T. (2004, March 5). France: Religious symbols banned. *The Spokesman.* Available online: http://www.msuspokesman.com/news/2004/03/05/WorldNews/France.Religious.Symbols.Banned-631074.shtml.

Agency for Cultural Affairs. (1972). *Japanese religion.* Tokyo: Kodansha International.

Akkara, A. (2001, December 12). New curriculum "tampering" with history, Indian churches protest. *Christianity Today.* Available online: http://www.christianitytoday.com/ct/2001/150/33.0.html.

American Jewish Community. (2003). *The west, Christians and Jews in Saudi Arabian schoolbooks.* Available online: http://www.ajc.org/In TheMedia/Publications.asp?did=744.

Ancient Roman education. (2005, downloaded). Available online: http://www.crystalinks.com/romeducation.html.

Arita, E. (2004, March 31). Teachers will be punished for not singing anthem. *Japan Times.* Available online: http://www.japantimes.co.jp/cgi-bin/getarticle.pl5?nn20040331a1.htm.

Asia Child Rights. (2003, June 25). Pakistan: Number of school-going children on the decline. *ACR Weekly Newsletter*, 2(26). Available online: http://acr.hrschool.org/mainfile.php/0133/161/.

Astier, H. (2004, September 1). The deep roots of French secularism. *BBC News*. Available online: http://news.bbc.co.uk/1/hi/world/europe/3325285.stm.

Attenborough, R. (2004). Mahatma Gandhi. Available online: http://www.engagedpage.com/gan1.html.

Australian Department of Immigration. (2004, March 11). *Key Facts in Immigration*. Available online: http://www.immi.gov.au/facts/02 key.htm.

Australian Dreamtime. (2005). *Crystalinks*. Available online: http://www.crystalinks.com/dreamtime.html.

Australian Education Council and Curriculum Corporation. (1993, June). *National science profile*. Carlton South, Vic.: Author.

Backgrounds: Spain religious freedom. (2004). *Countries of the world*. Available online: http://www.ncbuy.com/reference/country/backgrounds.html?code=sp&sec=religiousfree.

Baldauf, S. (2004, July 16). India considers historic rewrite. *Christian Science Monitor*. Available online: http://www.csmonitor.com/2004/0716/p06s01-wosc.html.

Barrett, D. B., & Johnson, T. M. (2004). Religion. In J. K. Sparks (Ed.), *Britannica 2004 Book of the Year*, p. 280. Chicago, IL: Encyclopaedia Britannica.

Blignaut, C. (2003, October 15). France's first Muslim school raises hopes and concern. *The Christian Science Monitor*. Available online: http://csmonitor.com/2003/1015/p07s01-woeu.html.

Bokhari, F. (2003, November 13). Pakistan's "madrassa" campaign can backfire in more ways than one. *Gulf News*. Available online: http://www.gulfnews.com/Articles/opinion.asp?ArticleID=102802.

Boston, R. (2004, December 2). When in Rome. *Americans United for the Separation of Church and State*. Available online: http://blog.au.org/2004/12/when_in_rome_ho.html.

Bradley, J. R. (2004, May 27). Waking up to the terror threat in Southern Thailand. *Straits Times*. Available online: http://yaleglobal.yale.edu/display.article?id=3985.

Bragg, R. (2001, October 14). Nurturing young Islamic hearts and hatreds. *New York Times*. Available online: http://www.rickross.com/reference/islamic/islamic34.html.

Breen, L. (2002, December 10). China: Can religion come out of the cold? *The Tablet*. Available online: http://www.thetablet.co.uk/cgi-bin/register.cgitablet 00672.

Brokaw, T. (2004, February 13). Pakistan madrassas. *MSNBC News*. Available online: http://msnbc.msn.com/id/4264215/.

Buhler, G. (1886). *The Laws of Manu—Manu Smriti*. London: Oxford University Press (volume 25 of *The sacred books of the east*).

Buripakdi, C., & Mahakhan, P. (1980). Thailand. In T. N. Postlethwaite & R. M. Thomas (Eds.), *Schooling in the ASEAN Region*. Oxford: Pergamon.

Caldwell, C. (2004). Veiled threat. *The Weekly Standard*. Available online: http://www.weeklystandard.com/Content/Public/Articles/000/000/003/583lxmcr.asp.

Cassidy, S. (2004, October 28). Schools instructed to provide atheism lessons alongside RE. *The Independent*. Available online: http://education.independent.co.uk/news/story.jsp?story=577134.

Catholic chaplains affected by French veil law. (2004, October 7). *Reuters*. Available online: http://www.reuters.co.uk/newsPackageArticle. jht ml?type=worldNews&storyID=598596&section=news.

Chan, K. (2004, December 15). Italian court rules against challenge to remove crucifix from classrooms. *Christian Post.* Available online: http://www.christianpost.com/php_functions/print_friendly.php?tbl_name=europe&id=329.

Charles II. (2004). *Britannia.* Available online: http://www.britannia.com/history/monarchs/mon49.html.

China. (2003, December 18). *International religious freedom report 2003.* U.S. Department of State. Available online: http://www.state.gov/g/drl/rls/irf/2003/23826.htm.

China refutes distortions about Christianity. (1995). People's Republic of China Embassy in the United States. Available online: http://www.china-embassy.org/eng/zt/zjxy/t36493.htm.

China releases bible smuggler from prison. (2002, February 10). *New York Times.* Available online: http://www2.kenyon.edu/Depts/Religion/Fac/Adler/Reln270/Bible-smuggler2.htm.

China steps up criticism on history textbook. (2004, August 29). *Japan Times.* Available online: http://www.japantimes.co.jp/cgi-bin/getarticle.pl5?nn20040829f1.htmå.

Chinese church, The. (2005). *OMF* (formerly *China Inland Mission*). Available online: http://www.omf.org/content.asp?id=9972.

Church history. (2004). *The Anglican Domain.* Available online: http://www.anglican.org/church/ChurchHistory.html.

Church of privilege, The. (2004). *The Centre for Citizenship.* Available online: http://www.centreforcitizenship.org/church1.html.

Clark, T. W. (1993). Reply to Haughness. *The Humanist,* 53(4), 22.

Clarke launches first national framework for religious education. (2004, October 28). *Qualifications and Curriculum Authority.* Available online: http://www.qca.org.uk/2586_9821.html.

ClickZ. (2004). Trends and statistics. Available online: http://www.clickz.com/stats/web_worldwide/.

Cline, A. (2004a). Southern Baptists. *About.* Available online: http://atheism.about.com/od/baptistssouthernbaptists/a/southernbaptist.htm.

Cline, A. (2004b). Evolution and creationism: Balanced presentation? *About.* Available online: http://atheism.about.com/library/FAQs/evolution/blfaq_evolution_jw.htm.

Constitution of India. (2004). Delhi: Ministry of Communications and Information. Available online: http://indiacode.nic.in/coiweb/welcome.html.

Constitution of Japan. (1946). Available online: http://tions/Japan/English/english-Constitution.html.

Constitution of the National Committee of the Three-Self Patriotic Movement of Protestant Churches in China. (2002, September 10). *Amity News Service.* Available online: http://www.amityfoundation.org/ANS/Articles/ans2002/ans2002.10/2002_10_8.htm.

Constitution of the People's Republic of China. (1982, December 4). Available online: http://english.people.com.cn/constitution/constitution.html.

Constitution of Thailand. (1991). Available online: http://www.parliament.go.th/files/library/b05-b.htm.

Cooper, S. (2004, October 6). Pennsylvania school district considers supplemental textbook supportive of intelligent design. *Discovery Institute.* Available online: http://www.discover.org.scripts/viewDB/index.php?command=view&id=2231.

Crabtree, V. (2002–2003). Religion in Britain. *Bane of Monotheism*. Available online: http://www.vexen.co.uk/religion/rib.html#UK.

Cummings, W. (1980). *Education and equality in Japan*. Princeton, NJ: Princeton University Press.

Daniel, A. (2004). Caste system in modern India. *Modern India*. Available online: http://adaniel.tripod.com/modernindia.htm.

Davis, A. (2004, October 29). School system forms the frontline in Thailand's southern unrest. *Jane's Intelligence Review*. Available online: http://www.janes.com/security/international_security/news/jir/jir041029_1_n.shtml.

Dean, C. (2004, October 26). Creationism and science clash at grand canyon bookstores. *New York Times*. Available online: http://www.times.com/2004/10/26/science/26cany.html?ex=1100581200&en=6fa918c90f114388&ei=5070.

Decide turban issue by Nov 5, French court tells school. (2004, October 22). *The Tribune* (India). Available online: http://www.tribunein dia.com/2004/20041023/main1.htm.

Defending the public display of the crucifix. (2003, November 9). *Catholic Online*. Available online: http://www.catholic.org/featured/headline.php?ID=480.

Dehousse, F., & Coussens, W. (2003). *Constitution of the European Union*. Available online: http://66.102.7.104/search?q=cache:oGmPVS6Aa 8oJ:www.irri-kiib.be/papers/Basic_Treaty.pdf+Constitution+of+the+European+Union&hl=en&ie=UTF-8.

Denzin, N. K. (1997). *Interpretive ethnography*. Thousand Oaks, CA: Sage.

Di Meglio, F. (2003). Debate: Has the crucifix become Italy's cross to bear? *Italianrus*. Available online: http://www.italiansrus.com/articles/ourpaesani/crucifix.htm.

Dord, O. (2003). Secularism: The French model under European influence. *Robert Schuman Foundation*. Available online: http://www.robert-schuman.org/gb/actualite/note24an.htm.

Dorman, C. (1996, January 30). McLean v. Arkansas Board of Education. *The Talk: Origins Archive*. Available online: http://www.talkorigins.org/faqs/mclean-v-arkansas.html.

Ehrlich, R. S. (2004, June 7). Wave of violence shakes Thailand. *Asia Times*. Available online: http://www.atimes.com/atimes/Southeast_Asia/FA07Ae03.html.

Eight Thai Muslims charged with rebellion. (2005, March 10). *Reuters*. Available online: http://www.alertnet.org/thenews/newsdesk/BKK28833.htm.

Elections in Spain. (2004). *Elections around the world*. Available online: http://www.electionworld.org/spain.htm.

Ergas, Y. (2004, August 19). When in Rome. *New Republic*. Available online: http://www.ocnus.net/cgi-bin/exec/view.cgi?archive=52& num=13630.

Europe: Religion: Church attendance. (2004). *Nationmaster*. Available online: http://www.nationmaster.com/graph-T/rel_chu_att/EUR.

European Commission. (2002, June). *Pakistan, education: Report of the EC Rapid Reaction Mechanism Assessment Mission*. Available online: http://europa.eu.int/comm/external_relations/cpcm/rrm/pakistan_02.htm.

Evolution and creationism. (1982). *United Presbyterian Church in the USA*. Available online: http://www.don-lindsay-archive.org/creation/voices/RELIGIOU/PRESS82.htm.

Evolution of Kathy Cox, The. (2004, May 2). *The Daily Whim*. Available online: http://www.photodude.com/article/2373/the-evolution-of-kathy-cox.

Faiola, A. (2005, April 6). Japan's OK of military textbooks stirs ire. *Arizona Republic*. Available online: http://www.azcentral.com/arizonarepublic/news/articles/0406japan-textbook06.html.

Filiatreau, J. (2000, June 29). Presbyterian science-and-religion group naturally selects a defender of evolution. *Presbyterian Church (USA) News*. Available online: http://horeb.pcusa.org/ga212/News/ga00125.htm.

Flag and the anthem: Enforcing Japanese patriotism, The. (2004, March 31). *The Asahi Shimbun*. Available online: http://japanfocus.org/103.html.

Flamini, R. (2004, October 7). Analysis: Spanish church battles new laws. *Washington Times*. Available online: http://www.washingtontimes.com/upi-breaking/20041007–045313–6360r.htm.

France: Constitution. (2004). *International Constitutional Law*. Available online: http://www.oefre.unibe.ch/law/icl/fr00000_.html.

French clerics oppose scarf ban. (2003, December 12). *BBC News*. Available online: http://news.bbc.co.uk/2/hi/europe/3309885.stm.

French schoolgirl expelled for headscarf. (2003, November 27). *Expatica*. Available online: http://www.expatica.com/source/site_article.asp?subchannel_id=58&story_id=2663.

French secularism. (2004, October 15). *BBC*. Available online: http://www.bbc.co.uk/dna/h2g2/A2903663.

Fuchs, D. (2003, December 21). *New York Times*, A1.

Ganley, E. (2004, January 17). Muslim women protest scarf ban. *Washington Times*. Available online: http://washingtontimes.com/world/20040117–112837–4357r.htm.

Genesis. (1611). *Holy Bible—King James authorized version*. Philadelphia: J. C. Winston (1950 edition).

Genetics Society of America. (2003, June). *Statement on evolution and creationism*. Available online: http://genetics.faseb.org/genetics/g-gsa/statement_on_evolution.shtml.

Gillard, D. (2001, December). Glass in their snowballs—The faith schools debate. *The Education Archive*. Available online: http://www.dg.dial.pipex.com/educ22.shtml.

Giroux, H. A. (1992). Border crossings: Cultural workers and the politics of education. New York: Routledge.

Glueckert, L. (2004). Papal states. In J. Chastain (Ed.), *Encyclopedia of 1848 revolutions*. Available online: http://www.ohiou.edu/~Chastain/ip/papal sta. htm.

God and Spain. (2004, September 25). *Telegraph*. Available online: http://www.telegraph.co.uk/opinion/main.jhtml?xml=/opinion/2004/09/25/dl2502.xml.

Groves, C. (2005). *The Groves collection*. Available online: http://arts.anu.edu.au/groveco.

Gurfinkiel, M. (1997, March). Islam in France: The French way of life is in danger. *The Middle East Quarterly*. Available online: http://www.meforum.org/article/337.

Gurumurthy, S. (1998, October 24). Vande Mataram then, Saraswati Vandana now. *The Observer*. Available online: http://www.hvk.org/articles/1098/ 0090.html.

Hammersley, M. (1992). *What's wrong with ethnography?* London: Routledge.

Hanna, J. (2005, April 27). Evolution-creation battle heats up again in Kansas schools. *Salt Lake Tribune*. Available online: http://www.sltrib.com/nationworld/ci_2687534.

Harrigan, S. (2004, November 25). Spain battles illegal Muslim immigration. *Fox News.* Available online: http://www.foxnews.com/story/0,2933,139511, 00.html.

Hart, A. (2005, January 14). Judge in Georgia orders anti-evolution stickers removed from textbooks. *New York Times.* Available online: http://www.nytimes. com/2005/01/14/national/14sticker.html.

Hasan, K. (2004, July 17). Pakistan backing away from promise to dismantle madrassas. *Daily Times.* Available online: http://www.dailytimes.com.pk/ default.asp?page=story_17–7–2004_pg7_34.

Hertz, T. (2002, August 7). Saudi Arabia blocks religious websites. *Christianity Today.* Available online: http://www.christianitytoday.com/ct/2002/130/ 31.0. html.

Hinsliff, G. (2004, February 15). Children to study atheism at school. *Education Guardian.* Available online: http://education.guardian.co.uk/schools/ story/0,5500,1148669,00.html.

Historians begin work with open mind. (2004, June 23). *Times of India.* Available online: 06/23/stories/2004062304001300.htm.

How many people go regularly to weekly religious services? (2004, November 22). *Religious Tolerance.* Available online: http://www.religious tolerance. org/rel_rate.htm.

Human population: Fundamentals of growth effect of migration on population growth. (2005). Population Reference Bureau. Available online. http://www.prb.org/ Content/NavigationMenu/PRB/Educators/Human_Population/Migration2/ Migration1.htm.

Hundreds of schools close in southern Thailand after teachers killed. (2004, December 23). *China Daily.* Available online: http://www.chinadaily.com.cn/ english/doc/2004-12/23/content_402758.htm.

Hurdle, J. (2005a, February 11). Advocates for teaching option to evolution in schools gaining. *San Diego Union-Tribune.* http://www.signonsandiego.com/uniontrib/ 20050211/news_1n11evo.html.

Hurdle, J. (2005b, August 4). Leading Republican differs with Bush on evolution. *Boston Globe.* Available online: http://www.boston.com/news/education/ k_12/articles/2005/08/04/leading_republican_differs_with_bush_on_evolution.

Hussain, A. (2003, July 29). No thanks. *The News International.* Available online: http://www.jang.com.pk/thenews/jun2003-weekly/nos-29–06–2003/spr. htm#3.

Hussain, Z. (2004, March). Much ado about nothing. *Newsline.* Available online: http://www.newsline.com.pk/Newsmar2004/cover1mar2004.htm.

India's supreme court allows religion in public schools. (2002, November). *Church & State,* 55(10), 21.

International migration: What prompts it? What problems arise? (1997, Fall). *UN Chronicle.* Available online: http://www.findarticles.com/p/articles/ mi_m1309/is_n3_v34/ai_20267841.

International migration expanding. (2004, November 29). *United Nations* (press release DEV 2495). Available online: www.un.org/esa/policy/wess/wess2004files/ part2web/wess04p2prel.pdf.

Iqbal, A. (2003, August 17). Mastering the madrassas. *Washington Times.* Available online: http: //www.washtimes.com/world/20030817–1239325826r.htm.

Iqbal, N. (2001, September 1). Pakistan gambles on change in school curriculum. *Asia Times.* http://www.atimes.com/ind-pak/CI01Df01.html.

Islamic era, The. (1994). *Encyclopaedia Britannica*, Vol. 18, pp. 15–17. Chicago, IL: Encyclopaedia Britannica.

Islam in France. (2004). *Wikipedia*. Available online: http://en.wikipedia.org/wiki/ Islam_in_France.

Islam is the fastest growing religion and the second largest religion in the world. (2005). *Statistics of Muslims' population around the world*. Available online: http://www.islamicweb.com/begin/results.htm.

Islamist schools are blamed for bloody uprising in Thailand. (2004, May 15). *Immigrants for America*. Available online: http://www.immigrantsforamerica. com/islamist.schools.are.blamed.for.bloody.uprising.in.thailand.05–14–2004. html.

Italian court bans classroom crucifix at Muslim's request. (2003, October 26). *Islam Online*. Available online: http://www.islam-online.net/English/ News/2003– 10/26/article08.shtml.

Italy—Constitution. (1948). Available online: http://www.oefre.unibe.ch/law/.

Italy president in crucifix row. (2003, October 27). *CNN*. Available on-line: http://www.cnn.com/2003/WORLD/europe/10/27/italy.President.crucafix. ap/.

Jacinto, L. (2004, January 15). Back to the future. *ABC News*. Available online: http://more.abcnews.go.com/sections/world/dailynews/madrassa020115.html.

Japanese national anthem (Kimigayo). (2004). Available online: http://www. japanorama.com/kimigayo.html.

Japan's modern education system. (1980). Tokyo: Ministry of Education, Science and Culture.

Kahn, S. (2004, December 9). Govt collecting data on madrassa funding, functions. *Daily Times* (Pakistan). Available online: http://www.dailytimes.com.pk/ default.asp?page=story_12–9–2004_pg7_25.

Kapisthalam, K. (2004, June 30). Learning from Pakistan's *madrassas*. *Asia Times*. Available online: http://www.atimes.com/atimes/South_Asia/FF23Df05. html.

Kendall, E. (2004, June 4). Japan: Watching Shinto nationalism. *World Evangelical Alliance*. Available online: http://www.worldevangeli cal.org/persec_japan_ 04june04.html.

Key statistics. (2004). *Christian Leadership World*. Available online: http://www.teal. org.uk/stats/key.htm#memtrend.

Lambert, T. (1998). Heresies and cults in China today. *China for Jesus*. Available online: http://www.chinaforjesus.com/heresiesandcults.htm.

Lawlor, R. (1991). *Voices of the first day: Awakening in the aboriginal dreamtime*. Rochester, VT: Inner Traditions International.

Lev, M. A. (2002, January 9). China jails member of "evil cult" for importing bibles by thousands. *Chicago Tribune*. Available online: http://www.beliefnet.com/ story/97/story_9739_1.html.

Lintner, B. (2004, November 24). A new battlefield in Thailand. *Yale Global*. Available online: http://yaleglobal.yale.edu/display.article?id=4922.

Liow, J. (2004, September 3). The truth about pondok schools in Thailand. *Asia Times*. Available online: http://www.atimes.com/atimes/Southeast_Asia/ FI03Ae04.html.

Lorenzi, R. (2004, April 28). No evolution for Italian teens. *The Scientist*. Available online: http://www.biomedcentral.com/news/20040428/04/n.

MacDonald, M. (2004, January 31). Evolution furor heats up. *Atlanta Journal Constitution*. Available online: http://www.ajc.com/saturday/content/epaper/editions/saturday/news_04b1651524aa00901040.html.

Madrassah schools in Pakistan remain entirely unreformed. (2004, January 25). *Para Pundit*. Available online: http://www.parapundit.com/archives/001907.html.

Madrassa muddle. (2005, January 2). *The News* (Pakistan). Available online: http://www.jang.com.pk/thenews/jan2005-daily/02-01-2005/oped/editorial.htm.

Mahmood, K. (2003, September 9). Muslims try to defuse tensions in South Thailand. *Islam Online*. Available online: http://www.islamonline.net/English/News/2003–09/14/article06.shtml.

Manhattan, A. (1949). *The Vatican in World Politics*. London: C. A. Watts. Available online: http://www.caphas-library.com/catholic/catholic_vatican_in_world_politics_chpt_9.html.

Maratos, J. (1995). Ideology in science education: The Australian example. *International Review of Education*, 41(5), 357–369.

Mason, J. (1996, April 21). Evangelical protestantism and the fundamentalist realignment in Latin America. *The Socialist International*. Available online: http://ww2.wpunj.edu/cohss/polisci/faculty/mason/jmevang.htm.

Mason, M. (2004, January 20). *Religious education: Could we do better?* Available online: http://www.ippr.org.uk/research/files/team23/project164/Marylin%20Mason%20Paper_doc1.PDF.

Max Muller, F., Williams, M., Stephen, R., & Childers, R. C. (1999). *Studies in Buddhism* (reprint). New Delhi: AES.

McElroy, W. (1998, June 1). The origin of religious tolerance. *The Independent Institute*. Available online: http://www.independent.org/publications/article.asp?id=153.

Moore, A. (2001). Saudi Arabia releases Christian leaders. *World New Daily*. Available online: http://www.worldnetdaily.com/news/article.asp?ARTICLE_ID=25853.

Moore, J. (1995). Some historical and conceptual relations among logical positivism, behaviorism, and cognitive psychology. In J. T. Todd & E. K. Morris (Eds.), *Modern Perspectives on B. F. Skinner and Contemporary Behaviorism*. Westport, CT: Greenwood.

Morello, C. (2005, January 23). Bible breaks at public schools face challenges in rural Virginia. *Washington Post*. Available online: http://www.washingtonpost.com/wp-dyn/articles/A29266–2005Jan22.html.

Mussolini and the Roman Catholic Church. (2004). *History learnings*. Available online: http://www.historylearningsite.co.uk/mussolini_roman_catholic.htm.

Nath, T. (2004, September 22). Sikh students can wear patka, says French envoy. *The Tribune* (India). Available online: http://www.sikh-history.com/cgibin/Ultimate/ultimatebb.cgi?ubb=get_topic;f=10;t=000624.

Nationality of popes. (2005). *Pope chart*. Available online: http://www.poprchart.com/facts.htm.

National Society (Church of England) for Promoting Religious Education. (2004). Available online: http://www.studyoverseas.com/re/re2. htm.

Number of adherents of world religions. (2005). *Religious Tolerance*. Available online: http://www.religioustolerance.org/worldrel.htm.

OMF. (2004). Three self patriotic movement churches. Available online: http://www.omf.org/content.asp?id=9979.

Ono, S. (1962). *Shinto, the Kami Way.* Tokyo: Bridgeway.

Or, E. (2004, September 23). Trust in religious institutions does not convey to church attendance. *Christian Today.* Available online: http://christiantoday.com/news/society/trust.in.religious.institutions.does.not.convey.to.church.attendance/106.htm.

Pakistan. (2004, September 15). *International religious freedom report 2004.* U.S. Department of State. Available online: http://www.state.gov/g/drl/rls/irf/2004/35519.htm.

Pakistan Constitution. (2001). *The Constitution of the Islamic Republic of Pakistan.* Available online: http://www.pakistani.org/pakistan/constitution/.

Panikkar, K. N. (2005). History textbooks in India: Narratives of religious nationalism. *International Congress of Historical Societies.* Available online: http://www.cishsydney2005.org/images/HISTORY%20TEXTBOOKS%20IN%20INDIA.doc.

Papal states. (2004). *Nationmaster.com.* Available online: .nationmaster.com/encyclopedia/Papal-States.

Papal states. (2005). *Wikipedia.* Available online: .org/wiki/Papal_States.

Party's secret directives on how to eradicate religion and ensure the victory of atheism. (2004, December 2). *Asia News.* Available online: http://www.asianews.it/view.php?l=en&art=2029.

Pennacchio, M. (2005). Traditional Australian aboriginal bush medicines. *HerbalGram (Journal of the American Botanical Council),* 65, 38–44.

Peri, S. (2004, October 1). Madrassas rising: Education, security, and US relations with Pakistan. *The Subcontinental,* 2(3). Available online: http://216.239.63.104/search?q=cache:J5CbxtSxJtUj:www.thesubconttal.org/public/journal/sPeri2.3.pdf+Pakistan+United+States+madrassas&hl=en&ie=UTF-8.

Philosophy of René Descartes, The. (2005). *The Radical Academy.* Available online: http://radicalacademy.com/phildescartes1.htm.

Pingree, G. (2004, October 1). Secular drive challenges Spain's Catholic identity. *Christian Science Monitor.* Available online: http://www.csmonitor.com/2004/1001/p07s02-woeu.html.

Pinto, D. (2004, January 7). The long, bloody path that led to French secularism. *International Herald Tribune.* Available online: http://www.iht.com/articles/124035.html.

Pomfret, J. (2002, December 24). Despite crackdowns, Protestant religious groups flourishing in China. *Washington Post.* Available online: http://www.religionnewsblog.com/1653-.html.

Pope Pius IX. (2005). *Catholic encyclopedia.* Available online: http://www.newadvent.org/cathen/12134b.htm.

Powell, C. (2004, March 11). Madrassas breeding grounds of terrorists. *Jihad Watch.* http://www.jihadwatch.org/archives/001120.php.

PSOE—Spanish Socialist Workers' Party. (2004). *Wikipedia.* Available online: http://en.wikipedia.org/wiki/PSOE.

Ramesh, R. (2004, June 26). Another rewrite for India's history books. *The Guardian.* Available online: schoolsworldwide/story/0,14062,1247860,00.html.

Rashtriya Swayamsevak Sangh. (2004). *Wikipedia*. Available online: http://en. wikipedia.org/wiki/RSS_%28politics%29.

Rebel teachers forced to get training to stand up for national anthem. (2004, August 3). *Japan Today*. Available online: http://www.japan today.com/ e/?content=news&cat=1&id=307355.

Religion. (1986). *Spain*. Available online: http://countrystudies.Us/ spain/44.htm.

Religion in Britain. (2004). *National Statistics*. Available online: http://www.statistics. gov.uk/cci/nugget.asp?id=293.

Religion in China. (2004, May 9). *International coalition for religious freedom*. Available online: http://www.religiousfreedom.com/wrpt/ China rpt.htm.

Religion in school. (2004, January 25). Available online: http://www.straughan.com/ italy/living/religion.htm.

Religious policy of the CCP—1949–1978. (2005). *Leiden University* (textbook passage). Available online: http://www.let.leidenuniv.nl/bth/aalderink/ policyb2.html.

Renou, L. (1961). *Hinduism*. New York: Braziller.

Rice, A. (2004, August 4). Evangelicals v. Muslims in Africa. *The New Republic Online*. Available online: http://www.tnr.com/doc.mhtml?pt= q8QXnEdoMTsh%2BvjvgnNq%2Bg%3D%3D.

Robinson, B. A. (2001, November 26). How many people go regularly to weekly religious services? *Religious Tolerance*. Available online: http://www.religioustolerance.org/rel_rate.htm.

Roe, M. (1994). Australia. In *Encyclopaedia Britannica*, Vol. 14, pp. 440–441. Chicago, IL: Encyclopaedia Britannica.

Rodríguez, L. J., & de Quirós, L. B. (2004, April 6). Who misled whom in Spain? *Cato Institute*. Available online: http://www.cato.org/dailys/04-06-04-2.html.

Rosenthal, E. (2002, January 29). China sentences man on reduced charge for importing Bibles. *New York Times*, A11.

Ross, F. H. (1965). *Shinto: The Way of Japan*. Boston: Beacon Press.

Ross, K. L. (2004). *The caste system and the stages of life in Hinduism*. Available online: http://www.friesian.com/caste.htm.

Rossiter, G. (1999). Finding the right balance: Religious education in Australia. *International Association for Religious Freedom*. Available online: http://www.iarf.net/ REBooklet/Australia.htm.

Sachar, R. (1999, January). Outlandish and illegal: Hindu prayers in government schools. *PUCL Bulletin*. Available online: http://www. pucl.org/from-archives/Religion-communalism/prayers.htm.

Saint Mark. (1611). *Holy Bible—King James authorized version*, p. 56. Philadelphia: J. C. Winston (1950 edition).

Sarfati, J. (1999). *Refuting Evolution*. Green Forest, AZ: Master Books.

Saudi Arabia. (2004). *World fact book*. Available online: http://www.cia.gov/cia/ publications/factbook/geos/sa.html.

Saudi Arabia—Constitution. (1993). Available online: http://www.concourt.am/ wwconst/constit/sarabia/sarabi-e.htm.

Saudi Arabia—International religious freedom report 2004. (2004). U.S. Department of State. Available online: drl/rls/irf/2004/35507.htm.

Saudi Arabia still detaining Christians. (2002, July 20). *Jesus Journal*. Available online: http://www.jesusjournal.com/articles/publish/article_251.htmls.

Science: A curriculum profile for Australian schools. (1994). Carlton South, Vic.: Curriculum Corporation.

Sciolino, E. (2004, February 4). Debate begins in France on religion in schools. *New York Times.* Available online: http://www.nytimes.com/2004/02/04international/europe/04FRAN.html?adxnnl=1&pagewanted=all&adxnnlx =1075968032cDMz4LqMm6521Zz3Fo9m+Q.

Sedgwick, R. (2001, November/December). Education in Saudi Arabia. *World Education News & Reviews,* 14(6). Available online: http://www.wes.org/ ewenr/01nov/practical.htm.

Sellers, J. M. (2002, April 22). Flogged and deported. *Christianity Today.* Available online: http://www.christianitytoday.com/ct/2002/005/26.82.html.

Sellers, J. M. (2005, January). Terrorizing ally. *Christianity Today.* Available online: http://www.christianitytoday.com/ct/2004/152/33.0.html.

Shaikh, H. (2005, February 23). OIC asks Thailand to end violence against Muslims. *The Muslim News.* Available online: http://www.muslimnews.co.uk/news/ news.php?article=8858.

Shinn, R. S., Folan, J. B., Hopkins, M. G., Parker, N. B., & Younglof, R. L. (1970). *Area Handbook for India.* Washington, DC: U.S. Government Printing Office.

Shouters is the Chinese version of the local church, The. (2004). *Apologetics Index.* Available online: http://www.apologeticsindex.org/s44.html.

Singer, P. W. (2001, November). Pakistan's madrassahs: Ensuring a system of education not jihad. *Brookings Institution.* Available online: http://www.brookings.edu/ views/papers/singer/20020103.htm.

Spae, J. J. (1972). *Shinto Man.* Tokyo: Orient Institute for Religious Research.

Spain. (2003). *International religious freedom report 2003.* U.S. Department of State. Available online: http://www.state.gov/g/drl/rls/irf/2003/24434.htm.

Spain—Constitution. (1978/1992). Available online: http://www.concourt.am/wwconst/ constit/spain/spaold-e.htm.

Spain under the Moors. (2004). Available online: http://www.sonhex.dk/under.htm.

Sparks, J. K. (2004). Religion. In *Britannica 2004 book of the year,* pp. 499–737, 767–769. Chicago, IL: Encyclopaedia Britannica.

Sparks, J. K. (2005a). Communications. In *Britannica 2005 book of the year,* pp. 818–823. Chicago, IL: Encyclopaedia Britannica.

Sparks, J. K. (2005b). Saudi Arabia. In *Britannica 2005 book of the year,* p. 688. Chicago, IL: Encyclopaedia Britannica.

Spillman, C. (2003, October 26). Furore as Italian court bans crucifix from school. *Clari News.* Available online: http://quickstart.clari.net/qs_se/webnews/ wed/be/Qitaly-religion.R-0d_DOQ.html.

Spirit, yes—priests, no, The. (1993, December 25). *The Economist,* 329(7843), 64.

Stalinsky, S. (2002, December 20). Special Report No. 12—Middle East Media Research Center. Available online: http://www.memri.org/bin/articles.cgi?Area= sr&ID=SR01202.

State v. John Scopes (the monkey trial). (2004). *University of Missouri-Kansas City School of Law.* Available online: http://www.law.umkc.edu/faculty/projects/ ftrials/scopes/evolut.htm.

Statement on creationism. (2005). *Australian Academy of Science.* Available online: http://www.science.org.au/reports/creation.htm.

Statement on science for Australian schools, A. (1994). Carlton South, Vic.: Curriculum Corporation.

Statement on the second appeal to the Tokyo Metropolitan Government demanding the retraction of the unjust punishment involving the Hinomaru and

Kimigayo. (2004, April 30). *The Organization of Reprimanded Teachers for the Retraction of the Unjust Punishment.* Available online: http://homepage3. nifty.com/yobousoshou/sakusaku/5_1.htm.

State-run Islamic schools in volatile south Thailand. (2004, September 29). *Jihad Watch.* Available online: http://www.jihad.watchorg/archives/003381.php.

Storm over Italy crucifix ruling. (2003, October 26). *BBC News.* Available online: http://news.bbc.co.uk/2/hi/europe/3215445.stm.

Taheri, A. (2003, January 7). A French church of Islam? *National Review.* Available online: http://www.nationalreview.com/comment/comment-taheri010703.asp.

Tarrow, N. B. (Ed.). (1987). *Human rights and education.* Oxford: Pergamon.

Teachers get choice on "intelligent design." (2005, January 8). *San Diego Union-Tribune.* Available online: http://www.signonsandiego.com/uniontrib/20050108/news_1n8nation.html.

Teaching of evolution, The. (2004). *National Science Teachers Association.* Available online: http://www.nsta.org/positionstatement&psid=10.

Tenets of scientific creationism. (1985). *Graduate School Catalog 1985–1987.* Santee, CA: Institute for Creation Research.

Thailand Islamic insurgency. (2004). *Global security.* Available online: http://www.globalsecurity.org/military/world/war/thailand2.htm.

Thailand: Rights groups deplore Thai carnage on Muslims. (2004, October 17). *The New Nation* (Bangladesh). Available online: http://nation.ittefaq.com/artman/publish/article_13406.shtml.

Thailand's restive south. (2004, December 23). *BBC News.* Available online: http://news.bbc.co.uk/1/hi/world/asia-pacific/3955543.stm.

Thomas, R. M. (1997). *Moral development theories: Secular and religious.* Westport, CT: Greenwood.

Thomas, R. M. (1983). Part I: The case of Japan. In R. M. Thomas & T. N. Postlethwaite (Eds.), *Schooling in East Asia.* Oxford: Pergamon.

Three-Self Patriotic Movement churches—history. (2005). *OMF* (formerly *China Inland Mission*). Available online: http://www.omf. org/content.asp?id=9979.

Today in China. (2004). *Lutheran hour ministries.* Available online: http://www. lhmint.org/facts/china/.

Tokyo school board adopts disputed history book. (2005, July 28). *New York Times.* Available online: http://www.nytimes.com/reuters/international/international-Japan-textbook.html?.

Tremlett, G. (2004, July 7). Spain being "taken back to Moorish times." *The Guardian.* Available online: http://www.guardian.co.uk/spain/article/0,2763,1255588,00.html.

Two Christian leaders arrested by Saudi Arabian authorities. (2001, July 30). *Christianity Today.* Available online: http://www.christianitytoday.com/ct/2001/131/13.0.html.

Two school boards push on against evolution. (2005, January 1). *New York Times.* Available online: http://www.nytimes.com/2005/01/19/national/19evolution.html/.

UNESCO Institute for Statistics. (2003). *Education/Culture & Communication Database.* Montreal: UIS. Available online: http://132.204.2.104/unesco/eng/ReportFolders/Rfview/Explorerp.asp?CS_referer=.

Universal Declaration of Human Rights. (1948, December 10). New York: United Nations. Available online: http://www.un.org/Overview/rights.html.

Vila, M. R. (2002). *International and regional migration trends, 1965–2000.* Available online: http://www.sela.org/public_html/AA2K2/eng/docs/Coop/migra/spsmirdi6–02/spsmirdi6–0.htm.

Weston, C. (2004, April 20). Japan: Symbols, schools, and nationalism. *Crikey.* Available online: http://www.crikey.com.au/columnists/2004/04/20–0004.html.

White, P. J. (2003, December 20). France's "new secularism." *Famsy.* Available online: http://www.famsy.com/salam/French%20secularism%201203.htm.

Wisconsin district to teach more than evolution. (2004, November 6). *CNN.* Available online: http://www.cnn.com/2004/EDUCATION/11/06/evolution.schools.ap/.

Worden, A. (2004, December 15). Civil liberties groups file lawsuit over teaching "intelligent design." *San Luis Obispo County Tribune*, A7.

Wyatt, K. (2004, November 9). Textbook disclaimer on evolution in Ga. Court. *Boston Globe.* Available online: http://www.boston.com/news/nation/articles/2004/11/09/textbook_disclaimer_on_evolution_in_ga_court/.

Ye, X. (2002, October 11). China's religions retrospect and prospect. Available online: http://www.china.org.cn/english/features/45466.htm.

Zia, L. (2003, May 22). 7 million girls not attending school in Pakistan. *The Nation.* Available online: http://lists.isb.sdnpk.org/pipermail/ngo-list/2003-May/003057.html.

Zindler, F. R. (1992). The wild, wild world of creationism. *American Atheists.* Available online: http://www.atheists.org/evolution/wild.html.

Index

About the Author

R. MURRAY THOMAS is Professor Emeritus at the Graduate School of Education, University of California, Santa Barbara. He is the author of *Moral Development Theories* (Greenwood), *Conducting Educational Research* (Greenwood), and many other books, articles, and book chapters.